Numb

Jaideep Varma created Impact
same year at the ICC Centena ... led him to work on the system full-time from 2010, and he has been its chief custodian since. Otherwise, he has been a filmmaker (both fiction and non-fiction) and a writer. His first documentary film on the music band Indian Ocean opened the Indian Panorama at the International Film Festival of India at Goa in November 2010, and later won the National Film Award. In February–March 2011, he also did a thirty-episode video diary on the Cricket World Cup for ESPN Cricinfo called 'Running Between the Cricket'.

Soham Sarkhel joined Impact Index in 2012 straight after a bachelor's degree in Media and Communication from Symbiosis, Pune. The acid test for him was how this system saw his two childhood heroes – Sadagoppan Ramesh and Roger Twose – both these stories figure in this book.

Nikhil Narain became a part of Impact Index in 2014 after stints at Citibank, the Commonwealth Games team, Cricbuzz and Star Sports, which he left in order to fully utilize his educational skill set of mathematics and statistics. He is an alumnus of St Stephen's College and the London School of Economics.

Aakash Chopra, one of the highest run getters in Ranji Trophy cricket, is a well-known former Indian cricketer and a popular television commentator and columnist. He is also the author of the critically acclaimed books *Beyond the Blues: A First-Class Season Like No Other* (HarperCollins, 2009), *Out of the Blue: Rajasthan's Road to the Ranji Trophy* (HarperCollins, 2011) and *The Insider: Decoding the Craft of Cricket* (HarperCollins, 2015).

Numbers ~~Don't~~ Lie

61 Hidden Cricket Stories

IMPACT INDEX

with

AAKASH CHOPRA

Illustrations by

VASIM MANER

First published in India in 2017 by Harper Sport
An imprint of HarperCollins *Publishers*

P-ISBN: 978-93-5264-385-1
E-ISBN: 978-93-5264-386-8

2 4 6 8 10 9 7 5 3 1

HarperCollins *Publishers*
A-75, Sector 57, Noida, Uttar Pradesh 201301, India
1 London Bridge Street, London, SE1 9GF, United Kingdom
Hazelton Lanes, 55 Avenue Road, Suite 2900, Toronto, Ontario M5R 3L2
and 1995 Markham Road, Scarborough, Ontario M1B 5M8, Canada
25 Ryde Road, Pymble, Sydney, NSW 2073, Australia
195 Broadway, New York, NY 10007, USA

Typeset in 11/14 Adobe Jenson Pro
by Jojy Philip, New Delhi

Printed and bound at
Thomson Press (India) Ltd.

CONTENTS

A NOTE ON THE BOOK

This book is a conversation between cricket analytics system Impact Index and former Indian Test cricketer and author Aakash Chopra.

Findings from Impact Index are elaborated upon and Aakash Chopra brings his perspective to bear on each of them. There are sixty-one findings here, sixty-one independent stories, with Aakash Chopra stepping in during the piece at times, and after it, mostly.

The Impact Index team comprises Jaideep Varma (JV), Soham Sarkhel (SS) and Nikhil Narain (NN). Each of them signs off on the pieces authored by them with their initials. As does Aakash Chopra (AC) when he interjects.

FOREWORD

AAKASH CHOPRA

As a cricket enthusiast and later as a professional cricketer this one question has perturbed me: Can the scoreboard alone tell the whole story? Sure, numbers don't lie, but do they give the whole picture, or only one slice of it?

When I tried to make sense of that question, I was usually advised to focus on the important details, the larger picture. But I couldn't quite come to terms with how completely we relied on the scoreboard to make sense of an innings or a player's game. Can a century scored on a featherbed in the subcontinent be equivalent to a century scored on the first day on a green and moist Gabba pitch? Should a century scored in the third innings of a Test match in Lord's be rated the same as a century scored in the fourth innings on a wilting pitch in Nagpur?

As an opener, I can vouch for the fact that there's less pressure while batting first in a limited overs game as opposed to chasing the target because of scoreboard pressure. Similarly, opening in Tests in the subcontinent is quite rightly considered to be much easier than doing so in England, South Africa or Australia. Dismissing the top order undeniably requires more skill, for quality batsmen are unlikely to throw their wickets away. But batsmen at nine, ten and eleven are known to give away easy wickets.

Yes, each individual innings and wicket is open to nuanced reading – anyone who's played the game or has followed the game ardently might put things in perspective there. However, it's impossible to do the same with a mountain of statistics accumulated over decades (in what is a decidedly statistics-heavy game). How can you ever know how many wickets in a bowler's career were of top-order batsmen in trying circumstances? The fact that a player is holding one end up for the team's success goes unnoticed over time. While scoring quickly does register, how many times it actually helped the team win a game is less easy to assess. There are simply too many things that conventional statistics have failed to address.

Sample this: In the Test match between India and Sri Lanka at Galle (2015), the hosts were trailing by 192 runs in the first innings and had been reduced to 95 for 5 in the second innings. The pitch had crumbled a little bit and the Indian bowlers were on top with an eye on wrapping up the match by the fourth day. In came Dinesh Chandimal and changed the complexion of the game in a few hours. His unbeaten 162 not just saved the ignominy of an innings defeat at home but also provided enough cushion for Rangana Herath and company to weave their magic. As it turned out in the end, India was bundled out for 112 chasing 175 in the fourth innings. Dinesh Chandimal had probably played one of the best Test innings of all time.

A couple of matches later, in Colombo, India was put in to bat by Angelo Mathews on a green and moist pitch. Murali Vijay and Shikhar Dhawan were both down with injuries in the first two Tests, and so India went in with a makeshift opener in Cheteshwar Pujara, who, incidentally, hadn't played a Test match for the last nine months. After a few middling tours of England and Australia, Pujara was dropped from the playing XI for the solitary Test match in Bangladesh and the first two Tests in Sri Lanka. When India lost Virat Kohli at 64 for 3, things started to look grim. Soon, half the Indian side was back in the hut with only 119 on board. Fortunately, Pujara was still battling on at one end and, with some help from Amit Mishra and Naman Ojha, took India's total to 312. He carried his bat through with 145 to his name. His knock was critical in shaping the Test match and since the series was locked at 1–1 before the last Test, his knock defined the series too. India won the closely contested series 2–1.

Both Chandimal and Pujara played out of their skins in what were, perhaps, the best Test innings of their careers. Their knocks must find a special place in the list of all-time great Test innings for the sheer odds stacked against them, and also for the impact their centuries had on the match and the series – in the case of Pujara, that turned out to be a series-winning innings. In record books based on conventional statistics, these knocks are just two Test centuries among so many.

Now, let's leave these knocks aside for a bit and look at another Test match from the same era – Australia vs West Indies, Down Under. The teams locked horns in one of the most lopsided series of recent times: one team was competing, the other merely participating. Australian batsmen piled on the runs against hapless Windies bowlers and Australian bowlers didn't break into a sweat taking those twenty wickets. Conventional statistics will give centuries scored in this series credence. Perhaps followers of cricket right now are informed enough to avoid reading too much into the numbers accumulated in this series; the same figures would read differently to a different generation twenty years down the line. Besides, such a series will unfairly inflate a cricketer's career numbers, and since there's no alternative system in place, you swallow the shortcomings of conventional statistics with a pinch of salt. I'm not suggesting that it's the Australian players' fault that West Indies was a poor opponent; it's a limitation of the prevailing system that it does not address the futility of these numbers.

This is why I have been following the findings of Impact Index so closely. The nuance of its statistics often has answers to the questions that have bothered me for long. Numbers appear cold, perhaps even limited, yet they seem definite. But if you delve a little deeper, numbers tell you stories that you didn't know existed. As you go through these pages, you will get to know in detail how Impact Index works. But it's worth mentioning that the key to its working is creating the right filters. One can contest, of course, that these filters are created by humans and therefore are susceptible to human bias. But can somebody argue that walking in to bat at 55 for 5 doesn't mean absorbing pressure, or that breaking a long partnership isn't worth a lot more than the numbers suggest?

While Impact Index's findings may not be the last word in cricket, they are certainly thought-provoking. They turn all conventional assumptions about numbers, and their role in conversations on the game, on their head. I participate in this project as a neutral observer – one who is both impressed and intrigued.

My contribution to this book is to put the stories in perspective from a cricketing standpoint. One can truly appreciate Peter May's career statistics only if we know how difficult it is to stitch together meaningful innings when the pitches are ever so challenging and your team is constantly losing wickets. Similarly, Anil Kumble's worth is a lot more than the 600-plus wickets he took, and V.V.S. Laxman could've ended with much better numbers had he batted at No. 3 all his life.

Then there's some anecdotal contribution about the players I played with or against, and the ones whom I had the chance of speaking to. There are far too many layers of conventional statistics and biases built over decades that don't let the real stories to come to the fore. The core philosophy of this book is to unearth those stories.

Another reason that I believe it is important to collaborate with Impact Index and probe its possibilities is that I think the system could be of great help for selectors who are combing talent in domestic cricket – both Ranji and age-group tournaments alike. It is humanly impossible for selectors to see all matches. What they need is a neutral algorithm that will point them in a certain direction.

The process of working on this book has been enjoyable and productive for me. I hope, dear reader, you find much to take away from it too.

INTRODUCTION

JAIDEEP VARMA

In March 2016, when Martin Crowe passed away at the age of fifty-three, Lawrence Booth of the *Daily Mail* published excerpts from an interview he had conducted with Crowe on Skype a few months before he died. In it, Crowe, who in the process of coming to terms with his cancer had found a clear-eyed and brutal honesty with which to judge himself, said this in response to a question if he would have scored more runs had he derived more pleasure from it: 'No, but I'd have scored better runs, more meaningful runs. I tended to shore up an end better than most, but I just always had this caveat that I was going to fall short – whether it be 299 (in a Test against Sri Lanka) or the semi-final of the World Cup (in 1992) or not quite reaching the goals of my career. I was just going to fall short. That's my over-thinking or fearful make-up getting in the way when it would have been nice for it to have flowed and allowed me to play a few more match-winning innings, which was the potential I had.'

This squarely explains one of Impact Index's findings that Martin Crowe wasn't New Zealand's highest impact Test batsman, despite being universally considered their greatest. There are actually four Kiwi batsmen who had a higher impact (minimum forty Tests), and the reason was Crowe's inability to influence important series results as regularly as a few others did. It took an exceptionally thoughtful version of a highly accomplished cricketer to admit this to himself, let alone the rest of the world.

It is worth asking here if a single cricket writer, anywhere in the world, ever arrived at this conclusion about Crowe's career. It needs no fancy stats system to identify this particular problem. Students of the game, let alone professional journalists or statisticians, who are paying attention, can sense this and confirm it by simply tabulating series results.

Here's another one. Between June 1972 and February 1976, Australia were the best Test team in the world, inarguably one of the great Test sides of all time. Their batting was led by Greg Chappell and Ian Redpath, while the likes of Dennis Lillee, Jeff Thomson and Max Walker dominated with the ball. The captain, famously, was Ian Chappell – who, in the thirty-five Tests during that period (which constituted nine Test series) averaged 50.30 with the bat, but was still behind five batsmen in the world when it came to batting averages during that period (minimum twenty Tests), including his brother Greg who averaged nearly 60. Despite this, Ian Chappell was the highest impact batsman in the world for that period, during which Australia did not lose a single series. One reason was his three series-defining performances (the most by any batsman in that period) – two batting performances that helped Australia draw series in England and New Zealand and one that enabled Australia to dominate Pakistan at home. Another reason was that he was the second batsman to absorb the most pressure (of falling wickets) in the world (after Keith Fletcher of England) in that period – clearly a critical contribution to the team that was at the summit then. Even if not quantified, this contribution is easily verified by just looking at the scorecards of the time. But look at any player profile of Ian Chappell on any website or magazine in the world – there isn't even a mention of this critical role he played as a batsman then, even though it was the most significant thing he ever did with the bat. His career batting average of 43.43 defines him in the eyes of these people.

One-dimensional thinking in cricket has resulted in stories being forgotten, sometimes never told – stories that are easily confirmed by looking at scorecards. Why are Inzamam-ul-Haq and Rahul Dravid Test cricket's biggest series winners ever? One would think this would practically define them as batsmen, but again, catch a single player profile on any website or periodical, even those that consider themselves 'custodians of the sport', mention this.

Impact Index tells stories about M.A.K. Pataudi and Roger Twose that nobody has spoken about before. Even our most surprising story – the one on Peter May – can be confirmed qualitatively by simply looking at the series scorecards of his era. That he comes up as the second highest impact Test batsman of all time after Bradman on our system is certainly not the main point, even though it may be a great hook to get your interest. But if you just accept that his significance as a player goes way, way beyond what his conventional stats suggest – even if you do not accept that he is entitled to the position after Bradman – the job we are really trying to do in this book is done.

That job is to tell stories that have not been told before, about cricketers in the context of what they accomplished for their teams. That, if you think about it, is the real point in a team sport. That these stories are untold is astonishing because it shows how little attention is given to a player's true value to the team. Or to looking at every performance in the context of a match, and also in the context of a series or a tournament. It is common sense and not anywhere near as subjective as some people think (or would like to believe it is). But once again, just look at player profiles on premier cricket websites. They highlight the numerically significant performances sans context, thus often glossing over the player's really important performances. We believe at least fifty-five of the sixty-one stories in the book comprehensively redefine the player profiles of each of those players.

The tragedy of the cricket world is that people pay more attention to the timing of a shot rather than the timing of the performance. Look at cricket highlight packages around the world – it is all about big shots and wickets, never about the context of the game, never about the struggle of the circumstances. Many of them will even focus on the exact moment a batsman scores a century (even if it is an inept edge to third man) and raises his bat to the crowd, rather than attempt to capture the essence of what was really special about the innings.

The smug romanticism that plagues cricket, besides being embarrassing, is damaging. It is responsible for a culture that hails false heroes, like that Mumbai schoolboy who made 1,009 runs; if you factor in context, his innings was disgraceful, and the manner in which he was hailed even more reprehensible.

Perhaps the tendency towards literary flourishes and romantic descriptions over actual insights has its roots in the 'Gentleman vs Players' mindset in England, where being an amateur 'gentleman' cricketer was seen as a higher pursuit than being a 'working class' professional player. This kind of thinking seems to manifest in England (and elsewhere too) even now, when petulant cries about the 'spirit of the game' rent the air. Add quintessential English understatement to this, and it perhaps explains why so much of modern-day cricket writing talks around the sport than get to the real essence.

Perhaps cricket coverage too needs to escape the realm of the amateur and enter the professional?

That simply means accounting for context – the most obvious element for measuring competitiveness. Which is why we stress on this again and again: Impact Index is not a stats system spewing out trivia (which is what the cricket world thinks the role of statistics is), it is a mindset. It is merely the process of seeing the bigger picture of every cricket performance, because there is no other way to measure competitiveness. That has to be the most important thing in any sport.

If anything, the system has much more to do with history, both immediate and distant, than statistics. Its findings do not churn numbers through complex algorithms, but identify events in careers (or series or matches) that have not been given deserved importance and uses an organic way to quantify them.

A system like this has to keep improving and evolving bit by bit (we do yearly updates). That also leads to a situation where findings sometimes get altered, very minutely, but that can still change positions. For example, even though Roger Twose absorbed the most pressure in ODI history as per Impact Index, Michael Bevan is very close at his heels, and even a small adjustment in a parameter that affects their ranking can make Twose the second or even third highest Pressure Impact batsman. The point is, that doesn't change the story in the least; it only changes the hook a little bit, that's all. The story of Twose's multiple heroics is still exactly the same – which is what leads to his high standing on Impact for absorbing pressure despite never being acknowledged for that quality. That is the point of this exercise. Even these changes happen only once in a while and most of them are minuscule in nature; it is very, very rare for a story to get transformed entirely due to these systemic improvements.

This is why we cannot stress this enough – *it is not the quantification that is significant but the identification of the event itself*. This is the most key thing about what we do, and about this book.

In future, hopefully, not only will Impact Index evolve further, but other analytics systems will further expand the horizons of this mindset. And perhaps reveal many other untold stories.

A few of the stories in this book were originally published on the Impact Index website in 2014 and 2015. We have updated them here and presented them in a form that allows Aakash Chopra to add another dimension to them.

It has been said that Impact Index is 'just another stats system' or 'yet another version of the truth'.

That is quite simply not true. Our findings are not trivia. They are absolutely essential, defining information about a player's importance to his team. Judging cricket performances without context is an inferior way of looking at the game – there is no plainer way to put it, regardless of whom it may offend. Frankly, rejecting the stories of events in this book could actually make one look like a climate-change denier. The only element of variance could lie in their quantitative importance, but even that is not as subjective as one may imagine.

In the end, this needs to be said: Impact Index is not here to provide the last word on this subject, merely the first thoughts in a new direction. Hopefully, the stories in this book signify that beginning.

HOW DOES IMPACT INDEX WORK?

This chapter is not essential reading to appreciate the sixty-one stories in the book. But if you want to know how we identified these stories and how these players stack up against each other through eras, this is useful.

Impact Index is based on a very simple idea – of accounting for every cricket performance first within the context of its match. And after that, the series or tournament the match is from.

Since every match has its own fingerprint, based on the context of the performances during the game, this system determines a base figure (in runs) for every match. This is done by using the innings totals.

Then, every performance in the match is measured as a ratio against this base figure, and the result limited to 5 in a career context (the Impact Index scale is therefore 0 to 5, up to two decimals). This limitation avoids the skews of conventional stats systems (like averages) where one big performance can cover for repeated failures thereafter. Take the example of a batsman who scores 0, 0, 0 and 160 in four ODI matches in a series. His batting average would be 40 which is pretty good – in fact, it is too good for someone who failed three out of four times. Here, his Impact would be 5/4=1.25 which is a much better representative measure. However, if that 160 helped his team draw the series from behind, its value would be considerably enhanced. Imagine doing this across careers; the results are very interesting. If we did not limit his Impact to 5 in that last game (in a match context its value may be considerably more), the skews from it would be very similar to what happens with averages.

All the information the system needs comes from the scorecard – no external inputs. Within a match context, it is able to measure all sorts of things never done till date. For a batsman, Impact Index can evaluate how much pressure (of falling wickets) he absorbed successfully (by using the 'fall of wickets' column), the impact of the partnerships he built (same principle) and, of course, the impact of his strike rate (which is different from the usual 'strike rate' numbers quoted for players, as this is in a match, context). For bowlers, it can spot Partnership Breaking Impact, Pressure Building Impact (when a bowler takes quick wickets) and, of course, Economy Impact (again, different from the usual 'economy' numbers used). It separates the lower-order wickets from the others. It also measures Captaincy, Fielding and Wicketkeeping Impact too. It measures the failure rate of all cricketers (impact of 1 or less in a match – which loosely means he could not even do the job of one player in the match).

To elaborate on some of this, let's take Runs Tally Impact, which calculates not just the number of runs the batsman scored but the proportion of runs scored by him in the match. For example, Herschelle Gibbs made 175 in that famous 438-run chase at Wanderers in 2006, but the Runs Tally Impact of Desmond Hayne's innings of 96 at Sydney against Pakistan in 1992 was higher. In the Wanderers match, Gibbs scored 20 per cent of the total runs in the match (Ponting, Smith, Hussey and Katich also made runs). In the Sydney game, West Indies scored 214 and Pakistan scored just 81. That run-scoring was tough in this match is perhaps exemplified by how many runs the second highest scorer in the match scored: 33. So, despite scoring 79 runs less than Gibbs, Haynes actually had a 33 per cent higher Runs Tally Impact.

Or Strike Rate Impact, which is a ratio of the batsman's strike rate against the average strike rate of the match (accounted for only in exceptional circumstances in Test cricket, if the performance helped the team win). This relative measure allows for the standards of its time to be accounted for organically, thus making cross-era comparisons easy. For example, A.B. de Villiers made 149 off 44 balls at Johannesburg in 2015, and South Africa finished with 439 while West Indies managed 291. In comparison, Viv Richards in 1984 scored 189 off 170 balls as West Indies finished at 272 (in 55 overs) and then England managed just 168. So, despite de Villiers's strike rate being 339 and Richards's 111, Richards actually had a higher Strike Rate Impact due to the context of the two matches.

The same principle operates when we calculate the Economy Impact for a bowler. For example, Nathan Bracken bowled for 5–67 off 10 overs in that same Wanderers match when South Africa chased down the score of 434. An economy rate of 6.7 is not considered good in ODI cricket, but given that the par economy in this match was 8.72, Bracken actually qualified as a restrictive bowler in this match.

To give you a taste of actual calculations, we take the example of a specific match, the 2011 World Cup final (a match that figures later too in the book) and calculate some real Impact numbers here.

- Sri Lanka batted first and scored 274 for 6 in 50 overs. India made 277 for 4 in 48.2 overs.

The base then comes to (274+277) ÷ 22 = 25

- Overs completed: 98.2. So, runs per over = 5.6. Runs per ball = 0.9
- Therefore, Jayawardene, who made 103 off 88 balls had this as his impact:

Runs Tally Impact: 103÷25 = 4.12

Strike Rate Impact is 0.96 which is calculated thus: If he had scored runs as per the runs-per-ball rate, he would have made 79 (which is 88 x 0.9). But he actually made 103. So, 24 (the difference) is divided by the base (25), which comes to 0.96.

- In ODI cricket, even doing these calculations on a match-by-match basis brings more clarity than exists currently in the sport.
- Meanwhile, elements like Partnership Building Impact and Pressure Building Impact are dependent on the expected proportion of runs from a non-tailender, which also determines

the value of each wicket (in two categories: 1–8 and 9–11 in ODIs; 1–7 and 8–11 in Tests).

- When all the parameters are added in batting and bowling, the impact of the player in the match is arrived at.

The series-defining performance (SD) is the most important measure in this system – a high impact performance (impact 4 or above) in a match that enables the player's team to win or draw level the series or (less often) change the momentum in a series. This also applies to other series where a player dominates more emphatically in two matches or more against a side not graded as a weak team (the player has to register at least two 5-plus impact performances in that series). A lot of stories in this book are about this aspect, because, in the Impact system, this is the true legacy of a player.

One of the criticisms against the SD measure is that it is valued too highly and, therefore, is subjective. But, given the importance of this in the overall context of a country's cricket history, it would be wrong to value it such that just a couple of high impact performances in less critical games make up for not delivering in these games. And, in a series (or a tournament, in limited overs cricket, where the play-off games are the tournament-defining matches), a player's consistency in other matches ought to also have a say in determining his impact in the series or tournament. We reckon that's an objective enough concern. So, besides rewarding the player for the high impact in the play-off game by giving him equivalent values in one more game (as if winning the series was like producing another high impact performance in the sequence), we add the Impact values of every match he has played in that series (or in a tournament, but only the stronger opposition is considered there, i.e., not minnows). This accomplishes both – makes the SD performance of sufficient value in a career context and also factors in consistency in series or tournament where he registers an SD performance. If you try to balance these two aspects, there aren't multiple solutions that you can arrive at; so, this is not as subjective as many may feel.

We have revealed far more of the methodology in this section than we ever have before. Too few people seem to be above plagiarizing other people's work. We worry about the weak intellectual property rights regime in India, which is, after all, where we operate from. Impact Index has been around long enough to see attempts to sneakily replicate its modest idea. Not revealing our entire calculation is not just self-preservation though. It is also to prevent the wrong debate to take centre stage, as there is a good likelihood for the conversation to move to hair splitting and everyone completely missing the big picture.

In the end, everything we do in this book is to identify aspects of the game and its players that haven't yet been told. Every time you question a conclusion in the book, do ask yourself if you got to know of any significant fact along the way, that you did not know about before. If not, given the evidence presented, why not?

All numbers in this book are updated till 5 November 2016.

The minimum matches considered with different observations keep changing in order to account for varying sample sizes in different time frames. We mention what the minimum number of matches considered are in brackets with every observation.

A GLOSSARY OF IMPACT INDEX TERMS

These are the parameters used in Impact Index. You don't really need to memorize them or anything like that; their usage in the book is minimal and in a context where you understand their essence. But, if you still want a more detailed overview of these parameters, you can refer back to them any time.

Batting

Pressure Impact or 'absorbed the most pressure'
This calculates the pressure of falling wickets each batsman successfully absorbs in the match within its specific context. It uses the 'fall of wickets' column to do so along with the match standards.

Partnership Building Impact
If two batsmen are involved in a partnership deemed significant within the context of the match (so, innings/match totals are accounted for), they are entitled to the Partnership Building Impact.

Runs Tally Impact
Different from regular runs tally in that here the runs scored are calculated as a ratio within the context of team totals in the match. This provides a much truer picture than plain runs tallies.

However, in circumstances where those runs assume a greater

importance due to the result of a match (for example, an innings victory), it assumes a higher value.

Strike Rate Impact

This measures the strike rate of a batsman as a ratio against the average strike rate of the match. In Test cricket, this gets measured in more exceptional circumstances than in limited-overs cricket (tied to the result of that match).

New Ball Impact

This measures the ability of a batsman to cope with the new ball, occupy the crease and score runs – usually the openers, but also No. 3 and occassionally No. 4 and beyond.

Chasing Impact

This measures the ability of a batsman to chase in the second innings of a limited-overs match.

Batting Impact

This is the sum of the Runs Tally, Strike Rate, Pressure, Partnership Building, Chasing and New Ball Impact values.

Impact of more than 1

An impact of 1 is mathematically the minimum impact a player has to accomplish in a match for it to not be considered a failure (in that match) – it loosely means he has done the 'job' of one player in that specific match. This is calculated, like everything else in the system, within the context of each match.

Failure Rate (Batting)

When a batsman has a batting impact of less than 1 it is deemed as a failure. So, failure rate calculates, as a percentage, all the times he produced performances below 1.

Bowling

Top–Middle Order Wicket Impact

If a bowler dismisses any batsman batting at positions No. 1 to 7, he is entitled to this impact in Test cricket. In limited overs cricket, this applies to batsmen batting in positions No. 1 to 8.

Lower Order Wicket Impact
If a bowler dismisses any batsman batting at positions No. 8 to 11 (or 9 to 11 in limited overs), he is entitled to this impact. On the rare occasions when a tail-ender scores runs proportionately higher (than an impact of 1), his wicket is treated as that of a top-order/middle-order batsman's in that match.

Partnership Breaking Impact
If a bowler breaks any partnership deemed significant within the context of the match, he is entitled to this value.

Pressure Building Impact
Taking more than one wicket within a narrow range of runs (determined by the match context) to put the opposition under mathematical pressure (of falling wickets).

Economy Impact
This measures the economy rate of a bowler as a ratio against the average economy rate of the match. In Test cricket, this gets measured in more exceptional circumstances than in limited-overs cricket.

Bowling Impact
This is the sum of the Top/Middle Order Wickets, Lower Order Wickets, Pressure Building, Partnership Breaking and Economy Impact values.

Failure Rate (Bowling)
When a bowler has a bowling impact of less than 1 it is deemed as a failure.

Series Defining Performance (SD)
The most important measure in this system – a high impact performance in a match that enables the player's team to win or draw level the series or (less often) change the momentum in a series. Also awarded to other series where a player dominates more emphatically in two matches or more against an A-grade team. This is the true

legacy of a player, in this system. In the limited-overs tournaments, play-off games assume the status of series-defining matches.

Match Impact
This is the sum of the Batting, Bowling, Fielding, Wicketkeeping and Captaincy Impact values.

Failure Rate (Match)
When a player has a match impact of less than 1 it is deemed as a failure.

Career Impact
This the sum of the Match Impact plus the Series-Defining/ Tournament-Defining value.

All-round Impact
For any player to qualify for an all-rounder impact, he or she should have a Batting Impact greater than 1 and a Bowling Impact greater than 1 (we give a 10 per cent leeway, to account for some variations sometimes).

Fielding Impact
Since everything is measured from the scorecard, this only accounts for catches and credited (or co-credited) run-outs.

Wicketkeeping Impact
Since wicketkeeping is a specialized function, the system gives this role a flat value, which is adjusted to account for the propensity of getting extra catches (calculated by looking at all of Test history). So, a wicketkeeper gets a slightly different flat value in Tests, ODIs and T20s, as per what its history suggests.

The value of byes (in a match context) is subtracted from this impact.

Grading
The strength of opposition is also accounted for by grading sides in A, B or C categories, based on recent previous performances and the performance in that series itself. A team, like say Sri Lanka in the early-1990s, may be A at home, but B away. The impact of big performances against B and C graded teams are valued lower than those against A graded teams.

1

ANIL KUMBLE IS THE SECOND HIGHEST IMPACT BOWLER IN TEST HISTORY IN HOME CONDITIONS

India is a batting country. The biggest cricket stars are batsmen or those remembered for their batting. And yet, no one even comes close to the impact Anil Kumble has had on Indian cricket, when it comes to winning matches and series. It seems fitting to begin this book with India's highest impact Test cricketer of all time, who was also India's most successful bowler.

Anil Kumble is the third highest wicket taker in Test history but is often regarded in a league below the two above him – fellow spinners Muttiah Muralitharan and Shane Warne.

Some say he took fewer wickets per Test, others that his away record is weak. While that is what conventional stats suggest, it is not the full story at all.

In the 139 years of Test cricket so far, Kumble is the seventh highest impact Test bowler of all time (minimum fifty Tests), after Muttiah Muralitharan, Dennis Lillee, Malcolm Marshall, Shane Warne, Richard Hadlee and Dale Steyn.

He is the tenth highest impact top/middle-order wicket taker, after Muralitharan, Lillee, Allan Donald, Glenn McGrath, Marshall, Steyn, Hadlee, Alec Bedser and Jeff Thomson.

AC: So, except Muralitharan, every one of these bowlers is a pacer. And Muralitharan was one of the two bowlers Sri Lanka had; he was bowling from one end early on anyway, and probably bowling 50 per cent of the overs. For 80 per cent of his career, he was the only dangerous bowler for Sri Lanka. It was never like that with Kumble – he was never a lone ranger. There were Srinath and Prasad, Chauhan and Raju, and later Zaheer Khan and Harbhajan – essentially, other wicket takers to share the numbers. For Kumble to be on a list like this means a lot more. It is the fast bowlers who pick up top/middle-order batsmen, not spinners, which only makes his record all the more remarkable.

Kumble is also the fourth highest impact lower-order wicket taker, after Muralitharan, Warne and Dale Steyn.

AC: India always had a problem with the tail. It takes a special skill to get the tail out cheaply before it wags. Kumble was that kind of a bowler. In fact, since Kumble has left the scene, India has had this problem again. That he is so high in Test history in this respect is a significant fact.

He is the second highest partnership-breaking bowler in Test cricket after Alec Bedser.

Most significantly, he has the second highest number of series-defining performances (SDs) in Test cricket history. Muralitharan has ten, Kumble has nine. One of Kumble's nine SD performances is actually for an all-round performance, so when it comes to just bowling, Kumble and Warne are level on that count.

This means that Kumble is actually the biggest series winner in Test cricket history after Muralitharan – that's Test cricket royalty.

It gets more interesting.

Mediocre traveller?

Anil Kumble took 619 wickets in 132 Tests at an average of about 29.6 apiece. Outside India, he took 269 wickets in 69 Tests at an average of about 36 apiece. This difference in away conditions has been used to temper the greatness ascribed to him.

After all, Muttiah Muralitharan averaged 28 in away games, Shane Warne 25.5, Daniel Vettori 32, Lance Gibbs 29, Derek Underwood 27 and Graeme Swann 31.5.

AC: All of them, except Muralitharan, got better conditions to bowl in abroad (for a spinner) than at home – it was the subcontinent that posed away conditions for them. Kumble, on the other hand, travelled to conditions which were less friendly to spinners.

The Holy Trinity of Indian spinners from the 1960s and '70s fared better too, but not by much – Bishan Bedi averaged 34, Chandrasekhar 33 and Prasanna 34 in away conditions. In this company, only Harbhajan Singh has been worse than Kumble abroad, with a bowling average of 39.

Therefore, despite being the third highest wicket taker in Tests after Muralitharan and Warne, Kumble has never been truly considered to be in their league.

But it is worth asking: What is the objective of competitive sport if not to dominate as a team, both home and away? Fine, India in the 1990s were a poor travelling team, winning just one Test series outside India. But what about what they did in India?

Uncompromising at home

The fact is, India did not lose a single Test series at home in that entire decade.

How is that significant? Let's see. Only three other Test teams have managed to do that after the Second World War: Australia in the 1960s, Pakistan in the 1970s (interestingly enough, although Australia and West Indies, the two best teams, did not visit them) and, unsurprisingly, West Indies in the 1980s. Even Australia's all-time great sides in the 2000s could not accomplish this (they lost to South Africa in 2008).

Some indigenous fans and even experts called it winning on 'doctored pitches'. As if the pitch and toss were manipulated by India to favour their players at different times during the game. As if both sides did not get the same surface.

AC: If you give a flat pitch to a batsman, there is still no guarantee that he will score a century, even if he is the best batsman in the world. But if you give a spinner-friendly pitch to Kumble, he won't just give you a five-wicket haul, he will win you a Test match. That's a huge thing.

Also, India did not play on doctored pitches during Kumble's time, not most of the time anyway. India often scored 350-plus on the same pitches that the opposition batsmen were struggling on. If only one team couldn't bat, you cannot call it a doctored pitch. It was just a spin-friendly pitch, which you should expect in India. People need to remember this.

India's unbeaten record in the 1990s set the standard for home performances in contemporary cricket. Even Steve Waugh, leading an all-time great Australian team to India in 2001, called it 'the final frontier'.

During this decade, Kumble was overwhelmingly the highest impact bowler in the world. McDermott, Warne, Akram and Muralitharan followed him. The big differentiator was the six SDs Kumble got in this period, more than anyone else. This is also why he was the highest impact Test cricketer in that decade, not just bowler.

He was the one who made India impregnable at home.

AC: Kumble was unplayable on pitches which had some bounce and on a day-four or day-five pitch. No one ever has been quite as unplayable in those conditions, with so much consistency.

This very significant legacy is why, to date, Kumble is the second highest impact bowler in the history of Test cricket in home conditions. It should not be hard to understand why Muralitharan is the highest impact: Sri Lanka has been a team very hard to beat at home. That said, they still do not have that unbeaten home series record in any decade.

Overseas conundrum

Kumble has always maintained that a big reason why his bowling (and Harbhajan's) was less effective abroad had to do with the non-performance of the batsmen, which put enormous pressure on the bowlers. This was certainly true in the 1990s. It is especially hard for spinners to lead a Test match abroad; the conditions usually work for them only in the second half of the game, by which time indifferent batting could have already put them on the back foot. When that didn't happen, the bowlers were that much more effective.

AC: Obviously, when you play in Australia, England, South Africa and New Zealand, pitches are much more seamer-friendly on the first two days, and spin really only comes into the picture as a wicket-taking option on days four and five. Unfortunately, the Indian batting was such in those conditions that matches didn't last that long. So, Kumble often did not even come into the game.

One thing that did go against Kumble in those conditions was that he did not deceive batsmen in the air, but off the pitch. He was not like Warne or Vettori or Swann, or even Muralitharan to some extent. Muralitharan could spin the ball on a glass top, which was an ability Kumble did not have. He did not turn the ball much, especially for a perceived leg-spinner, and that was a clear disadvantage. He had nothing going for him on day one and two of a Test which had nothing to offer. Harbhajan, for example, still beat people in flight and, therefore, could have more of a say than Kumble in the first innings. Which is also why Ganguly preferred him over Kumble a lot of the time in overseas Tests.

An example of what Kumble was talking about manifested during India's tour of Australia in 2003–04. When India took the lead in the second Test, the pressure was on Australia and Kumble took 5 wickets in an innings in three consecutive Tests. In the last Test, buoyed by India's total of 705, Kumble finished with 12 wickets, where Australia survived by the skin of their teeth (and a Steve Waugh special, playing his final Test innings). If someone else had helped him a bit with the wickets (or had taken catches consistently behind the stumps), or had left him with more time to dismiss Australia, that would have been an overseas SD for Kumble (pushing him up even higher on the all-time list).

The lack of consistently successful fast bowlers abroad also set India back – Javagal Srinath and Venkatesh Prasad notwithstanding. It led to a situation where Kumble was often the stock bowler, trying to contain scoring, instead of looking to take wickets.

The primary spin-off was another problem. Indian batsmen did not appear to have sufficient experience against the rising ball, and this led to many an embarrassing collapse.

Having said that, here are the two occasions when Kumble provided India with two famous overseas wins.

Vs Sri Lanka, Colombo, 1993: *The only Test match India won outside Indian shores in the 1990s. After Indian batsmen put up a substantial 366, Kumble's 5–87 resulted in a 112-run lead for India – the crucial moment of the game. He took 3 wickets in the second innings too as Sri Lanka chased a well-nigh impossible target.*

Vs West Indies, Jamaica, 2006: *Series level as the fourth and final Test began on a difficult batting pitch. Rahul Dravid's brilliance in both innings saw India post totals of 200 and 171. Harbhajan Singh (5–13) and Kumble (6–78) took charge in each innings to ensure India still won by 49 runs. Significantly, Kumble's 45 with the bat in the first innings almost separated the two teams in the end – a classic all-rounder's effort from him. And India won a Test series in West Indies after thirty-five years.*

These were Kumble's two overseas SDs, both hugely significant. The remaining seven, all in India, bookmark recent Indian Test history memorably.

Vs England, Kolkata, 1993: *A stunning innings of 182 from Mohammad Azharuddin changed the complexion of the match, and eventually the series. The spinning trio of Kumble–Raju–Chauhan did not allow the English any space to manoeuvre – Kumble was the highest impact bowler, not just in this match, but the series. The clean sweep of*

3–0 against a highly regarded English side was inarguably one of India's most significant Test series results ever. It set the foundation for what was to follow that decade, as Kumble stamped his authority as the leader of India's bowling pack.

Vs South Africa, Kanpur, 1996: *The series was level, and the final Test was shaping up to be a humdinger. From 160 for 2, India had been dismissed for 237. The same happened to the South Africans – from 121 for 3, they were dismissed for 177, Kumble's 4–71 calling the shots again. Nightwatchman Kumble then came out to bat at 2 for 1 and stayed long enough to give India stability, with a two-and-a-half-hour 42. Thereafter, a stunning 163 from Azharuddin pretty much finished off the match. The other bowlers put in the finishing touches and India won the series 2–1.*

Vs Australia, Chennai, 1998: *A classic Test match, in which Tendulkar's 155 in the second innings appeared to change the course of the match and the series. Kumble's 8 wickets in the match (and a valuable 30 runs in the first innings) played a big part. He went on to take 8 wickets in the next Test at Kolkata too, which decided the series.*

Vs Pakistan, Delhi, 1999: *Kumble's most famous moment, when he got 10–74 in the second innings. He had also got 4–75 in the first innings and dominated the match so much that no one remembers S. Ramesh's hugely impressive 60 and 96 in only his second Test match. India came back to level the series 1–1 in a tacky sequence. The next Test (which India lost) was part of the Asian Test Championship, because of which this Test assumed an SD status.*

Vs New Zealand, Kanpur, 1999: *Kumble's 4–67 and 6–67 helped India win comfortably. Experts take these kinds of performances for granted because the opposition is unfancied (though this was the strongest Kiwi side of that era). It is worth remembering, therefore, that this was the only result Test of the series. The Kiwis competed hard in the other two, and a drawn series had seemed fairly probable.*

Vs England, Mohali, 2001: *Kumble's 8 wickets in the match and Harbhajan's 7 along with a uniformly strong batting performance from India (including 37 as nightwatchman from Kumble) won this on a canter* *for India. Kumble was Man of the Match, and this turned out to be the only result Test of the series.*

Vs Pakistan, Delhi, 2007: *In his first Test match as captain, Kumble took 4–38 in the first innings and 3–68 in the second (all top order wickets) in a moderate-scoring thrilling game as India sped home by 6 wickets. His 24 with the bat in the first innings contributed too. Once again, the only result Test in the series, and hence an SD.*

After Harbhajan's 2001 Performance

From Kumble's Test debut in August 1990 till Harbhajan's sensational series in March 2001 (for which Kumble was injured), Kumble was the highest impact Test bowler in the world. Harbhajan's once-in-a-lifetime series performance of 32 wickets in 3 Tests against Australia, then the best team in the world (when Kumble was injured) changed the equation somewhat. Kumble took some time to get back to full throttle after that injury, and Harbhajan strongly established himself in the meantime.

After Kumble rejoined the team, even though Harbhajan and he combined brilliantly off and on, when only one spinner could be picked, captain Ganguly often preferred Harbhajan Singh. Partly, it had to do with Kumble being lethal after the pitch had gone through wear and tear, while Harbhajan did not necessarily rely on that as much.

AC: It rarely happened that both Kumble and Harbhajan were at the peak of their powers when they played together. While Anil was going great, Harbhajan was coming back from injury and hence didn't have form on his side, and when Bhajji (Harbhajan) got his form back, Kumble either got hurt or lost a little bit of form. It's rather unfortunate that the two best Indian spinners didn't produce enough results even when they played together.

Despite this, Kumble ended up playing marginally more Tests than Harbhajan from that landmark 2001 series until the end of his career in November 2008. This is due to Harbhajan's own issues with injury. Kumble also had a slightly higher impact than Harbhajan in that period. Both were the fifth and sixth highest impact bowlers in the world then (with Muralitharan, Warne, McGrath and Danish Kaneria occupying the top four spots; minimum forty Tests), which explains why India were a force to reckon with (and of course, there was Rahul Dravid, at the height of his powers).

There is also no doubt that both ate into each other's impact during that period too, as it happens in strong teams.

Yet, after Kumble's retirement, and till October 2015, Harbhajan was again India's second highest impact bowler, after Zaheer Khan this time.

Timing perhaps plays a larger part in sporting careers than all others. But the greatest sportsmen, like Kumble, tend to give time a lesser say.

AC: Anil Kumble made his Test debut barely ten months after Tendulkar had (during which time Tendulkar played just two away series in Pakistan and New Zealand). Yet, both had different goals. One guy was trying to prove people right – which was Tendulkar, as the child prodigy, trying to live up to the expectations people had of him. The other, Anil Kumble, had to prove people wrong. He started as a leg-spinner who couldn't spin the ball as much, and therefore was destined to fail rather than win. A bowler who wore specs and did not bowl the kind of balls we were used to seeing from a leg-spinner. As Mukul Kesavan observed in his book *Men In White*...

JV: That's one of the great cricket books, truly, and perhaps the biggest inspiration for Impact Index. The writing is great, of course, but I admire it primarily for Kesavan's ability to arrive at so many fresh observations.

AC: Yes, absolutely. So, Kesavan writes there, and I paraphrase, it was a failure of people to understand Kumble's craft. He was viewed as a leg-spinner, which led to a lot of confusion because you did not see the drift or dip or prodigious turn you expected. What was Kumble bringing to the table? We did not really acknowledge his craft. And he had to keep proving people wrong. First, at home, when people said that he was only fit to bowl on certain surfaces and then, of course, overseas. Towards the latter part of his career, he found his mojo there as well, so that average of 36 would have looked much worse if he had finished earlier. He found other things to do; he got that googly going, he started bowling slower in the air so there was some amount of dip. But with his height, there was obviously a problem getting that kind of parabola dip that other leg-spinners could get. His trajectory was generally flat but, within that restriction, he did some pretty impressive bowling, and eventually proved a lot of people wrong. He probably took 600 wickets more than what people thought he could.

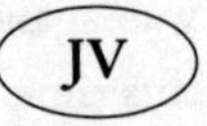

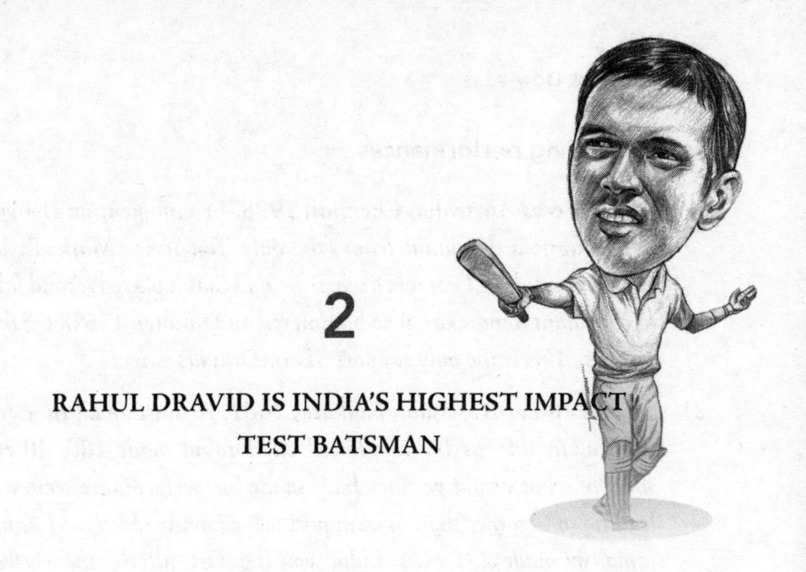

2

RAHUL DRAVID IS INDIA'S HIGHEST IMPACT TEST BATSMAN

No Indian batsman has produced more high impact performances in critical circumstances (in a series context) than Dravid. In fact, in all Test cricket, only Inzamam-ul-Haq has as many series-defining performances as him (eight). Between 2001 and 2006, Dravid was the second highest impact batsman in the world after Inzamam-ul-Haq. In that period, India made considerable strides in world cricket (including notable overseas wins), and it is uncanny how Dravid played the leading role every single time in those landmark wins.

Dravid also has the second highest batting consistency in Indian Test history after Sunil Gavaskar. He has the highest Runs Tally Impact (proportion of runs made in every match relative to the match standard, with a higher value on 'tough runs') and Partnership Building Impact (self-explanatory) in Indian cricket history. And the fourth highest Pressure Impact (of falling wickets) after Gundappa Viswanath, Chandu Borde and V.V.S. Laxman.

Interestingly, he even has the fourth highest New Ball Impact (ability to see off the new ball). There are only three batsmen ahead of him, all openers: Gavaskar, Gautam Gambhir and Navjot Sidhu. This is an indication of what a reliable No. 3 batsman he was. Combine all that with his longevity (163 Tests in sixteen years, second only to Tendulkar), and his place cannot be disputed.

Series-defining performances

1) ***52 and 56 vs Australia, Chennai, 1998.*** *In a momentum-changing Test against a dominant team (the only Test series Mark Taylor's Australian side did not win), where he and Sidhu played second fiddle to a brilliant Tendulkar, who hammered an unbeaten 155 in the third innings. This is the only support SD in Dravid's career.*

2) ***25 and 180 vs Australia, Kolkata, 2001.*** *Against an all-time great Australian side, as India followed on, Dravid made 180, 20 runs short of what would perhaps have made his performance seem a co-leading role (rather than as a support act, as many see it), as Laxman famously made 281 runs. India won the Test, utterly unexpectedly, drew the series 1–1 with it, and then went on to win the series. This was the performance that gave birth to a batting legend. For the next five years, Dravid would be the second-highest impact batsman in the world after Inzamam-ul-Haq (minimum forty Tests). And he would repeatedly produce the most critical performances for his team.*

3) ***148 vs England, Leeds, 2002.*** *In treacherous batting conditions, he came out to bat at 15 for 1. The series was on a knife's edge, but he conquered it all (with Sanjay Bangar, who made 68) – a viciously swinging ball, uneven bounce for a while and the all-important first day's batting. When he finally departed at 335 for 3, for 148, the match had probably already been won. India made 628 and won by an innings (thus drawing the series 1–1). Even though Tendulkar made 45 runs more than him, it was Dravid who won the Man of the Match award.*

AC: Thing is, India won the toss and batted first on a pitch that was supposed to do a lot, so they went in with that knowledge, and then Sehwag got dismissed cheaply. The ball was doing a lot, like a lot, because the pitch was also soft and, every time the ball was pitching, it was creating dents on the pitch which actually makes batting very tough. There are things you account for as a batsman, like swing, and a lot of it is guesswork based on past expereince. The good batsmen are just better at that guesswork. But it was very tough that day on that pitch, and hard to guess what the ball was going to do, especially because Indian batsmen hardly ever got those kind of conditions to bat in.

Bangar's innings was equally important, because things can go wrong very quickly in those circumstances. I still think of the first day in the second Test against Pakistan at Lahore in 2004. Dravid was captain then and, when I went out to bat, he told me that the first hour or two would be crucial. If we could see that through, we'd be fine. But we lost four wickets by lunch, and were behind right through the match after that, and eventually lost it comprehensively. At Headingley, Leeds, things could have gone like that too, if India were 45 or 50 for 4 at lunch. Those divots on the pitch became quite menacing in the end, and Harbhajan and Kumble exploited it well. But, really, they wouldn't have been able to if the match hadn't gone into the fourth or fifth day.

So, that partnership was hugely significant, and then Dravid laid the foundation for a big score. That performance changed everything; India drew the series because of that moment. That innings is worth its weight in gold. It also demonstrated how technically competent Dravid was.

4) ***233 and 72 not out vs Australia, Adelaide, 2003.*** *Replying to Australia's 556, India were 85 for 4, having lost 3 wickets in less than half an hour. Then, Dravid and Laxman put on 303 in six hours, and Laxman was finally dismissed for 148. Dravid went on to make 233. Australia collapsed in the second innings and, chasing a tricky 230 to win, Dravid walked back in at 48 for 1. He anchored the innings with an unbeaten 72 in four hours of batting as India won by 4 wickets and took the lead in Australia for the only time in their Test history before or since. Either of Dravid's innings would have been the stuff of legend. The series was drawn 1–1, but India had turned a significant corner.*

AC: All Indian cricketers grow up believing Australia is the pinnacle, the toughest opposition and the toughest place to play cricket, and Rahul Dravid was no exception. He had gone there in 1999 and failed – and it was bound to be on his mind, even though he was there on the back of some outstanding performances in the past two-three years. That's exactly what happened after the first Test match, where he got some inconsequential runs at the fag end of the drawn Test, and he hadn't done well in the warm-up game as well. He felt a lot of pressure at that stage, and a lot of it was probably self-inflicted.

That was his mental state before the Adelaide Test. And I remember John Wright, the coach, asked him to skip a practice session two days before the game, which was quite huge for Dravid who followed the very strict routine that he had formed over the last decade. Given how significant that Test match was deemed to be, it needed a leap of faith on Dravid's part to actually heed John on this. Anyway, at that last stage, there isn't much a cricketer can set right – it is all mind management. He went for a movie with Viru (Virender Sehwag), which was in English, which Viru did not understand much (probably because of the genre as well), and he ensured that he told Rahul that.

And so, that's how he played the Adelaide Test. I remember it was very hot in Adelaide, and I wore sunglasses while fielding for the first time in my life; I'd never worn them in matches before, not even in India, but if I hadn't there, I would have had a headache. Australia made 550-odd and all of us were tired when we came out to bat. At one stage it was 85 for 4, which is when, nine out of ten times, you will collapse. Even if you don't collapse, you're conditioned to believe that you will fall short by 200 runs. Then the match would be over very quickly. So, we needed to avoid the follow-on. That's when Dravid went out there, and he did not commit a single mistake. That was the most remarkable thing – that he did not commit a single mistake in that innings, except the shot that got him to his century, which was a top-edge...

JV: Which went for the only six by an Indian in that match!

AC: Yes, it went for six, and it was his only lapse in concentration, despite the relentless Australian bowlers. Shane Warne's absence helped; Stuart MacGill wasn't as consistent. And who knows whether that would have been Glenn McGrath's series; he may have been absent, but Jason Gillespie was at the peak of his powers then and Brett Lee was very much there too (though not in this particular match), and they had a very able support cast. Also, given how much pressure their batting could put you under (which made bowling attacks seem that much more potent too), it was still a very tough series. And playing these two outstanding innings in the same match was a superhuman effort.

JV: There's a small Impact Index oddity here. Given that 1,059 runs were scored in the first innings by both teams, at an average of 54 a wicket, whereas the second innings average for both sides was 27 a wicket, exactly half, and given that it was a fourth-innings chase, always the toughest time to bat in a Test match, the second-innings unbeaten 72 is actually of marginally higher impact than the first-innings 233.

AC: That is an oddity because without that 233, that 72 would not have happened.

JV: Of course it wouldn't have, but fourth-innings performances like that are also very rare. In fact, even rarer than double centuries in high-scoring games, which that match was at that point.

AC: So, you're saying that if Laxman had scored those 233 runs in the first innings, and done nothing in the second innings, Dravid's would be the match-defining innings?

JV: No, no, they had almost the same impact; only, the 72 was very marginally higher. And it wouldn't affect their career numbers anyway (because Match Impact is capped at a point on a career level, regardless of how much more it is, to prevent skews). But what it does is bring attention to how rare that 72 was in the context of Test cricket. This fourth-innings shepherding is as rare as any double century, if not rarer.

AC: I would still rate that 233 higher, simply because there would be no 72 to make without it. That 233 allowed you to fight, it allowed you to dream, and come back into the fight. It is fitting then that Dravid produced both these innings.

5) ***270 vs Pakistan, Rawalpindi, 2004.*** *This is straightforward. Series drawn at 1–1. Deciding Test. Pakistan 224. India 0 for 1, when Dravid walked in. India 593 for 9 when he walked out, after a twelve-and-a-half-hour 270. India won the match by an innings, and the series 2–1.*

AC: This was a tough pitch, damp,. and it is good that India didn't bat first. But Sehwag was out first ball, and Dravid was back to batting as an opener again. Though the pitch had eased out, it was still a greenish pitch. With the kookaburra ball, anything could have still happened. Parthiv batted well (he made 69) and all credit to him for that; he probably did here what Bangar did at Leeds in 2002.

But there is a story here, the stuff of legend, really. At the end of that day's play (India were 23 for 1), Rahul was having dinner with some people, including journalists. He left early, saying, perhaps in jest, that he had to sleep earlier than usual because he had to bat the whole day tomorrow. He ended up doing exactly that.

Also, one important thing had happened before that match. John Wright told us that, while we had done very well to win Test matches abroad, like at Port-of-Spain, Leeds and Adelaide, we had to now make an extra effort to win the series as well. We were all aware that we were on the cusp of making history here – and Dravid pretty much was the key figure.

6) ***80 and 47 not out vs South Africa, Kolkata, 2004.*** *Replying to South Africa's 305, India were 17 for 1 when Dravid walked out to join Sehwag. Together, they produced the most significant partnership of the match as both got eighties in their own styles. The middle order played well and India got a lead of 106. Kumble and Harbhajan combined brilliantly again and India soon had 117 to win. At 15 for 1 again, it was up to Dravid to reduce the loss of Sehwag's wicket to a hiccup. India won by 8 wickets and the series 1–0.*

7) ***81 and 68 vs West Indies, Kingston, 2006.*** *After failing to finish off three close Tests, in the final match, India won the toss and were 3 for 2 on a difficult pitch when Dravid came in. It became 58 for 4, soon 78 for 5 and then 91 for 6. After an unlikely partnership with Kumble (45), Dravid was eighth out at 197, and India was all out 3 runs later. Then, West Indies collapsed from 42 for 1 to 103 all out, thanks to Harbhajan Singh's 5–13. Out walked Dravid again at 6 for 2, which was soon 76 for 5. This time he took the score to 154 before being dismissed. India were all out 13 runs later. Then Kumble got 6–78 and India won the match by 49 runs and the series 1–0: their first series win in West Indies after thirty-five years. It is no hyperbole to say Dravid had done it single-handedly with the bat – after all, Dravid had occupied the batting crease longer than the entire*

West Indian team in both innings combined, on one of the toughest batting pitches of his career.

However, Dravid's golden run was destined to end here. During these five years, every single significant Indian series win had a major contribution from him. No Indian batsman has ever come close to this kind of domination. It is worth repeating – he was the second highest impact batsman in the world (minimum forty Tests) in these five years after Inzamam-ul-Haq.

AC: It is noteworthy how Dravid consistently managed to raise his game for the really big games. The credit for that goes to his discipline. The toughest thing to do on big days is to 'be yourself', and Dravid's biggest asset was his 'set in stone' routine, irrespective of the importance of the game. He would prepare the same way for every single game – both on and off-field. His morning rituals before the game, and the way he started or built the innings, would never change. When that's the case, you can stay neutral in most compelling circumstances too. If you're a consistent player, the law of averages ensure that you end up with good numbers in crunch games too, but if you put too much pressure on yourself for certain games, the numbers will reflect that too. Perhaps that was the case with some of the greats who don't feature really high on Impact Index.

Curiously, for the next five years, despite the occasional gutsy contribution (like 93 at Perth, 2008), Dravid's form was well below the standards he had set. Well below – during this period, he was India's lowest impact specialist batsman.

Still, his story had a fairy-tale ending of sorts. Five years later, when India toured West Indies again (with an injury-depleted side), the first Test was at Kingston – the same venue where they had played their last West Indian Test match. On a slow pitch, Dravid produced a déjà vu performance.

8) ***40 and 112 vs West Indies, Kingston, 2011.*** *Dravid top-scored for India again in a low-scoring game that they won by 63 runs, only*

their fifth Test win ever in West Indies. The next two Tests were hard-fought draws, giving this match an SD status.

Immediately after that, India toured England for a much anticipated tour, but lost 0–4, the most humiliating Test series defeat in Dravid's career. And yet, he was easily India's highest impact batsman, with three centuries, two as an opener, once carrying his bat through. It was a stunning comeback – and a last hurrah. Soon after, India lost 0–4 in Australia and Dravid decided to call it quits.

AC: In 1996, my first memory of seeing Rahul Dravid had been of someone who was primarily an on-side player, someone who could not really time the ball that well. Tendulkar and Ganguly looked far better in this respect at the time. But then, gradually, we saw an evolution of Dravid as a batsman. And, in 2011, when Dravid had an outstanding series in England, it was noticeable how well he played on the off side really well. Of course, this was partly because bowlers were also bowling the off stump line to him, because on-side play was such a strength for him, but also it was his determination to keep evolving and improving, right till the end. Like how he cut down the shuffle, which was so important to his batting, that trigger movement, which enabled him to play so freely in England. But the technique backfired in Australia a bit, preventing him from having a second line of defence, which is why he was bowled so often. If it had not been his last series, he probably would have found an answer to that too. That was the hallmark of a player who began as an on-side player, finished as an off-side player and evolved right through.

Curiously, if both Dravid and Tendulkar had retired from Tests at the end of World Cup 2011, they would both be neck and neck on impact, with nothing really to choose between them. This is interesting because Dravid had the worst period of his career between 2006 and 2011, whereas Tendulkar's highest impact phase in his career came between 2008 and 2011.

After the World Cup, Tendulkar had a horrifying fall; that 100 international 100s hype turned out to be a curse and ostensibly ate him up, as he himself admitted. He was India's second-lowest impact specialist batsman (after Gautam Gambhir) from then till the end of his career with an unreal 61 per cent failure rate.

Dravid, on the other hand, in the fourteen Tests he played since that World Cup till the end of his career, was India's highest impact batsman with a failure rate of 29 per cent. So, despite the hype around Tendulkar's farewell Test, and despite that poor series in Australia, it was actually Dravid who went out on a high.

If we take career figures, the comparison is less obvious. Tendulkar's batting average of 53.78 in 200 Tests is favourable to Dravid's 52.31 in 164 Tests. Tendulkar also has a colossal 51 centuries and 68 half-centuries to Dravid's 36 centuries and 63 half-centuries.

But if you look at the overview of Dravid's Test career, you can clearly see why he influenced India's series results more than anyone else. In our book (and the Impact system), that makes him India's most significant batsman.

Here's something interesting. Since the early 1980s, Sunil Gavaskar was emphatically India's highest impact batsman. Tendulkar never overtook him in the 1990s, not even in the period he was considered to have been at his best (1996–99), which has quite a bit to do with team results also, of course.

Gavaskar's impact was overtaken only in 2003–04 by Rahul Dravid. And then, in the period between 2008 and 2011, when Tendulkar had the highest impact period in his career (that's the only time he has been the highest impact batsman in the world), he overtook Gavaskar. But he could never overtake Dravid. Which means, Tendulkar has never actually ever been India's highest impact Test batsman of all-time. Rahul Dravid still is.

AC: In January 2016, I did a Twitter poll by asking who would have had more impact on Test matches/series and gave four options. A total of 3,418 people voted and I got this as the result: Gavaskar: 6 per cent, Tendulkar: 17 per cent, Dravid: 43 per cent and Sehwag 34 per cent. To me, this means that people who follow cricket understand Dravid's contribution only too well.

JV: It could also have something to do with how their respective careers ended. Dravid's career ended on a high, while Tendulkar's ended with people asking why he had not retired a year ago. How people remember, for example, a film often has to do with what note it ended on. So, maybe life is not very different from a film.

AC: Sehwag coming in second here is also very interesting. People seem to see him as a big game changer. Also, let's not forget that Gavaskar featuring so low might have something to do with the fact that he played in the pre-Internet era.

3

VIRENDER SEHWAG, DESPITE HIS SEEMINGLY CAREFREE DEMEANOUR, PERHAPS HAD A PROBLEM WITH EXPECTATION

Many people around the world would pick Virender Sehwag as the most exciting batsman in the last twenty years. It is astounding that he accomplished so much despite playing as he did: carefree and without effort or artifice.

The manner in which he graduated from being a middle-order batsman in domestic cricket to becoming an opening batsman in international cricket is the stuff of legend. When asked by Ravi Shastri once why he goes hell for leather right from the beginning, when opening batsmen are supposed to be watchful and see the new ball off, Sehwag had replied, 'Since the new ball is my weakness, I like to make it old as soon as possible.' He was not being flippant; that was actually his strategy – a very successful one at that.

AC: Test opening can actually be divided into two eras: BS and AS (before and after Sehwag). He actually rewrote the rules. The way he batted defied logic, defied our perceptions of the game itself. Given the big daddy hundreds he scored, he not only had an impact on the scoreline, but also on the minds of people he played against. Players are seldom able to sustain that kind of hitting for too long, but Sehwag did it for three, four, five hours at a time.

This method-in-madness approach was the foundation of a lot of what Sehwag accomplished. He was a blind spot for quite some time when it came to Indian Test cricket; his high failure rate in One-Day International (ODI) matches had suggested that he was a slapdash player in Tests as well. Then, the **big hundreds** began to come, one after the other, then the triple and double hundreds. In fifteen of his twenty-three Test hundreds, Sehwag crossed 140; four times he crossed 200, twice 300. Not surprisingly, his batting average reflects this high rate of scoring – 49.34 in 104 Tests. That is the score of a considerable overachiever, especially for someone who was considered an iffy batsman with no footwork. What it does not reflect is how he made that score.

The conventional **strike rate** number of 82 is just an indication of how fast he scored those runs. On Impact Index, he is the fifth highest Strike Rate Impact batsman in Test history (minimum fifty Tests) after Adam Gilchrist, Ian Botham, Chris Cairns and Viv Richards. This picks out the batsmen whose high strike rate actually helped affect the result of that match. That's how decisive Sehwag was – the first opening batsman on this list. (David Warner is close on his heels – he was the second man in that genre of batting. Curiously, when Warner first played for Delhi Daredevils under Sehwag's captaincy, he hadn't even played much first-class cricket. Yet, Sehwag predicted to him then that he would have great success in Test cricket, much in the same way that he had had. Warner was surprised, to say the least. But, clearly, Sehwag is an unusually astute cricketer.)

AC: People say Sehwag was happy-go-lucky, see-ball-hit-ball kind of player but that wasn't the case. He had natural talent, of course, but he was someone who started as an off-spinner who could bat a bit but struggled against fast bowlers. I know him from those days, and he worked very hard. He was often the first one to get into the nets and the last one to leave. Those hard yards tend to go unnoticed.

He was also very shrewd at what he did. For example, he never tried to hook a fast bowler or sweep a spinner – he knew he couldn't do these things well. But he was also acutely aware of what he could do, and he went the whole hog then. His biggest strength was his courage of conviction. I have seen people tell him to change; he refused because he knew he would succeed only his way. Thank God for that! Cricket would have been poorer if he had changed his game. But at the fag end of his career, he should have changed and adapted. That lack of adaptability became a bit of an issue, but then again, that is what made him successful in the first place. You live and die by the sword; he was that kind of a player.

Sehwag was also a very street-smart player. I remember one instance when we were playing a Ranji Trophy game on a bad pitch (the match lasted only two-and-a-half days or so), and even Basant Mohanty, who was bowling at 115 or 120 kmph, was unplayable because of the pitch. I was at the non-striker's end, and I saw Sehwag step out and go for a wild slog and miss the ball. I went down and asked him to calm down. He said, relax, I have done this on purpose, now he will bowl short. He did, and Sehwag smacked him for fours off two consecutive balls.

Truly, he had the ability to play with the bowler's mind. The second Test against New Zealand comes to mind. Paul Wiseman, I think, was bowling. I barely got to play one or two balls of his spell of six or seven overs. He took all the strike, and jumped from 50 to 80, and at times diligently kept getting beaten deliberately outside the off stump, playing inside the line of the ball, so that the captain would give him a couple of more overs. He would tell me, you're being foolish to take a single, now watch the drama. And then he would smash him.

Similarly, against Australia at Sydney, 2004, when we were batting, Brett Lee was swinging it a lot in an eight-nine over spell. And he barely faced two or three balls then. Later, he told me, 'Good that I didn't come that side because I would have got out.' He was happy to be at the non-striker's end, despite scoring 195 in the last game.

He was a very good partner to have. Even in that Sydney match, when he didn't want to face Brett Lee, he never said no to any single that I wanted. It's another story that I couldn't rotate strike as much as I wanted. But he was always selfless in that respect.

He had no ego when it came to fast bowlers, but with spinners, oh yes, he had an ego. That again was smart play; he knew what he could or could not do.

JV: John Wright used to say that after Sehwag is set, I have my heart in my mouth whenever the spinner comes on, because I know he will take serious risks now.

AC: But Sehwag won that battle more often than not against the spinners. And he never took fast bowlers on in that manner because he did not have the hook in his armoury.

JV: All this you're describing suggests an absolutely unique temperament. What was he like as a teammate?

AC: He was brutally honest, with you and himself as well. He would say, 'Aakash, six innings have gone by, and if you want to stay in the team, you'd better deliver now.' He would say that about himself as well – referring to himself in the third person, 'Sehwag's time has come to be dropped; if he doesn't score now, he's certain to be dropped.' I remember he once told Ajay Sharma, his Delhi captain, during his first year in first-class cricket, 'Sharmaji, rest all is fine, but you were struggling against the fast bowlers.' He would just say it directly. He told Sourav Ganguly once, 'Dada, if you don't score runs, people will write, right? See, I didn't score runs and they wrote about it. Now, they are saying Sourav Ganguly is not scoring runs, so his time is up.' He was always like that.

JV: Did people like that?

AC: See, there was no malice. He was as transparent as can be. At times, you don't like what he says, because it is just ... impolite. I mean, when you're going through a bad patch, you don't want your friend to come and say you don't deserve a place in the side. But then, he would treat himself like that also. The thing is, he genuinely wanted your good. I have seen him at his happiest when others have done well.

But even more interesting is his **failure rate**. Sehwag's 45 per cent failure rate is lower than many other batsmen who have never really been associated with inconsistency. Ricky Ponting, Allan Border, Steve Waugh, Martin Crowe, Michael Clarke and Gautam Gambhir, for example, all have higher failure rates than Sehwag in Tests.

Yet, on a list of the highest impact Indian Test batsmen, Sehwag is below Viswanath (who averaged 41.93) and Azharuddin (who averaged 45.03). The reason is simple – they were both more emphatic big-match players than Sehwag. This may seem odd, given the kind of highly photogenic impact Sehwag's destructive batting had.

On closer examination, though, this is also what comes out: not a single one of Sehwag's ten highest impact batting performances happened outside the subcontinent. Sehwag produced three SD performances in his career – all in India.

Vs England, Chennai, 2008: *India were set 387 to win in about four sessions and it really seemed a game of survival, rather than a realistic attempt on a target that had never seen anything like this accomplished in Test cricket in India. It wasn't clear what the expectations from Sehwag were, but they certainly weren't what transpired. In an hour and forty-odd minutes, he had transformed the match, with 83 off just 68 balls. He was out in the 23rd over of the innings and from 117 for 1, India suddenly began to see new possibilities. India eventually won by 6 wickets, with Tendulkar, Yuvraj and Gambhir sharing impact with him. India eventually won the series 1–0.*

Vs Sri Lanka, Kanpur/Mumbai, 2009: *First, an innings of 131 out of India's 642 to effect an innings win. Then, a bordering-on-insanity 293 off 254 balls as India again won by an innings, and the series 2–0. Both Muralitharan and Herath played this series, so this was no rookie attack.*

Vs South Africa, Kolkata, 2010: *To South Africa's 296, India replied with 643 for 6, which pretty much finished the match. Sehwag top-scored with 165 (off 174 balls), while Tendulkar, Laxman and Dhoni also got centuries. This innings win levelled the series 1–1.*

Additionally, against the West Indies at home in 2002, Sehwag dominated the first Test and was the highest scorer in the first innings of the next Test, all of which helped India take a 2–0 unbeatable lead in the series.

These were all high impact performances. However, his performances were always dominating in nature, never the sort where he had to fight hard to get his team out of a tough spot. While this is also because he set the tempo as an opening batsman, it does not explain why he has a poor fourth-innings average of just 31.

This is partly the reason why he has the **lowest Pressure Impact** (absorbing the pressure of falling wickets as per the circumstances of the match) in Indian Test history when it comes to specialist batsmen. Opening batsmen anyway tend to absorb less pressure than middle-order batsmen as they begin the innings, but it is curious that not a single opening batsman in Indian Test history absorbed less pressure than Sehwag. Bizarrely, even if we account for all-rounders, or wicketkeeper batsmen, only Kiran More (who averaged 26 as a batsman) absorbed less pressure than him.

This leads to a rather curious thought: Did Sehwag have a problem with the pressure of expectation? He was brilliant when he had the licence to play his natural game, but when the match situation required him to take his team out of a rough spot, he rarely seems to have done so.

Perhaps this explains why an explosive batsman like him, given the licence to kill from the very first ball, had a lower success rate in limited-overs cricket than in Tests. Perhaps it may also explain why, despite some famous performances, Sehwag actually achieved the least in T20s, relative to the other two formats.

In fact, in T20 cricket, Sehwag played in eleven knockout games (World T20, Indian Premier League, Champions League and English T20 Cup) and his failure rate was 82 per cent, which is rather staggering. In the IPL, his team (Delhi Daredevils and later Kings XI Punjab) played seven knockout games, and lost six. He failed five times and played only one big innings (122 off 58 balls in an IPL 7 semi-final, which also came against expectation as he had failed right through the tournament; he promptly failed in the final as well).

In ODI cricket, it is a little better. He played twenty knockout innings, failed in nine of them, and produced middling performances in seven others. He never made a century and had an average of 29.60 in these matches. His highest score of 82 came in the World Cup final of 2003 against Australia, where the match was seen as lost pretty early on and there were no expectations from him at that point. In the other World Cup final he played in 2011 against Sri Lanka, he was out off the second ball.

Perhaps it explains why he has just one series or tournament-defining (TD) performance in ODI cricket, and none in T20 cricket, which would have been seen as his natural habitat.

Maybe this also explains why he so often failed to put away the free hit in limited overs cricket – this happened too many times for it to be a mere coincidence. You'd think he would be the ideal batsman to face it.

AC: I don't know ... he treated almost every ball as a free hit. He played just one way. But, come to think of it, this is a very good observation actually. Numbers do suggest something; his numbers were phenomenal when there was no baggage. He scored centuries against every team, in every country (except New Zealand). He could bat on bad pitches, so it wasn't that he was a flat-track bully. Yet, there was a decline in his game in certain circumstances. He averaged 62.50 in the first two innings, 29.69 in the third innings and 31.06 in the fourth innings. So, there is no question that there was something there. But it had nothing to do with the quality that he had. Cricketing conditions did not induce that kind of failure rate from him. You are right, perhaps there is something here.

4

V.V.S. LAXMAN, DESPITE PLAYING SOME OF THE GREATEST INNINGS IN INDIAN TEST HISTORY, IS NOT AMONG INDIA'S HIGHEST IMPACT BATSMEN

If we take a minimum of fifty Tests, India's highest impact Test batsmen are Rahul Dravid, Sachin Tendulkar, Sunil Gavaskar and G.R. Viswanath. As an oddity (we will come to that in a later chapter), Navjot Sidhu comes up after this, followed by Mohammad Azharuddin and Virender Sehwag.

It is unsettling that Laxman comes in after them. His batting average of nearly 46 complements some of the high impact innings he played – which are among the greatest innings in Indian Test history. Those innings palpably affected the series as well.

In fact, Laxman's series-defining performances are all classics. Enough has been said about the 281 against Australia in 2001; it turned a match and a series on its head.

> **AC:** This remains the greatest Test series India has ever played in and this innings the greatest Test innings by an Indian. Triple centuries have been scored, of course, but nothing came close to the quality of this innings. In fact, even if you took away the context of the innings, just the sheer quality of the performance was unbelievable.

Then, there were two famous innings in 2010 – his other two SDs (both came away from home).

The first, in Sri Lanka in the deciding Test in August, as India chased 258 in the fourth innings: Laxman came out at 62 for 4 and joined Tendulkar. After a century stand, Tendulkar departed but Laxman's hallmark fluency had lifted his team's confidence enough for Suresh Raina to stay with him right till the end. In almost three-and-a-half hours of batting, Laxman stayed not out with 103, and India levelled a series in Sri Lanka after thirteen years.

The second, in South Africa in December, as India trailed in the series: after top-scoring for India with 38 in what was set up to be a low-scoring Test, Laxman saw Harbhajan Singh and Zaheer Khan destroy South Africa for 131. Still, when he came out to bat again, India were in trouble at 48 for 3, which soon became 56 for 4. Batting for almost five hours, Laxman played one of his finest innings, to be last out for 96. India won by 87 runs and drew the series – the only time they could do that in South Africa.

> **AC:** V.V.S. Laxman was one of those players who would hit you for a four and you wouldn't feel the hurt. He'd cut you and you wouldn't bleed. I remember playing against him in a Duleep Trophy game where he scored 175 or so for South Zone; from time to time, I found myself applauding the shots he was playing, even though they were coming against my own team. There was some kind of poetry in his batting; he'd hit you for three fours and you wouldn't realize you'd been taken for 12 runs in an over.

In between these two, Laxman played another classic innings, at home against Australia, where, set 216 for a win in the fourth innings, India were 124 for 8. Along with Ishant Sharma (31) and Pragyan Ojha (5), India scraped home by 1 wicket, with Laxman 73 not out off 78 balls. This was the first Test and India went on to win the next Test too, and the series 2–0.

There are two other high impact innings Laxman played – both somewhat forgotten.

Against South Africa, on his Test debut in 1996, India were 82 for 4 when Laxman came out to bat in the second innings of the opening

Test of the series, with India just 61 ahead. Dravid was dismissed 9 runs later, and the long tail was exposed. But Laxman batted for almost three hours, top-scored with 51 and took India to a relatively challenging 190. Srinath and Kumble ran through South Africa and India won by 64 runs. They would go on to win the series 2–1.

Against Australia in 2004, after the series had already been lost at home, India were 14 for 2 in the second innings on a difficult pitch, 85 runs behind Australia, and perhaps even looking at an innings defeat. But a counter-attacking 69 (with 12 fours) from Laxman led the way, and despite setting Australia a meagre 107 to win, India won by 13 runs. The series was still lost 1–2.

Laxman produced most of these classics against Australia, indisputably the best side of the era, and South Africa.

Unfortunately, his consistency did not match his ability. A high failure rate of 51 per cent kept him from achieving the sort of greatness a player like him should have attained at the international level. Only Vengsarkar, Sidhu and Azharuddin (in that order) had higher failure rates than him when it came to the ten highest impact Indian batsmen who played over fifty Tests.

Still, he absorbed the fifth most pressure (of falling wickets) in Indian Test history (after M.A.K. Pataudi, Vijay Hazare, G.R. Viswanath and Chandu Borde) – a huge contribution given that, unlike the others, he played during the golden age of Indian cricket.

It is safe to say that Indian cricket history would have been quite different without V.V.S. Laxman.

AC: Laxman's career suffered because of the era he played in. First, he was made to open in Tests, a position he had never batted in during his first-class career. He did well there but, at some point, he put his foot down and said that that he would rather not play for India than open. The problem now was that Nos. 3 and 4 were not available to anyone, thanks to Dravid and Tendulkar. So, that's why he was drafted into the middle order. Now, with all the skills that he had, he was not an ideal No. 5 or 6 either, and in any case, Ganguly was often No. 5 as well. Laxman was a touch player who did not run that well between the wickets. There are two things you need as No. 5, 6 or 7, as you bat with the tail a lot of the time. One, you need to have the ability to be a big hitter and clear the field when needed, or muscle the ball to the fence because when the fielders are deep, it is not that easy to find the gaps. And two, you have to be a good runner between wickets, to convert ones into twos, keep strike and so on. And these qualities he did not really have.

Really, I am not surprised that he had a high failure rate in those positions. In fact, he failed as an opener before that, so he was shunted in and out of the side. He was one of those unfortunate players who was dropped very quickly, and perhaps not with enough thought about the consequences to the player himself.

The problem also was that he was purely a Test cricketer and did not really play the other formats. In that situation, your failures tend to get magnified quite a bit, but your successes often get forgotten because, when there are no Test series for six months, people have to jog their memories to come to the conclusion that someone is still in form. Meanwhile, if another batsman, say Yuvraj Singh, did really well in one-day cricket, suddenly there was a compelling case to include him in the side, and Laxman became the scapegoat. This happened far too many times in his career.

JV: Did it make him bitter?

AC: I don't think he is bitter now, but he must have felt unhappy from time to time, and would have been absolutely justified in feeling so, especially given the match-winning innings he produced. If he had batted regularly at No. 3, he would have in all probability scored more centuries and also a higher proportion of runs, because he had the ability to play long innings. At the positions he batted in for most of his Test career, he could not score double centuries from there; one, he didn't have enough time, two, he didn't have the game for those positions.

Frankly, numbers will never do justice to the talent that the man had. If he wasn't there as one of the pillars, Indian cricket would just not be what it is today.

JV

5

SACHIN TENDULKAR IS THE GREATEST SUPPORT ACT IN THE HISTORY OF TEST CRICKET

It is curious that Sachin Tendulkar's highest impact performance through our system was against Australia in a dead-rubber match in 2004 (the final Test at Mumbai after the series had been lost 0–2), when he made 55 on a very difficult pitch and helped put India ahead in a match where they were trailing badly. India went on to narrowly win the match, as Australia couldn't even make the 107 it needed to win. The highest impact batsman in the match was V.V.S. Laxman.

Tendulkar's second highest impact performance is at least a famous one, from five years before that, that chanceless 136 he made against Pakistan at Chennai in 1999, which still could not prevent a 12-run defeat.

You'd be hard-pressed to find any other batsman in the pantheon of greats in any era of Test cricket who has this particular distinction: the two highest impact performances of his career in losing causes (from a series perspective), and not even as a leading act in one.

But this is only a part of the story. The better-known part is, of course, the tally records he holds – of runs, centuries and matches played – the highest in the history of Test cricket. His success against the best team in the world, Australia, both at home and in away conditions, has also been well documented. However, in the context of all his performances, these two parts mesh to tell an interesting new story.

Let's look at the results in every Test series that India won or drew from 1990 onwards. We will not include series in which India were expected to win and dominated in – like against Bangladesh or Sri Lanka in India (forget winning a bilateral series in India; Sri Lanka have never even won a Test match here), unless the series result was close. Please note: this includes every series thus defined; there is no cherry-picking here.

Indian cricket in the 1990s

During this decade India were unbeaten at home (in a series context) and did not win anything outside the subcontinent. Let's look at the high points of the 1990s, only from India's batting point of view. The names in bold are of the batsmen who played an emphatic leading role.

1) **January 1993:** India beat England 3–0 at home. It all began with a singularly dominating innings of 182 by **Mohammad Azharuddin** in the first Test at Kolkata, out of a team total of 371, that appeared to change the series momentum decisively for India. Sachin Tendulkar produced the goods in the second Test and Vinod Kambli dominated in the last Test.
2) **July 1993**: India's only overseas Test and series win in the whole decade came in Sri Lanka where they won 1–0 in a three-match series. Navjot Sidhu and Vinod Kambli were India's main batting stars in the sole deciding Test.
3) **November 1994:** India drew a series with West Indies 1–1 at home. In the first Test at Mumbai, the only match India won, Tendulkar and Sanjay Manjrekar scored the most runs for India (119 and 117 respectively, in both innings) while Mongia (80) and Srinath (60) also produced crucial innings. Overall, **Tendulkar** was India's leading batsman in the series.
4) **October 1995**: India beat New Zealand 1–0 in a three-Test, rain-hit series. Azharuddin and Ajay Jadeja were India's stars with the bat in the sole result-producing Test.
5) **November–December 1996:** India beat South Africa 2–1 in a home series. Laxman, Azharuddin and Dravid scored the most

runs for India in the first Test, which India won. In the third, and deciding Test, **Azharuddin**'s 163 decidedly took the match away for India.

6) **March 1998**: India beat Australia 2–1. In the first Test in Chennai, Sidhu and Dravid got 50s in both innings, and Tendulkar produced one of the finest innings of his career (an unbeaten 155) to beat Australia by 179 runs. In the next Test at Kolkata, Sidhu and Laxman scored near-centuries and Azharuddin scored 163 to KO Australia – series won here itself. Tendulkar did score 177 and 31 in the last Test, which India lost, but it was a dead rubber by then anyway.
7) **January–February 1999**: India drew 1–1 with Pakistan at home. Tendulkar produced arguably his most famous innings of 136 but India lost the match. In the next Test that India won, S. Ramesh shone with the bat.
8) **October 1999:** India beat a strong New Zealand side (which had just beaten England in England) 1–0 in a three-Test series. In the only result Test, Devang Gandhi and S. Ramesh (with 88 and 83 respectively) were India's batting stars.

So, in these eight Test series, Tendulkar played a leading role in one series (West Indies) and a significant shared role (Australia).

On the other hand, Azharuddin emphatically led the way in two of those series (against England and South Africa) and played two significantly shared roles. Sure, Tendulkar was more consistent, but Azharuddin was the more categorical big-match player. People who harp on about Tendulkar being in a weak side in the 1990s might want to give that a thought.

The story does not change very much in the years that follow.

Indian cricket in the 2000s

1) **November 2000**: India beat a decent Zimbabwe side 1–0 at home. In the sole result Test, **Dravid** overwhelmingly led the way with two unbeaten innings of 200 and 70.
2) **March 2001:** The legendary turnaround against an all-time great

Australian side happened through **V.V.S. Laxman** and **Rahul Dravid** at Kolkata (both were leading roles, as they depended entirely on the other for the match to stay alive). And in the deciding match at Chennai, Tendulkar scored the most runs for India (143 in two innings) followed very closely by Laxman (131), as Dravid, Ramesh and S.S. Das produced useful performances too.

3) **June 2001**: India drew 1–1 with a strong Zimbabwe side in their backyard. In the Test India won, S.S. Das led the way, with strong support performances by Tendulkar and Harbhajan Singh.
4) **December 2001:** Against England at home, Deep Dasgupta top-scored with 100, while Dravid and Tendulkar both got runs (86 and 88 respectively) as India won the Test, and later, the series 1–0.
5) **August 2002:** Trailing 0–1 in the series in England, India won the toss and batted first in difficult conditions. An outstanding partnership between Sanjay Bangar (68) and Rahul Dravid (148) laid the foundation for mayhem once the pitch flattened out. Ganguly (128) and Tendulkar (193) made merry on that pitch as India won by an innings. Although Tendulkar made more runs, Dravid rightly got the Man of the Match award.
6) **October 2002: Virender Sehwag** top-scored in two consecutive Tests as India won the three-match series 2–0 against West Indies. Sanjay Bangar and Rahul Dravid were the next two biggest contributors in these two Tests.
7) **October 2003:** India drew 0–0 with New Zealand at home. Dravid's 222 helped India dominate in the first Test, but V.V.S. Laxman's 104 and unbeaten 67 saved India the blushes in the next Test.
8) **December 2003:** India took the lead in a series in Australia for the only time in their history, through **Rahul Dravid's** superhuman efforts of 233 and 72 not out in the match. V.V.S. Laxman's 148 and 32 constituted the next most important contribution. In the deciding Test at Sydney, Tendulkar produced 241 and

60, Laxman made 178, while Sehwag and Dravid contributed adequately too, but India ran out of time and the match ended in a draw, leaving the series at 1–1 too.

9) **March–April 2004:** Sehwag made 309 in the first Test in Pakistan, Tendulkar an unbeaten 194. India won, but Pakistan pulled it back in the next match. In the deciding Test, **Rahul Dravid**'s 270 fundamentally differentiated the sides as India won a Test series in Pakistan.
10) **November 2004:** Sehwag and Dravid led the way with 88 and 80 respectively, as India won the second Test against South Africa at home to win the series 1–0.
11) **March 2005: Dravid**'s 110 and 135 led the way for a win over Pakistan at Kolkata. Pakistan came back to level the series 1–1 though.
12) **March 2006: Dravid**'s 95 and 42 led the way a year later at Mohali against England this time, to help India win. Like the previous year, India lost the initiative as England won the last Test to draw the series 1–1.
13) **July 2006:** With 81 and 68 on a tough batting pitch, in the deciding Test of the four-match series, **Dravid** led India to their first series win in West Indies after thirty-five years.
14) **July 2007**: Dinesh Karthik scored the most runs in the match (99 in two innings) for India, Tendulkar produced 91, Ganguly 79, while Jaffer and Laxman got fifties too, as India won the second Test at Nottingham, and eventually the series 1–0, their first series win in England after twenty-one years.
15) **November 2007:** Wasim Jaffer made the most runs (85 in both innings together) for India in the first Test against Pakistan at home, while Laxman produced the most sparkling innings (72 not out) and Tendulkar made a useful 56 in the fourth-innings chase of 203, as India won the only Test in the three-match series.
16) **April 2008: Sourav Ganguly** made an outstanding 87, and Laxman a half-century, as India went on to win the third Test against South Africa at home, to draw the series 1–1.

17) **October–November 2008:** M.S. Dhoni and Gautam Gambhir got the most runs in the second Test at Mohali against Australia, while Virender Sehwag did that in the fourth Test at Nagpur (followed by Tendulkar and Dhoni) as India won again, and the series ended at 2–0.
18) **December 2008:** Sehwag played a blitzkrieg innings (83 off 68 balls), while Tendulkar got 103 and Yuvraj 85, as India beat England in a record fourth-innings chase of 387. This was the only result in a two-Test series.
19) **March 2009: Tendulkar** led the way with 160, as Gambhir and Dravid also got runs in the first Test in New Zealand. India won the match, and thanks to Gambhir's heroic 137 and Laxman's fluent 124, managed to save the second Test. The third Test was drawn (after another marathon from Gambhir) and India won a series in New Zealand after forty-one years.
20) **February 2010: Sehwag** got 165 (in 174 balls), Tendulkar 106 and Laxman 143, as India beat South Africa by an innings at Kolkata and drew the series 1–1.
21) **August 2010: V.V.S. Laxman's** 56 and unbeaten 103 in a fourth innings chase of 258 gave India a 5-wicket win in the third Test, which helped them draw a series in Sri Lanka after thirteen years. Tendulkar played well in that Test too, and also, along with Sehwag, was India's leading batsman in the series.
22) **October 2010:** In the opening Test against Australia at Mohali, V.V.S. Laxman, who was injured in the first innings, produced an outstanding unbeaten 73 in a fourth-innings chase of 216, after India were reduced to 124 for 8 at one stage. He missed the next Test, but **Tendulkar** who had had a good first Test too (with 98 and 38) produced an even bigger performance in the next one (214 and 53 not out) to help win the two-Test series 2–0. As it happens, this was the highest impact series of Tendulkar's career.
23) **November 2010: Rahul Dravid**'s 191 took the match away from New Zealand in the final Test, which also led to an innings victory and a 1–0 series result in the three-match rubber.

24) **December 2010: V.V.S. Laxman** finished a remarkable year for himself, as his 38 and 96 helped India beat South Africa in the second Test at Durban, to level the series 1–1. Tendulkar and Gambhir (160 and 157 runs in both innings respectively) were India's highest scorers in the deciding Test, which ended in a draw, thanks to Jacques Kallis's century in both innings.
25) **June 2011: Rahul Dravid**'s 40 and 112 helped India win a low-scoring Test at Kingston, Jamaica, eerily reminiscent of a more famous win five years ago. This was the sole result Test in a three-match series.
26) **February–March 2013:** India trounced Australia 4–0 at home, and their new guns were the stars for the most part, thus clearly demonstrating the direction forward. Dhoni scored a double hundred in the first Test, but it was Murali Vijay, Cheteshwar Pujara and Shikhar Dhawan who led the way with the bat in the series.

From 1990 to 2013 (till Tendulkar retired), there are the thirty-four highlights for Indian cricket, both home and away. This is not to say that series defeats led to no gains – in terms of experience and newly discovered talent – but surely it would be churlish to argue against series wins and hard-fought draws being the most important steps forward?

In these thirty-four Test series then:

» Rahul Dravid played the lead nine times and a support role seven times (sometimes, very significantly, like his 148 at Leeds, 2002, which actually brought him the Man of the Match award, but let's assume it was a support role for this argument).

» Sehwag played the leading role twice and a supporting role six times.

» Laxman played the leading role thrice and a supporting role nine times.

» Tendulkar played the leading role thrice and a supporting role fourteen times.

You don't even need any special analytics or statistics system to see any of this. A straightforward series tabulation will throw up the same results (which is why we say over and over: Impact Index is a mindset more than a stats system).

AC: But list all the others too, so that the case you're trying to make is clear. Otherwise, it really seems as if you're cherry-picking.

JV: All right. These are the series India lost, or won in easier circumstances (and, once, drew in a rain-hit series) – one-off Tests not included.

February 1990: India lost 0–1 in New Zealand; Tendulkar did make an 88 in a washed-out Test. Azharuddin was India's leading batsman in the series.

July–August 1990: India lost 0–1 in England; Tendulkar produced an outstanding unbeaten 119 to save the second Test, and India dominated the last Test (thanks to Ravi Shastri's 187) but could not level the series, where Azharuddin was India's best batsman.

1991–92: India lost 0–4 in Australia; Tendulkar made two centuries – an unbeaten 148 and a 114 on a difficult Perth pitch that brought him international attention. Tendulkar and Shastri led the Indian batting.

1992–93: India lost 0–1 in South Africa; despite scoring a century, Tendulkar was inconsistent in the series, but he and Kapil Dev were still India's leading batsmen.

January 1994: India beat Sri Lanka 3–0 at home. Azharuddin was the star of the series.

June–July 1996: India lost 0–1 in England; Tendulkar scored heavily, but in circumstances when defeat was imminent and later in a high-scoring draw. He was the leading scorer in the series.

1996–97: India lost 0–2 in South Africa; Tendulkar produced one great innings at Cape Town where India lost heavily but was middling in the final Test at Johannesburg when India came close to winning the Test. Dravid was the leading batsman overall, with Tendulkar close behind.

March 1997: India lost 0–1 in West Indies; Dravid dominated for India, with Tendulkar the next best.

November–December 1997: India drew 0–0 against Sri Lanka in a rain-hit series; Ganguly dominated the series, followed by Dravid.

1998–99: India lost 0–1 in New Zealand; Dravid dominated the series, followed by Tendulkar.

1999–2000: India lost 0–3 in Australia; the only Indian batsman to play relatively consistently was Tendulkar, who averaged 46 in the series.

2000: India lost 0–2 to South Africa at home; Tendulkar averaged just 36.5.

November 2001: India lost 0–1 to South Africa (away); Tendulkar and Sehwag got centuries in the first Test that India lost and Dravid and Deep Dasgupta saved the next Test with the bat.

February 2002: India beat Zimbabwe 2–0 at home, with Tendulkar dominating in the first Test, Ganguly in the second.

April 2002: India lost in West Indies 1–2. Laxman was India's best batsman in the series, and in the Test India won. Dravid and Tendulkar the next best.

December 2002: India lost in New Zealand 0–2; Dravid was India's best batsman, followed closely by Tendulkar.

October–November 2004: India lost 1–2 to Australia (at home); Sehwag made the most runs for India but Laxman and Tendulkar produced two fine innings to win the last Test for India (in a dead rubber).

December 2004: India beat Bangladesh 2–0; Tendulkar feasted the most among the Indian batsmen – his highest Test score of 248 not out came in the first Test.

December 2005: India beat Sri Lanka at home 2–0; Irfan Pathan, Laxman and Tendulkar had a good series with the bat.

January 2006: India lost in Pakistan 0–1; Tendulkar had a poor series.

2006–07: India lost 1–2 in South Africa; Ganguly was India's best batsman, with Tendulkar, Jaffer and Laxman not far behind.

May 2007: India beat Bangladesh 1–0, with the first Test rain-hit. Four Indian batsmen got centuries in the second Test, including Tendulkar, who feasted on the bowling in the first Test too.

2007–08: India lost 1–2 in Australia, Tendulkar made the most runs in the series. Though Laxman and Dravid scored the most runs for India in the sole Test win for India.

July–August 2008: India lost 1–2 in Sri Lanka; Tendulkar had a poor series.

November–December 2009: India beat Sri Lanka 2–0 in India; Sehwag dominated the series.

January 2010: India beat Bangladesh 2–0; Tendulkar feasted on the bowling and topped all batting lists.

July–August 2011: India lost 0–4 in England; Tendulkar had a very poor series. Dravid shone with three centuries in the series.

November 2011: India beat West Indies 2–0 at home; Dravid and Laxman led the way with the bat for India.

2011–12: India lost 0–4 in Australia; Kohli and Tendulkar had a middling series in a disaster zone overall.

August–September 2012: India beat New Zealand 2–0 at home; Tendulkar averaged 21.

November–December 2012: India lost 1–2 to England at home; Tendulkar averaged 19.

October–November 2013: India beat West Indies by an innings twice to win 2–0 at home. Rohit Sharma and Cheteshwar Pujara were India's dominant batsmen.

So, in these thirty-two series, Tendulkar played the major leading role eight times; three of them were against Bangladesh.

Of course these other matches mattered too, even in the series India lost, but again, would you disagree that the list of thirty-four series that India won or drew mattered more? Would you disagree that the matches in those series determined Indian cricket history to a greater extent, just as knockout games matter more in limited overs tournament? Of course, the bowlers had to take all the opposition wickets for India to win, but equally, if not for these batting performances, the bowlers wouldn't accomplish wins either.

Tendulkar chimes in with his high consistency rate – almost an omnipresent support act.

Even though Tendulkar's tally of six SDs places him joint sixth on a Test list of series-defining tallies – after Inzamam-ul-Haq, Rahul Dravid, Graeme Smith, Kumar Sangakkara and Jacques Kallis – it is useful to remember that no one played as many Tests as Tendulkar.

His massive tally of Tests does not lead to a high SD–match ratio (which also reduces his career impact overall).

Even more curiously, five of his six SDs in Tests came as a support act when someone either took the lead (Leeds, 2002; Chennai, 2008) or scored more than him (Colombo, 2010; Mohali, 2010) or contributed with him (Chennai, 1998). Tendulkar's was a consistent and significant support act for most of his career in matches that really mattered to his team from a series-defining angle – except for the 2008–11 phase, which was the best phase of his career, even more so than the 1996–99 phase, which is widely considered his greatest period. In fact, as mentioned before, the 2008–11 phase was the only period when Tendulkar was the highest impact batsman in the world.

AC: It is quite fascinating that Tendulkar has shared that impact with others when India has done well. Of course, you cannot hold it against him that others have also done well, sometimes better, when he has contributed significantly. But questions will remain, like why there is not an instance where he has scored 60 per cent of the runs his team has made, or why he has never scored a triple hundred. Or that he never made 500 runs in a Test series; that's a huge oddity for someone who has scored as many runs as he has. In the end, it shows that, even though Tendulkar produced superman-like numbers, he was also human.

JV: There was an interview of Brian Lara with Ian Frazer sometime back, where Lara was asked why he got such big scores but Tendulkar didn't. Lara said that Sachin was a one-pace player, and played the same no matter who bowled and whatever the situation of the game, whereas Lara picked bowlers and moments when he could get a burst of runs, and then he would pace himself until an opportunity for another burst came along.

This is fascinating, because it matches the macro picture as well. Tendulkar was, of course, incredibly consistent, but could it be that he did not raise his game when the big moments came, and played in the same mode all the time?

AC: See, most players will tell you that no one really thinks in terms of Test series that sharply. It is different in knockout games (in limited-overs cricket) where it is do or die. It is hard to identify what that do-or-die equivalent is here. So, when you're batting in the first innings, you have no idea what its place will be in the end. Similarly, you're in the second Test of a series and you have no idea that this performance of yours will determine the series outcome. So, it is easy to join the dots in retrospect, but as a player, that is very hard to do. Once in a while, you do know that the series is at 1–1, and this is the last Test match, but not often.

And, look, he has been remarkably consistent, he has a 50 every 2.75 innings, which is incredible. Being a support act so often is very remarkable, right?

JV: Can God be a support act?

AC: But who says he is God? His peers don't. All of us treat him as a great player. But we have all seen him fail, as everybody does – that is the nature of the beast. Also, you must remember that, until the late 1990s, Tendulkar did not have the reassurance of having Dravid in the team, which also made a difference.

JV: But interestingly, Tendulkar's best phase in his career (2008–11) came when Dravid was having his worst phase. Which also means he was coming in sooner to bat.

AC: So, yes, he probably got more of a chance to make an impact then.

JV: Could the advent of T20 cricket also have had anything to do with Tendulkar's best phase? After all, IPL began in 2008 too, and picked up during Tendulkar's incredible second wind. Interestingly, Tendulkar's impact for Mumbai Indians was the highest with the bat for that team, till 2011 (and if you leave out big matches, he was the second highest impact batsman in the IPL, which is remarkable). He redefined his role as a sheet anchor's, scoring a high proportion of runs and building partnerships at the cost of a lower strike rate. But could this fresh exciting format have made his juices flow again, and rekindled his desire to score runs in other formats too? More importantly, could that changed role at Mumbai Indians have permeated his thinking on the international stage too?

AC: It makes a lot of sense, for new challenges bring out the best in champion players. T20 cricket came really late in Tendulkar's career but it's worth remembering that the first avatar of Tendulkar we saw (way back in New Zealand, batting at Nos. 5 or 6) was ideal for this format. Tendulkar was an aggressive player at heart. Also, since the T20 format was in its infancy, and therefore the role of an anchor was still around.

And yes, a new challenge can get you going all over again. You start thinking about reinventing your methods and that's when you become a kid again.

An interesting reason why Tendulkar played a support role is that he batted in the easiest position in Test cricket history – proved both by impact and batting average (No. 4 has the highest batting average among all positions in Test history, despite the colossus Bradman batting mostly at No. 3). The challenges he avoided at that position were actually also opportunities he missed to register a greater impact on the game, a role Dravid and Laxman flourished in. This is camouflaged by the volume of runs he made and the statistical monuments he built. (It is easy to also forget that his highest Test score of 248 not out is against Bangladesh.)

In most great Test teams, the best batsman comes in at No. 3. Tendulkar did not. The role that the openers and No. 3 played in making his work easier cannot be underestimated here, and they never get credit for it. Tendulkar stuck to No. 4 for his entire career. It is curious that he opened only once in his career (and that too to garner quick runs in the third innings, so it doesn't really count), despite having accomplished that very successfully in ODI cricket. He might have had a higher impact from there and the team might have been considerably stronger too, given the middle-order talent India was blessed with at the time. Meanwhile, a number of hapless middle-order batsmen had their careers jeopardized by being forced to open, including Yuvraj, Dravid, Sehwag and even Laxman. Ganguly, if he wasn't captain, would have been forced to open too. India could have lost many of these batsmen forever, but were lucky that Sehwag made such a great fist of it.

AC: It is true that No. 4 is an easier batting position than others. Opening the batting is tough, especially in overseas conditions – the bowlers are fresh – and No. 3 is tough for much the same reasons. Down the line, Nos. 5 and 6 have it tougher too, because the ball gets a bit softer, run-scoring is a little less easy, and you also run out of partners sometimes.

Obviously, it also matters what the resources around you are. The great thing that worked for Sachin was that he had Dravid at No. 3, which made things much easier for him. But the important argument here is that Tendulkar earned that spot. He batted lower down earlier in his career, and through sheer performance climbed up the order and settled at No. 4. So, you can't begrudge him that position. Just like Virat Kohli in the current team, who batted lower down but now will stay at No. 4 all his life.

JV: Sure, but if Tendulkar opened, and made a success of it (which he probably would have), not only would he have a higher impact in Test cricket, but the Indian team would have done much better.

AC: The team felt it was important to protect their best batsman, because that was good for them collectively. He was their strongest asset and they wanted to manage him that way. What is wrong with that?

JV: But why does he need to be protected? He was easily the best batsman. It is the same thing with the idea of nightwatchmen in Test cricket, which is now being questioned.

AC: But that's what the team wanted, for him to get the best position because he was likely to produce results more than anyone else. For example, why you don't ask your best one-day batsman Virat Kohli to open and give him fifty overs to bat? You don't want to expose him to two new balls. That's how it works in Test cricket; you don't want to put him up front because you know whatever you get after he gets out is of inferior quality, relatively speaking. It's a team's call, what they think is best for them, no one else's.

JV: That seems like a defensive way of playing, really, if someone refuses to play out of his comfort zone. The Australians, for example, would never do this, would they?

AC: Did they ever make Ricky Ponting open?

JV: But that team was not struggling with opening batsmen like India was.

AC: Recently, they were struggling, before they got Chris Rogers, but they didn't make Michael Clarke or Steve Smith open. In any case, every team plays a different brand of cricket, so let's not go there. Australia doesn't fear failure because they have seen enough success, whereas India then was not a team that had seen nearly enough success. And you remember what India's overseas record was in the 1990s.

Also, you cannot penalize Tendulkar for being the best player in the side. All his life he had batted at a certain number, one he was comfortable at, and he had earned that right. Would you, for instance, say the team doesn't have fast bowlers, so learn fast bowling?

JV: But so many other middle-order batsmen were being forced to open, weren't they? Why were they made scapegoats?

AC: Most of them found a spot where they were at least comfortable, like Dravid and Laxman. And Sehwag would have too, if he had not been this successful as an opener. That's just how these things work. And you have to see Indian cricket and Sachin Tendulkar through that nuanced point of view, where the best batsman doesn't open.

JV: So, basically, you are saying that the best batsman in the team earns the right to not face the biggest challenges, even if he is the best equipped to handle it?

AC: I'd say that the best batsman in the team earns the right to bat at the position where he's most likely to perform consistently and better than the rest. Of course, he could either open or bat with the tail also, but that would also mean marginalizing your best. Just like Australia did with David Warner in the WT20, 2016. Just because he could play the spinners better than the other three openers, he was sent down the order – and that, you might remember, proved counterproductive.

Curiously, Tendulkar did the same in ODI cricket. The position of an opener would have been most productive for him to bat in that format. With the field up and the ball hard in the powerplay, openers have the best opportunities for scoring and playing a long innings. However, at least in ODIs, he was an all-time great player; the fifth highest impact batsman ever after Viv Richards, Dean Jones, A.B. de Villiers and Hashim Amla (though theirs is an ongoing career and could fall away).

Tendulkar's ODI accomplishments and the tally landmarks in Tests both tend to blur the picture when it comes to judging him in the main format of the sport. Comparisons with Bradman are wholly superfluous (Tendulkar's impact is a mere 51 per cent of Bradman's) as are even comparisons with Lara (Tendulkar's impact is 83 per cent of Lara's).

So, what does all this mean in the end? All the evidence suggests that Tendulkar played more or less at the same level right throughout his career (those few moments of bad form excluded; that happens with everybody). His game was the same, regardless of the challenges his team faced, or lack of them. It was almost metronomic in its consistency.

That makes Sachin Tendulkar the greatest support act in Test cricket history. This is a significant contribution, of course, but perhaps not the contribution people associate with him.

6

THE HIGHEST IMPACT BATSMAN IN TEST HISTORY AFTER BRADMAN AVERAGED BARELY 47

This is perhaps Impact Index's most significant finding.

The batsmen that are invoked – after the rightful name of Don Bradman – on a list of the greatest Test batsmen of all time include the likes of Sachin Tendulkar, Brian Lara, Greg Chappell, Ricky Ponting, Viv Richards, Kumar Sangakkara, Len Hutton and Jack Hobbs.

Here's how they all look on a list, in descending order of conventional batting averages (minimum fifty Tests). The last column provides their impact (as per Impact Index) relative to Bradman, whose impact is taken as 100.

Position	*Name*	*Matches*	*Batting Average*	*Batting Impact (per cent)*
1	Don Bradman	52	99.94	**100**
2	Herbert Sutcliffe	54	60.73	**55**
3	Ken Barrington	82	58.67	**55**
4	Wally Hammond	85	58.45	**54**
5	Garry Sobers	93	57.78	**58**
6	Kumar Sangakkara	134	57.4	**59**
7	Jack Hobbs	61	56.94	**61**
8	Len Hutton	79	56.67	**60**

Position	*Name*	*Matches*	*Batting Average*	*Batting Impact (per cent)*
9	Jacques Kallis	166	55.37	57
10	Younis Khan	110	53.98	64
11	Greg Chappell	87	53.86	62
12	Sachin Tendulkar	200	53.78	51
13	Brian Lara	131	52.88	62
14	Javed Miandad	124	52.57	51
15	Rahul Dravid	164	52.31	55
16	Mohammad Yousuf	90	52.29	43
17	Ricky Ponting	168	51.85	53
26	A.B. de Villiers	106	50.46	61
28	Viv Richards	121	50.23	53
31	Inzamam-ul-Haq	120	49.6	61
51	Peter May	66	46.77	65

Note: Impact numbers of only Tests with a minimum of two innings are included. Batting impact is expressed on a scale of 0 to 100, with the maximum (100) assigned to the highest impact batsman (Don Bradman). All other batsmen are scaled relative to that.

The conventional measure of the batting average has Peter May at 51 on batting averages but the second highest impact batsman after Bradman (with 65 per cent of the impact Bradman had). What exactly is going on here?

Why are we saying that Peter May, who barely averaged 46.77 for England with just thirteen centuries in sixty-six Tests is higher impact than all those other great batsmen?

Let's lay out the big picture first.

Peter May played in the toughest decade in a hundred years to score runs in

In the last 100 years, the 1950s were the toughest on batsmen; the average runs per wicket is considerably lower than any other decade after the First World War. In fact, if an adjustment for this is made (using the general rule of thumb), May crosses an average of 50 quite easily (and many others would have their batting averages reduced for the same reason).

It was also the lowest scoring decade in England (post-1920). Yet, Peter May averaged 60 in that decade and 57 though his career there (1951–61) in thirty-nine Tests.

July 1957. Fourth Test vs West Indies, Leeds. *Peter May makes 69 (the highest scorer for his side) against West Indies. England make 279 and actually win by an innings.*

AC: Why was the 1950s the hardest decade to bat in?

JV: In England, there seems to have been a concerted effort to prepare result-oriented pitches as the post-war period had produced enormously high-scoring matches. Curiously, the 1940s, or the half that saw Test cricket, was the highest scoring decade in Test history (and remains so). This resulted in bowling-friendly pitches in the 1950s, and the entire cricket world seems to have taken England's lead in this.

AC: Now, this has made it very interesting, for batting and bowling averages have headed north in the last few decades. The best batsmen in the 1980s were averaging in the 40s, but now, the best are touching 60s. That's where cold numbers aren't a good indicator for when we are going back in time. Pitches have since become flatter, bats have become bulkier and a lot of effort is spent on making the ball go farther. Can you make a rough calculation – what would May's average look like if he played during the 2000s, and Tendulkar's or Viv Richards's if they had played in the 1950s?

JV: So, May's batting average in the 2000s translates to 54.50 while Tendulkar's average in the 1950s would come down to 46.24 while Richards's average would be reduced to 44.32.

AC: Great revelation. Bringing parity to the table provides the numbers with a context.

England, during this period, had their longest unbeaten streak in Test history

From 1951 to 1958, England played fourteen Test series (via 62 Tests) in Australia, New Zealand, West Indies, India, South Africa and, of course, at home. They did not lose a single one (won 10, drew 4). Inarguably, they were the best team in the world then. In the 139 years of Test cricket so far, that was English cricket's finest moment.

Peter May played in forty-nine of his sixty-six Tests during this period.

Peter May was the second highest impact player in the world in this period

During this heady period, when May played most of his international cricket (his career ran from 1951 to 1961), he was the highest impact batsman in the world by a distance. More significantly, he was the second highest impact player after Richie Benaud (minimum thirty Tests).

The latter is particularly interesting because only in very exceptional cases is a batsman amongst the top two or three highest impact players – understandably, quality bowlers and bowling all-rounders almost always have a higher impact than batsmen in the Test format – and there were more than a few in his time. Despite having bowlers like Jim Laker, Alec Bedser, Tony Lock, Fred Trueman, Brian Statham, Frank Tyson and Roy Tattersall and an all-rounder like Trevor Bailey in his team at various times, May had higher impact than all of them during those triumphant years. A batsman being the second highest impact player in the world over eight years is remarkable, almost Bradmanesque.

Conventionally, May had a batting average of 48 in this period and Clyde Walcott, Garry Sobers, Everton Weekes and Len Hutton (who finished his career in a blaze in 1955) were ahead of him on averages. But the fact that the greater proportion of May's runs were made in low-scoring matches and his best performances came when the team needed them the most – and they made the biggest difference in several series – makes his impact higher than everybody else's.

This amply reveals the extent of May's role in his team reaching the summit amongst Test teams.

July 1956. Third Test vs Australia, Leeds. *Having lost the previous Test and trailing 0–1 in the Ashes, England are 17 for 3. May's 101 and Washbrook's 98 change the course of the match as their team reaches 325 in difficult conditions. Australia collapse for 143 and 140. Series 1–1. England win the next Test and go into the deciding Test 2–1 up.*

August 1956. Fifth Test, The Oval. *At 66 for 3 things look shaky, before May and Denis Compton take charge. May stays unbeaten at 83 as England are dismissed for 247 – a very good score in these conditions. Australia 202. Another unbeaten 35 from May in the second innings leaves Australia with too much to do in two hours of play. In 38 overs though, they do plummet to 27 for 5 before play is called off. Series and the Ashes to England.*

AC: A batsman having the most impact in a decade where batting was tough? Well, I'd say that is only natural, because good bowling numbers would cancel each other out, and wickets would get distributed evenly, in bowling-friendly conditions. If both teams have managed only 150, bowlers from both sides would have great returns and that's where a big knock would make all the difference.

JV: Yes, and perhaps because of how low- scoring the pitches were, and also because caution became the prevalent mindset that decade, with low scoring rates, it wasn't exactly the decade of spectacular batsmanship. So, could that be the reason why not many Test innings are remembered today from that period? And could that be the reason why batsmen from the era are not rated as highly as those who came in later periods? The romantics tend to remember only what is spectacular, perhaps?

AC: Fair point. It was also the pre-television era, so since cricket from that era is available mostly in text form (cricket was yet to be broadcast on television), we are thus totally dependent on people who saw it first-hand and then on what they chose to write about it. To be honest, even for many cricket fans, this era didn't exist, for we tend to eulogize batting performances a lot more.

Peter May absorbed more pressure than any Test batsman ever

In the history of Test cricket, no one absorbed the pressure of falling wickets more than May (minimum fifty Tests; if we reduce it to forty, only M.A.K. Pataudi comes over him).

This is a massive point. Typically in Test history, it has been the batsmen from relatively weaker teams (Andy Flower, Brian Lara, Angelo Mathews, Kane Williamson, M.A.K. Pataudi) who absorb pressure because they often run into circumstances where they need to stabilize the situation due to wickets falling around them.

But to do it in a team that was the best in the world for the majority of May's career suggests that his team's – the best of its time – dependence on him was huge. Bowlers may win matches but runs have to be scored too. The number of times May turned things around for his team as a batsman was actually the single most important reason why England dominated so decisively in that decade. This finding is absolutely extraordinary.

In fact, the game in which May absorbed the most pressure was also the one that resulted in his highest Test score (not a common occurrence at all; most batsmen get their highest scores in easier circumstances; Hanif Mohammed, Brendon McCullum and Martin Crowe are the only exceptions that place above him).

June 1957. Opening Test vs West Indies, Edgbaston. *Mystery spinner Sonny Ramadhin takes 7 for 49 and England crash for 186. West Indies put up 474 and England are 65 for 2 when May walks in, which is soon 113 for 3 (two wickets to Ramadhin and all set up for an early finish, with almost two days to go). But after ten hours of batting, May emerges 285 not out. England declare 295 ahead and reduce a shaken West Indies to 68 for 7 before captain John Goddard bats out time. But the tide has turned emphatically. Ramadhin takes only 5 more wickets in the next four Tests and England win three of them by an innings.*

Peter May is the highest impact third-innings batsman in Test history

Averages start telling slightly truer stories when you break them down further. Here is a list of the best third-innings averages in Test history, in descending order (minimum twenty innings) – top five as they are, then some famous names and their positions.

Position	*Name*	*Innings*	*Batting Average*
1	Peter May	21	68.05
2	Jacques Kallis	67	65.26
3	Denis Compton	31	65.2
4	Allan Border	76	63.83
5	Damien Martyn	25	63.31
12	Garry Sobers	48	57.9
13	Kumar Sangakkara	65	56.76
19	V.V.S. Laxman	53	54
33	Vivian Richards	37	49.5
44	Sachin Tendulkar	72	46.81
78	A.B. de Villiers	39	42.23
93	Brian Lara	56	40.42

It has to be mentioned that Bradman and Sutcliffe averaged more – Bradman 130.41 in just 15 innings and Sutcliffe 74.75 in 16 innings.

Even this chart belies May's true significance. What averages do not show (unless you search for that) is how many times May stabilized his side from behind and helped save the game, or win it (win: four times in 1954–55 when he was at his peak; drew, twice post-1958). On most of these occasions, his performance changed the course of the series. No other batsman produced such a high proportion of rearguard fightbacks that transformed series.

December 1954. Second Test vs Australia, Sydney. *Australia have won the first Test by an innings, dismissed England for 154 here, taken a lead of 74 and reduced England to 55 for 3 with an attack comprising Ray*

Lindwall, Ron Archer, Alan Davidson, Bill Johnston and Benaud bearing upon them aggressively. But Peter May takes charge with some help from Colin Cowdrey at first, then John Edrich. His five-hour 104 (second highest score 54) gives England a 222-run lead. Despite Neil Harvey's heroics, Australia fall 38 runs short. The series is 1–1.

Next Test, Melbourne. *England 191. Australia 231. England 40 for 1 as May walks in. He makes 91 (next highest score 42) as England get a lead of 239. Frank Tyson takes 7 wickets and Australia are dismissed for 111. Series 2–1.*

England go on to win the series 3–1.

AC: When his team is either following on or trailing by a huge total, a batsman may intend to ignore the scoreboard and focus on the next delivery, but I assure you it's almost impossible to not acknowledge the position that you are in. Your response to the next delivery is certainly altered because of it. You know that you cannot make a single mistake. Playing percentage cricket is paramount. Even while you're scoring runs, you aren't making tangible progress. Until you wipe off the deficit, you haven't moved an inch. It's only when the scores are level that you start moving forward. Also, this provides a great opportunity to the fielding captain to attack relentlessly and most batsmen would tell you that a wicket is often the outcome of this. Once you're set, the captain puts a few fielders in defensive positions at the cost of fielders in catching positions, and that's when a thick edge goes through where the third slip or gully would've been stationed. Third-innings heroics are also different from fourth-innings performance for the same reason – since it's only the third innings, as the fielding team attacks a lot more on the field because their team will have one more opportunity to bat. On the contrary, there's no such luxury in the fourth innings and, therefore, prudence demands a more conservative approach.

Peter May was the biggest series winner with the bat from his era

May had three series-defining performances in his career, more than any batsman, bowler or all-rounder in that time frame (1951–58). When he stopped playing Test cricket (1961), only two players had gone past him: all-rounders Richie Benaud (five SDs) and Alan Davidson (four SDs). But no batsman. Again, this exemplifies the huge impact May had in his time despite being a single-skill player.

Furthermore, in the three series that May accomplished his series-defining performances, his SD value (which is also dependent on the player's consistency in that series) is very high. With the sole exception of Bradman (and if we take forty Tests as a minimum), no one had a higher series-defining value in Test cricket history. This essentially means that May had been consistent across his career: his big match performances were not aberrations. This is the main reason why May is ahead of Hutton on impact despite being almost 10 runs behind on conventional averages, even though Hutton is marginally ahead of May on almost every other batting parameter.

June 1955. Second Test vs South Africa, Lord's. *After beating South Africa in the first Test (where May and Don Kenyon lead the way with the bat), England struggle here. All out for 133, conceding a lead of 171 and then 9 for 1 when May walks in. He makes 112 (second highest score is 69) and England get a lead of 182. Brian Statham takes 7 wickets and England are 2–0 up.*

Then, South Africa win the next two Tests (a third-innings 117 and a fourth-innings 97 by May in vain – both are highest scores for his team). The series is at 2–2.

August 1955. Fifth Test, The Oval. *England 151. South Africa 112. England 30 for 2 when May walks in, match and series in balance. Wickets fall regularly but not his. A five-hour unbeaten 89 from him, last man standing, when England are dismissed for 204. A target of 244 on that pitch with Laker and Lock to face proves too much, and England win the match by 92 runs. And the series 3–2. May has contributed significantly in every single match.*

Peter May is the third most consistent batsman in Test history

Only Don Bradman (27 per cent) and Len Hutton (30 per cent) have lower failure rates than Peter May (33 per cent) in Test cricket history (minimum fifty Tests). Given that nobody considers May in the same league as Bradman and Hutton, and the luminaries below him on this list, this is one of the more surprising findings.

His consistency and the circumstances in which May played (the lowest-scoring decade in 100 years) also has him placed sixth on the list of Runs Tally Impact (proportion of runs made by batsman in a match-by-match context; minimum forty Tests) after you-know-who, Jack Hobbs, Neil Harvey, Joe Root (an ongoing career), Matthew Hayden and Brian Lara. The fact that Harvey averages less than 50 and is, therefore, not clubbed with the all-time great batsmen is further evidence of how urgently we need to reassess conventional statistics. Like May, he too played in an era where run-scoring was not as easy, and produced the goods more emphatically in challenging circumstances.

The 'home vs away' comparison will always come up in the end, but in this instance it is an argument that lacks nuance. True, May averaged 57 at home (39 Tests) and 36 away (27 Tests). More importantly, he averaged 40 in Australia (ten Tests) and 35.5 in West Indies (eight Tests) and produced important contributions in both countries. His one truly bad away series happened in South Africa where he played five Tests for an average of 15 (a series England could not win, but drew 2–2). He did not play in the subcontinent – in all probability, that would have been an opportunity to bolster his average. May contributed immensely to keeping England – not an easy place to bat – dominant at home against strong opposition, and in a decade that was particularly tough for batsmen. Besides, nobody has a perfect away record, except Bradman, and he only played in Australia and England all his career.

May's departure from the scene in 1961 coincided with England slipping from its position of pre-eminence as a post-Bradman Australia, West Indies and South Africa asserted themselves. During his career, May even captained his side forty-one times (winning twenty and losing ten, he was an influential captain) and was at his peak as a batsman during this period.

In the end, it is a tragedy for cricket that the contributions of Peter Barker Howard May have remained unrecognized: an all-time great batsman who helped change his country's cricket history. Often with his back to the wall.

AC: As a rule of thumb, batsmen only set up matches and bowlers win them. But if you happen to play on pitches where there's a little too much for the bowlers, batsmen play defining roles. The thing going in Peter May's favour is the period in which he played, for batting averages were poor across the board.

There is one other thing to keep in mind here: When you play on bowler-friendly pitches, form does not help you as it should. You never hit a purple patch. As a batsman, you're never set, and just because the previous ball behaved according to your expectation and hit the middle of your bat doesn't mean that the following ball will do the same. A lot of people might tell you to forget what happened on the previous ball, but the fact is that nobody does that – and, perhaps, nobody should. While obsessing about the previous ball is not recommended, taking valuable lessons from it is a must. All batsmen condition themselves to make use of that important first-hand information, because it allows you to prepare well. But if the pitch is misbehaving, you can't rely on the data that you've received. You must unlearn the habit of taking cues from the previous ball and that can't be easy.

Additionally, if you don't stitch a lot of high-scoring innings together, you'd never save enough for the inevitable dry patch. Considering all this, suddenly, the average of 47 seems a lot more than the number itself suggests.

I am glad Impact Index unearthed this particular story. Perhaps more than anything else within these pages, it redefines how we look at cricket history. In the recent past, I've spoken to many former Indian Test cricketers about it, and not even one thought that Peter May would feature this high on the list – most hadn't even heard his name before.

JV

7

UNTIL RECENTLY, THE HIGHEST IMPACT ASIAN TEST BATSMAN OF ALL TIME WAS INZAMAM-UL-HAQ

Whenever Imran Khan was asked to choose between Brian Lara and Sachin Tendulkar, he usually steered the conversation to Inzamam-ul-Haq. 'No one plays fast bowling better than Inzamam,' Imran would say. He would talk about Inzamam's capacity for playing valuable knocks at crucial times. Inzamam, declared Imran, was the batsman he would want to bat for his life. The interviewer would politely nod and move on.

But Imran was not shooting in the dark.

He had seen some of it as Inzamam's teammate and captain. In fact, Inzamam's international career began with this special quality right at the fore – though in a different format. As a fresh-faced twenty-two-year-old, he made 60 in 37 balls in the 1992 World Cup semi-final with Pakistan needing 123 runs in 15 overs – a near-unthinkable equation at that time. Accomplishments like those often turn out to be flashes in the pan (think Collis King, Mike Veletta) but for someone as young as him to do it on the biggest stage in the world was perhaps a sign of much more to come. As it turned out, Inzamam did it again and again in limited-overs cricket and, more significantly, in Test cricket. It turned out to be his hallmark as a batsman.

AC: Imran Khan used to say, 'Inzy, you will win the World Cup for me,' and people would laugh. Since Imran was at the fag end of his career, a lot of people called him senile behind his back. They used to say, 'Why is he supporting this fatty, he is a waste of time.' Inzamam kept failing and still Imran kept his faith up.

JV: He had also grandly announced that Pakistan would win the World Cup, on the very day they were saved by rain from being eliminated.

AC: He would say such things. Now, it is the stuff of legend, of course. That's what he said to Inzamam before that semi-final against New Zealand.

JV: This is pretty amazing. Sometime back, when we interviewed him, Inzamam said, 'Imran always backed those who played for the team. If someone made just 10 or 12 runs and got out early playing for the team, he would back that player over someone who scored 70 but played for himself.' It was, therefore, a lesson he imbibed very early on. He said he was always very conscious of the match situation and what the team required right through his career.

It is this quality of delivering at the big moments that made him the highest impact batsman from Asia in Test cricket history until August 2016, when Younis Khan overtook him. Remarkable for a batsman whose average did not touch 50 in these high-scoring times.

The conventional angle

If you look at conventional batting averages of batsmen in matches that their teams won, after Superman, sorry, Bradman, it is Inzamam at number two – with an average of 78 in 49 matches won (minimum 40 innings). Given that Pakistan was not among the top two Test sides in the world during a lot of Inzamam's career, that again provides an indication of an extraordinary career. But then again, the doubt about how many of these matches might have been in dead rubbers or one-sided series, or who the opposition were, always remains.

This is where Impact Index comes in handy, as all its measures are relative and everything is in a match and series context.

The Impact angle

In the Impact Index system, series-defining performances are the true legacy of a player.

As it transpires, no batsman in Test history has more SDs in his career than Inzamam-ul-Haq and Rahul Dravid – eight each. Dravid did it in 164 Tests, Inzamam in 120.

Moreover, the only Asian batsman with a higher impact than Inzamam is Younis Khan (who has six SDs in 110 Tests). Younis Khan's is an ongoing career though, and the usual tapering-off at the fag end might lead to a loss of impact.

AC: Inzamam was in a team where many batsmen had flair and there was some amount of chaos in the side. But he was the calming influence. He just slowed things down in his inimitable, subtle style, making the game move at a slower pace, simply because of the time he had to play. He often changed the tide with this quality. In that sense, he was a momentum changer, like a sage in a commotion.

He was not a quintessential Pakistani player of the sort Osman Samiuddin described in a piece on the Pakistani cricket ethos; he was not a maverick, didn't have that flair.

JV: The one where he compared their cricket ethos to a Qawwali, 'haal', 'which can set fire to eternity'? One of the finest pieces, on cricket or otherwise.

AC: But Inzamam was not that at all. He was unfazed at all times, unless he was running between wickets, which he did very little of.

The Pakistan angle

Inzamam is the second highest impact Pakistani batsman after Younis Khan (because of the latter's phenomenal performances in 2015–16). In conventional terms, both Younis Khan (54) and Javed Miandad (53) have higher batting averages than Inzamam (50). But it wasn't just the difference in the number of SDs or Inzamam's big-match quality that made his impact higher.

He also absorbed the most amount of pressure in Pakistan's Test history after Younis Khan and Azhar Ali (minimum fifty Tests).

He built the most partnerships in Pakistan's Test history. Interestingly, his propensity to get his partner run out (often in delightfully ludicrous ways) more than any other contemporary batsman did not come in the way of this quality.

He has the third highest Strike Rate Impact (higher strike rate than match standard in winning Tests) after Wasim Akram and Misbah-ul-Haq.

AC: For someone who did not really rotate strike, he had this uncanny ability of hitting fours off good balls. With him, you always kept the field slightly deep because you knew he was not going to run. But even then, he managed to pierce the gap, which is not an easy thing to do when the fielders are standing deeper. If given a choice between rotating strike or scoring boundaries, even if they resulted in a similar number of runs, you would always choose boundaries because that has the additional effect of deflating the opposition. That forces the fielding team to do something else and releases the pressure off your non-striker as well. This is what Inzamam did so well, and this, in fact, explains why his Partnership Building Impact is so high.

He had the fourth lowest failure rate (when a batsman is unable to register an impact of 1, it suggests that he could not do the job of even one player) among Pakistani Test batsmen, after Azhar Ali, Mohammad Yousuf and Younis Khan.

Inzamam dominated right through his career as evidenced below.

Pakistan vs Australia, Karachi, 1994. *Australia had not won in Pakistan for thirty-five years. Pakistan had never lost at National Stadium, Karachi, not for thirty-nine years. Nor had they ever chased down a total like 314 to win in the fourth innings. And yet, this moment was upon both sides – chasing this highly improbable total, Pakistan were 258 for 9. Inzamam was joined by Mushtaq Ahmed. All was forgotten then, Saeed Anwar's twin fifties (85 and 77) in the match, Michael Bevan's impressive Test debut of 82, Steve Waugh's high-octane 73, David Boon's unbeaten century in the* *second innings, the bowling of Wasim Akram, Waqar Younis, Mushtaq Ahmed, Shane Warne and Glenn McGrath, all consigned to the past. Twenty-four-year-old Inzamam, who had come in at 179 for 6 (which inevitably became 184 for 7), took charge and along with an inspired Mushtaq Ahmed (who made 20), wrapped up the match in 8.1 overs in a pulsating finish that saw the rapidly swelling crowd chant 'Allah-o-Akbar'. This was just the first Test of a potentially classic series. However, in a successful attempt to sit on the lead, Pakistan prepared two featherbeds, which led to drawn matches (even though Pakistan had some anxious moments in the second Test).*

AC: What set Inzamam apart as a batsman is that he had a lot of time. Even though he was not very flexible, he always had more time than the others. Unlike A.B. de Villiers, who moved a lot in the crease to get into the right place, Inzamam was in position with minimal movements, so was rarely off balance – a quality that I have perhaps only seen in Rohit Sharma since then. Batsmen like him have the option of playing on the back foot or front foot equally, so the short and full ball can both be handled without any commitment. This is what gives the impression that they have a lot of time to play the ball.

***Pakistan vs Zimbabwe, Harare, 1995**. It was 1–1 in the series when the final Test began against a Zimbabwe side hard to beat at home. Inzamam made 101 in Pakistan's 231 against a rampant Heath Streak. Zimbabwe got a slight lead and Pakistan were 88 for 3, so the match was dead even. But Inzamam's stabilizing 83 (out of 250) took the match away for a second time. Pakistan set Zimbabwe a target of 239 and won comfortably on a pitch not so easy to survive on.*

***Pakistan vs England, Manchester, 2001**. In an oddly constructed two-Test series, England had won the first Test by an innings. Pakistan were 39 for 2 in this match, with Andy Caddick and Darren Gough on fire. Inzamam and Anwar counter-attacked, but another mini-collapse later, it was 92 for 4. Then, along with Younis Khan (65), Inzamam (114) guided the team through an exciting first day that yielded 370 runs and set the tone for a classic Test match that went back and forth. Inzamam's 85* *was the highest innings score in the second innings too, which would enable Pakistan to set England a target of 370 and win by over a hundred runs, to draw the series 1–1.*

> **AC:** For an Asian batsman, he played swing remarkably well. He would play the second line superbly – the assumed line where the ball is going to end. Better players of swing will always play the second line, and Inzamam was absolutely outstanding at this. Where he acquired that ability, I don't know, but he was brilliant at it. He was very different from any other Asian batsman I have seen, in terms of playing late and in the second line.

Pakistan vs New Zealand, Wellington, 2003. *Trailing 0–1 in a two-Test series, Pakistan were crawling back after the first half of the second Test, 170 behind. Then Shoaib Akhtar changed everything with a scintillating burst – his 6 for 30 knocked out New Zealand for 103 and set Pakistan a not-easy 274 to win. But Pakistan batted superbly. Inzamam walked out at 156 for 3, with an assured Yousuf Youhana at the crease. They took it home brilliantly from there, fighting rain, cold, wind and seam – Youhana unbeaten on 88 and Inzamam on 72. Interestingly, this is the only series-defining performance in Shoaib Akhtar's and Yousuf Youhana's (Mohammad Yousuf's) careers.*

Pakistan vs West Indies, Kingston, 2005. *Trailing 0–1 in a two-Test series, Pakistan were precarious at 43 for 2 when Inzamam came in and made a fifty, which along with Younis Khan's century and a few other contributions, took them to a seemingly safe 374. But West Indies hit back hard with a consummate 153 from Lara, and took a 30-run lead. Then, after a good start, Pakistan had a mini-collapse when Inzamam came out at 119 for 3. With Younis Khan and Shahid Afridi (43 each), Inzamam proceeded to comprehensively take the match away from West Indies. He was unbeaten with 117 when the innings ended. Despite the seemingly achievable 280-run target, the fight had left West Indies, and they collapsed for 143, as the somewhat unlikely pair of Shabbir Ahmed and Danish Kaneria finished them off.*

These were five of Inzamam's eight SDs. It's not like he didn't perform otherwise too.

Pakistan vs New Zealand, Hamilton, 1993. *A humdinger in a single Test series that had Pakistan under the pump – a deficit of 48 in the first innings, and 25 for 4 in the second innings when Inzamam took guard. Soon it was 39 for 5, and Rashid Latif joined Inzamam. Together, they got Pakistan out of the toughest pressure situation in their Test history, given what followed. Latif stayed for more than an hour and a half, grinding out 33 while Inzamam stayed an hour longer when he was finally dismissed for 75 with the team total at 158. Pakistan had 127 runs to play with as New Zealand came out to bat. The Wasim-and-Waqar show ensured they only needed 94. Inzamam was the highest impact player in the match by a mile, but Wasim Akram got the Man of the Match award.*

Pakistan vs West Indies, Antigua, 1993. *Facing West Indies' 438, Pakistan were 108 for 4 when Inzamam walked in. And it was 323 for 9 when he walked out five hours later with 123. It saved the match and prevented a clean sweep by West Indies.*

Pakistan vs England, Lord's, 1996. *It was 12 for 2 when Inzamam walked in to bat and 267 for 7 when he was bowled, after 148 of the most impressive runs that summer, at the time his highest Test score. It helped Pakistan get a lead, and a buoyed Pakistani batting, with another 70 from Inzamam, set England a highly unlikely 408, which they predictably failed to get close to. Waqar Younis got the Man of the Match award but Inzamam was higher impact than him.*

A giant from any angle

Inzamam's finest batting patch coincided with the first six years of the new millennium. He was comfortably the highest impact batsman in the world then (2000–05), followed by Rahul Dravid, Graham Thorpe, Younis Khan and Matthew Hayden. Pakistan won nine series in that period, drew five and lost eight. Inzamam got five of his eight career SDs in this period. But it wasn't just that.

Inzamam's Runs Tally and Partnership Building Impact was

amongst the highest in the world along with Hayden in this period. He also had the highest Pressure and Strike Rate Impact amongst the twenty highest impact batsmen of that period. Even though Inzamam had a marginally higher failure rate than Kallis, Jayawardene, Hayden and Lara, by and large he was indestructible (even if his team wasn't).

Pakistan vs Bangladesh, Multan, 2003. *A low-scoring Test match appeared to have reached its end, a historic Bangladesh win was beckoning and Pakistan was at 132 for 6 chasing 261 for victory. Inzamam played one of his classic innings, an unbeaten 138 – shepherding the tail-enders, farming the strike and scoring the runs, to take Pakistan to a famous 1-wicket win.*

AC: Another thing that set him apart was his ability to sweep. I have seen this from very close, at short leg. I have never seen anyone sweep Anil Kumble with that much authority. He could sweep fine, full or square, and he was never cramped, which is very unusual.

Whenever exercises are done on the greatest batsmen of the last two or three decades, Inzamam is just another name added to a list that includes Brian Lara, Sachin Tendulkar, Steve Waugh, Ricky Ponting, Matthew Hayden, Jacques Kallis, Kumar Sangakkara, Mahela Jayawardene, Shivnarine Chanderpaul, Rahul Dravid, Graeme Smith, Mohammad Yousuf, Younis Khan, A.B. de Villiers and Hashim Amla.

It is sad that Inzamam is seen as just another big-scoring batsman, because on our system, in this mindset, only two batsmen come up with higher impact than Inzamam from this list: Younis Khan and Brian Lara.

But this one's about Inzamam-ul-Haq and what a giant he has been, not just for Pakistan cricket, but also the game in general, in so many respects.

AC: It is interesting that India is known as a batting country, but the highest impact batsmen of Asia (Younis and Inzamam) do not come from there. While Pakistan, which is known for its fearsome bowling, did not produce the highest impact bowler (it is Muralitharan, then Kumble). I guess that's because the powerful batsmen in India's line-up kept sharing impact, and the same with Pakistan's bowling – they had so many wicket-taking bowlers?

JV: Absolutely right. And also because these two batsmen (Younis and Inzamam) absorbed a lot of pressure and bore a lot of responsibility, which is also why they throughly deserve this particular ranking.

JV

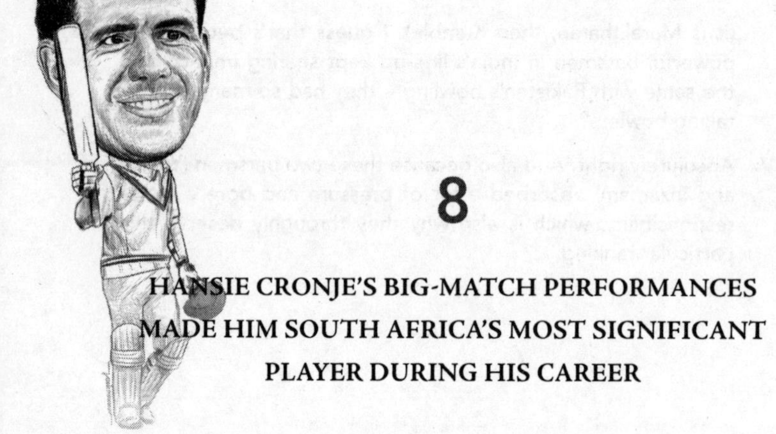

8

HANSIE CRONJE'S BIG-MATCH PERFORMANCES MADE HIM SOUTH AFRICA'S MOST SIGNIFICANT PLAYER DURING HIS CAREER

This story had a well-known and tragic ending – a public confession of match fixing, disgrace and an untimely death at the age of thirty-two. Hansie Cronje's place in cricket is acutely identified with infamy.

Our system, unprejudiced by reputations, identifies him as a high impact player. The thing is, even when he was at his peak, his real value as a player had never entirely been understood. Sure, he was hailed as an influential captain, but not as a batsman. His Test batting average of 36.41 suggested that he was mediocre, his ODI batting average of 38.64 that he was pretty good, but not much more. And his bowling was deemed a support act in both formats.

No one seemed to notice how he influenced South Africa's cricket history.

Third Test, South Africa vs India, Port Elizabeth, 1992. *This was South Africa's first full series after readmission. The series was still at 0–0. South Africa won the toss, put India in and knocked them over for 212. Captain Kepler Wessels was out before he could score and, at 0 for 1, Cronje walked in, playing his third Test, batting at No. 3 for the first time. A 117-run partnership with Andrew Hudson promised much, but a collapse saw the Proteas teetering at 185 for 6. Twenty-three-year-old*

Cronje batted for almost nine hours and was last out for 135, as South Africa took a decisive 63-run lead (India were 31 for 6 in the second innings before Kapil Dev's century made it relatively respectable), and won by 9 wickets. This was the only result match of the four-match Test series, so Cronje had an SD in his very first full series.

In his very next Test series in Sri Lanka (very hard to beat at home even then), Cronje again top-scored with a century from No. 3 as South Africa won by an innings, in the only decisive Test of the series. An SD in his second Test series too. Against New Zealand in 1994–95, with the series at 1–1, in the deciding Test, Cronje top-scored with a century and helped his team win the series 2–1.

So, Cronje had three SDs in his first six Test series, which is jaw-dropping. But his batting average of 37 in those nineteen Tests did not let any of this on.

South Africa's rise in world cricket

Those six series were also South Africa's first after their readmission. The early wins set the tone for the country's glorious run in Tests since. As for Cronje, he did it again soon:

Third Test, South Africa vs Pakistan, Port Elizabeth, 1998. *The deciding Test with South Africa 0–1 down. On a difficult pitch where Pakistan would muster only 106 and 134, Cronje walked in at 81 for 4 and top-scored with 85 to put South Africa decisively ahead in the game, and thus, along with his bowlers, accomplish a 1–1 series result.*

South Africa firmly established themselves as the second-best side in world cricket after Australia (in both Tests and ODIs) by the end of the millennium. It was stunning, given their lack of international exposure. Cronje played a major role in this rise. In fact, South Africa's win/loss ratios in both Tests and ODIs were better than Australia's in the 1990s.

Importantly, this ascent also included conquering the subcontinent. South Africa won in Pakistan in 1997, and though Cronje failed to click solely as a batsman, he made up for it with his all-round efforts. In the deciding Test in Faisalabad, Cronje scored 30 runs (in a low-scoring game) and picked up the wickets of the two Pakistani top scorers within a space of five runs. He didn't produce an SD but played an important support role in the series win.

There was India – unbeaten at home for over a decade. And then, this happened.

First Test, India vs South Africa, Mumbai, 2000. *India won the toss, batted first, but were dismissed for 225 on the first day, with the Proteas' attack sharing wickets; Cronje got 2 middle-order wickets too. South Africa were dismissed for 176 – a seemingly substantial lead for India on that wicket. Shaun Pollock then devastated India; Cronje got 3 wickets too, including the prized wicket of Tendulkar. South Africa chased 163 and won by 4 wickets; Cronje's 13 in about an hour's batting calmed things down for a while, even though his bowling contributed much more in this match. It was a very significant loss for India, as the momentum shifted dramatically. India lost the next Test by an innings, and were vanquished for the first time in a home series in over a decade. To date, Cronje remains the only South African captain to win a series in India.*

Cronje's place in history

During the course of his career (which ended in March 2000), Cronje was the third highest impact Test player for South Africa after Allan Donald and Shaun Pollock. And the third highest impact ODI player, after Pollock and Lance Klusener. In ODIs, Cronje had impact as a bowler as well, and was an all-rounder himself. In Tests, he was more than half a bowler and had some notable moments to show (as recounted above).

Most significantly, Cronje got more SDs than any other South African in both formats in that period. His five SDs as a Test player constituted four purely as a batsman, twice that of the next best (Gary Kirsten). Cronje's tally of six SDs as an ODI player was twice that of Shaun Pollock (though Kirsten again got four, all as batsman).

As captain, Cronje's significance is inarguable. On the Impact Index scale (which is admittedly limited when it comes to judging captains), Cronje comes up as the second highest impact Test captain ever after Graeme Smith, as also in ODIs, after Clive Lloyd.

To date, Cronje is also the fifth highest impact South Africa Test batsman (minimum fifty Tests) after A.B. de Villiers, Graeme Smith, Jacques Kallis and Gary Kirsten. Forget them, even the four batsmen after him on this list – Daryl Cullinan, Hashim Amla, Herschelle Gibbs and Ashwell Prince – all have higher averages than Cronje.

In ODI cricket, where Cronje was a genuine all-rounder, he is the fourth highest impact South African player ever, after Jacques Kallis, A.B. de Villiers and Shaun Pollock.

All of this is because of his propensity to produce the big performances when his team needed it the most, regardless of the opponent, place or format.

The punishment Cronje received, both earthly and otherwise, more than fit the grave crime of match fixing. But it is only fair then that his reputation also matches what he did in the middle as a player for South African cricket during its crucial readmission phase.

If anything, this only amplifies the tragedy.

AC: Howsoever ironic it may sound, Hansie Cronje is a classic case of doing the right thing at the right time. Otherwise, he was not a consistent big-score batsman or 5-wicket bowler. He scored only 6 centuries, took only 43 wickets in 68 Tests, and that is simply not enough to make people sit up and take notice. He would contribute in most games that he played but not with performances that were big enough to draw attention. Our memories and conventional numbers are aligned to remember the really big (defined by the number of runs and wickets) performances and, therefore, consistent, medium-sized performances slip under the radar.

The other thing that might have gone against Cronje was the fact that his batting neither gave the impression of Kallis's solidity nor Gibbs's flair. Nor was his bowling style eye-catching, for his biggest strength was luring batsmen into false strokes, bowling gentle outswingers along the fifth stump line all day. Surprisingly, he wasn't as slow as he looked – his pace didn't allow batsmen to treat him as a release bowler.

The one thing that no one contests is Cronje's impact as skipper. He was hugely respected (something he took unfair advantage of) within the team and was able to rally his troops against some of the toughest opponents.

Having said all that, I feel a bit uncomfortable about this piece glorifying him for his cricketing deeds. I am of the opinion that the records of match fixers should be expunged.

JV: The point of this book is not to glorify anybody. We are presenting facts that conventional statistics failed to acknowledge or understand. If Cronje did not indulge in match fixing and retired as this player, it would make for a very important story, wouldn't it? The cricket discussed here was clearly not fixed. As far as punishing him for match fixing goes, he paid for his crime with a lifelong ban, which should be enough, shouldn't it? If a writer of excellent books commits a murder, he should absolutely be punished for it, but why should his books go out of print? Some people may choose not to read them, but others may wish to separate the work from the person. That's all this piece seeks to do.

JV/SS

9

NEIL HARVEY AVERAGED BARELY 48 BUT IS THE THIRD HIGHEST IMPACT AUSTRALIAN TEST BATSMAN EVER

Neil Harvey averaged 48.41 in seventy-nine Tests with 21 centuries and a highest score of just 205, and yet, he is the third highest impact Australian Test batsman of all time (minimum fifty Tests) after Don Bradman and Greg Chappell.

The majority of his Test career played out in the 1950s (1948 to 1963, to be exact), which is still the lowest-scoring decade after the First World War. Like Peter May, who also played in the same period for England, Harvey scored a very high proportion of runs for his team, in fact, even more than May. In all of Test history, only Bradman and Jack Hobbs scored a higher proportion of runs than he did (minimum 50 Tests) – a stunning fact for someone who averaged less than 50.

Vs South Africa, Brisbane/Sydney, 1952–53. *In the opening Test, Harvey produced 109 out of Australia's 280 and 52 out of 277 as Australia prevailed by 96 runs. In the third Test, responding to South Africa's 173, Australia were 49 for 2 when Harvey walked in. It was 374 for 7 when he walked out, with 190 dominating runs, which pretty much decided the match. Thus Harvey was the highest impact player in both the matches Australia won in a 2–2 series.*

Harvey's batting failure rate of just 38 per cent is the lowest in Australian Test history after Bradman, David Warner, Doug Walters and Ian Redpath (minimum fifty Tests). He had three series-defining performances in his career, the first two (against South Africa in 1952–53, West Indies in 1955) directly the result of his consistency, when he notched up two high-impact performances in each series. The last one was against England in 1962–63:

Vs England, Sydney, 1963. *Down 0–1 in the series and responding to England's 279, Australia were 14 for 1 when Harvey walked out to join Bob Simpson. Together, they took Australia to safety, then a position of dominance, with a 160-run stand, the biggest in the match. Simpson made 91, Harvey 64, and Barry Shepherd's 71 further helped Australia to a lead. Then, it was the Davidson–McKenzie show as they demolished England for 104, and a comfortable 8-wicket win secured. This levelled the series, and as it happened, 1–1 was the final series score as well.*

All this make Harvey Australia's highest impact batsman by a distance in the post-Bradman period when Australia reasserted themselves and gradually became the world's best team again (from 1953 to 1958, England was the main stumbling block). During this period, Neil Harvey led the way with his consistency and his ability to score from the crucial No. 3 position in any kind of condition.

Harvey played in eighteen Test series for his country; Australia won thirteen of those, lost three (all to England, between 1953 and 1956) and drew just two – a stunning record.

AC: Test Cricket is perhaps the only sport where much of the competition happens bilaterally between countries rather than as multi-nation tournaments. The result of the series should generally be what matters the most in a player's career, but that is rarely the case. The focus generally is on individuals, how many runs have been scored, centuries and so on. The focus is never on how many series have been won or lost. We don't even do that for captains; instead of calculating how many series have been won under his captaincy, we look at how many Test matches have been won. Someone may have won more Tests as captain but not as many series, which is revealing. It is ironic that we belittle international engagements in this manner. If we're just going to remember aggregates of a player at the end of his career, what is the point of having series?

JV

10

RICHIE RICHARDSON'S IMPACT IN TEST HISTORY WAS ALMOST AS MUCH AS VIV RICHARDS'S

Viv Richards averaged 50.23 in 121 Tests while Richie Richardson averaged 44.39 in eighty-six Tests. How did our system arrive at this then?

The answer lies in two things: the dynamics of an all-time great side where players tend to share impact, and the bigger opportunities (and challenges) that being at No. 3 brings. Richardson replaced Richards at No. 3 in the last year of Clive Lloyd's captaincy. Richards went down to No. 4 and later, even No. 5, which reduced his impact.

Richards became captain of West Indies in 1985 and, from then on, West Indies would remain the world's best Test team till mid-1995, when Australia triumphed in a classic contest. That's a whole decade of dominance. And Viv Richards would not even be there post-1991.

In fact, from 1985 until the end of his career in August 1995, Richardson was West Indies' highest impact batsman, and the second highest batsman in the world after, curiously, Mark Taylor (we'll come to that too). This in turn means that Richardson was the highest impact batsman for West Indies longer than Richards was.

A lot of Richards's legend has to do with his ODI exploits – he remains the highest impact ODI player of all time – and the characteristic swagger with which he played his many dominating innings.

Richardson contributed substantially in many innings but never played the sort of high-scoring innings that Richards did. In fact, Richardson never even scored a double-century in his career. Nor did he use the opportunities to score heavily against weaker teams (which explains his batting average).

Still, Richardson scored a higher proportion of runs than Richards between 1985 and 1995 (in which he played seventy-five Tests; Richards forty-eight), was marginally more consistent than him (with just a 39 per cent failure rate), and had one SD more than him (in his entire career, Richards had one SD more than Richardson though).

Series winners

Vs India, 1989: *West Indies won a home series against India 3–0, who were not abject travellers at the time. They'd in fact beaten England at home in their last overseas assignment, though almost three years had passed since then. In that period, they had actually drawn with West Indies in India, albeit on turning tracks.*

After the first Test had been rained off, in the second Test at Bridgetown, thanks to Sanjay Manjrekar's 108, India made 321. Gordon Greenidge (117) and Richardson (93) gave West Indies the foundation to reach 377. An outstanding 107 by Ravi Shastri and 50 by wicketkeeper Kiran More helped an otherwise ordinary Indian batting to compile 251. Greenidge went for 6 as West Indies chased 196, but Des Haynes (112 not out) and Richardson (59) pretty much finished off the match.

At Port-of-Spain, Gus Logie and Richardson scored the most runs for West Indies, but it was Malcolm Marshall's show as he took 11 wickets to destroy the Indian batting.

In the final Test at Kingston, from a precarious position of 32 for 2, Richardson produced 156 and Richards 110 to effectively end India's fight. Richardson was the Man of the Series.

Vs Pakistan, 1990: *West Indies were 0–1 down when the second Test began at Faisalabad. In conditions offering movement in the air and off the pitch, Pakistan made just 170 in the first innings. Wasim and Waqar* *then wrecked West Indies for 195; Richardson top-scored with 44. In the second innings, from 145 for 4, Pakistan crashed to 146 for 9, as Marshall took 4 wickets in 13 balls. Chasing 130, West Indies were 34 for 3 at one stage. Inexplicably, against the run of play, Richardson crashed 70 off 86 balls and finished off the game to level the series. Despite a stunning performance by Carl Hooper in the last Test, the match ended in a draw. The series thus ended 1–1 against the second-best side of that period in their backyard.*

Vs Australia, 1993: *When the fifth Test began at Perth, the series was at 1–1. Curtly Ambrose destroyed Australia for 119. And when Haynes retired hurt with the score at 34, there was everything at stake. Richardson (47) joined Phil Simmons (80) and put West Indies almost at par with Australia by the time their partnership ended. That foundation pretty much decided the match, as West Indies went on to win by an innings.*

Of course, Richardson was aided by the bowling – Curtly Ambrose, Courtney Walsh and Ian Bishop among others – and the presence of Richards and Haynes (both had almost the same impact post-1984) and later Lara.

It is also easy to forget Richardson's contribution to West Indian cricket, given those who had just come before him. Even now, the legendary West Indian team is seen as the one Lloyd harnessed, not the ones Richards and Richardson led. It is easy to forget that Lloyd was captain of the best team in the world for the first eight years only. Thereafter, Richards was captain for seven years (during which period Richardson was the star batsman) and then Richardson was captain for four years.

Of course, in a side like that, with batsmen like Greenidge, Haynes and Lloyd as their teammates, both Richards and Richardson shared their impact but it is a measure of Richards's greatness that he was actually more consistent down the order than he had been at No. 3, and had a slightly higher impact playing there than he had before.

Given Richards's longevity though, his impact is only marginally higher than Richardson's. And that, in itself, is quite a story.

AC: Clive Lloyd's era was built around four fast bowlers and a barrage of bouncers. The one-bouncer-an-over rule was put in place in 1991 and there were attempts to prepare pitches to combat it too. But, undoubtedly, it is remarkable that the West Indies stayed on top for so long.

This story is particularly interesting for what it tells you: that memory can mislead. Impressions are made from what we hear and see, like the documentary *Fire in Babylon*, but that is not the entire story. Sure, Clive Lloyd set the template for what was to follow, but Richards's captaincy is perhaps not remembered as much as it should be. True of Richardson as player and captain too: he is as much a part of that era as anyone.

11

IAN BISHOP WAS A HIGHER IMPACT BOWLER THAN AMBROSE AND WALSH

His conventional numbers – 161 wickets in 43 Tests at 24 apiece – suggest a very good bowler. But Impact Index finds that he achieved greatness that these figures camouflaged rather than revealed.

Remarkably, he did this despite a career beset with injury. First, at twenty-three, after playing just eleven Tests. Then, again at twenty-five, just seven Tests later. He came back strongly two years later and lasted another three years, playing his last Test at the age of thirty. Everyone could tell that a career that promised greatness had been cut short, but no one fully gauged what he achieved anyway.

Bishop is the third highest impact bowler in West Indian Test history.

Surreal, yes. A full ten West Indian bowlers have a higher aggregate of wickets than Ian Bishop. Four of them have a better bowling average. Three of them have a better strike rate.

Despite this, Ian Bishop is the third highest impact bowler in the history of West Indies Test cricket (minimum thirty Tests), coming in after Malcolm Marshall and Andy Roberts – above the likes of his contemporaries Ambrose and Walsh and even the fabled Michael Holding and Joel Garner.

There is one, straightforward reason for this: Bishop was a serious big-match player. He has three series-defining performances in just forty-three matches. This is what gives him a greater impact than bowlers like Ambrose or Holding, who did better than him in most other bowling impact parameters, and, overall, were undoubtedly better bowlers.

In fact, three out of Bishop's four highest impact bowling performances in a match context are series-defining performances, which is quite a rarity. It suggests he had a rare sense of occasion.

Series winners

Vs England at home, 1990: *The Wisden Trophy (1989–90) was at stake. With the series tied at 1–1 after the first four Tests, it all came down to the fifth and final Test at St. John's, Antigua.*

Ian Bishop, playing only in his eighth Test, ran through the English middle and lower order (5–84). The visitors, from 167 for 3, collapsed to 260 all out. Gordon Greenidge and Desmond Haynes put together a mammoth opening stand of 298 which was largely responsible for West Indies' first innings score of 446. Then, Bishop picked up three crucial wickets in the second innings (3–36) to become the highest impact bowler in the match. West Indies thrashed England by an innings and 32 runs to win the series 2–1.

Vs Australia in Australia, 1993: *After the West Indies accomplished a thrilling 1-run victory over the hosts which levelled the series at 1–1, the Frank Worrell Trophy (1992–93) was at stake in the fifth and final Test at the WACA. Allan Border's decision to bat first spelt doom for the home side.*

Bishop first got rid of Justin Langer and Steve Waugh before Ambrose ran through the side, skittling them out for 119. Bishop shared the new ball with Ambrose and kept the batsmen on a tight leash. West Indies took a significant lead after posting 322 in their first innings.

Then Bishop and Ambrose reversed roles, as the former terrorized the Australian batsmen with his pace and picked up 6–40, cleaning up the hosts for 178, giving the West Indies victory by an innings and 25 runs and with it the series 2–1. Ambrose had a higher impact in the match and the series, but Bishop's contribution was immense too – he was the second highest impact player in the match.

Vs India at home, 1997: *After draws at Kingston and Port-of-Spain, India and West Indies headed to Barbados for the third Test of the five-Test series. Good knocks from Dravid and Tendulkar had helped India take a slender 21-run lead after West Indies had posted 298 in their first innings. Bishop was the most economical of the West Indian bowlers and returned with figures of 3 for 70 off his 28 overs (including the wickets of Dravid and Tendulkar). The Indian pacers bowled out the home team for 140 in the second innings. India needed a mere 120 to win on a day that remains the biggest nightmare of their careers for all Indians who played that day. Bishop picked up 4 for 22 in 12 overs (including Tendulkar, at his peak as a player then, for the second time in the match) and along with Ambrose and Franklyn Rose, cleaned up India for a paltry 81, giving West Indies a 38-run victory. The remaining two Tests ended in draws and the West Indies took the series 1–0.*

Bishop was the sixth highest impact bowler in the world during his career (minimum twenty Tests), after Shane Warne, Craig McDermott, Allan Donald, Wasim Akram and Anil Kumble.

He was also the highest impact bowler in the Caribbean (even ahead of Ambrose) during the period his career ran.

It is to Ian Bishop's credit that he beset the huge disappointment of a truncated career as a player by becoming one of the game's finest commentators, known for his balance and reason.

Perhaps these are the qualities that enabled him to perform at his best when his team needed it the most.

AC: I've spoken to people who have seen Ian Bishop before the injury and after it. They said he was quite simply the fastest bowler they had ever faced before his injury happened. And very few have had to go through what he did. He had to change his action so much that he came back as a different bowler. So, there are actually two Ian Bishops who have played international cricket. It was like learning a new language, building from scratch. Others who had back injuries like his just petered away or became trundlers. L. Balaji is a good example; after his injury, the Balaji we saw in Pakistan in 2004 disappeared as if he did not exist. But Bishop came back, and that too as a force – if not the same force. It's a what-could-have-been career that promised so much.

As far as SDs go, it is slightly easier for bowlers to raise their game to the next level, simply because they are allowed to fail. If one spell doesn't work, they can still come back and produce a match-changing spell later, in the next session. With a batsman, not so – their entire life depends on one mistake. So, when the stakes are higher, most batsmen tend to play percentage cricket because they know they cannot afford to make even one mistake. Bowlers also have the added advantage of people around them telling them that things are going wrong, and sometimes there is an opportunity to get them going right in the same game, same innings, maybe even the same spell.

12

THE SECOND HIGHEST IMPACT ENGLISH BOWLER IN TEST HISTORY: DARREN GOUGH

Eleven Englishmen have taken more wickets, six amongst these have a better bowling average. Tales of the greatness of several others in their 139-year-old Test cricket history have been extensively documented.

Yet, Darren Gough emerges as the second highest impact English bowler (minimum fifty Tests), only after Fred Trueman (who is even conventionally considered England's finest bowler by many).

This also means that Gough is the highest impact English bowler in the last fifty years.

He registered three series-defining performances in fifty-eight Tests. In English cricket history, only six bowlers have three or more SD performances – Graeme Swann, Darren Gough, Fred Trueman, Ian Botham, Bobby Peel and Derek Underwood (the latter three have four each).

What is special about Gough is his matches to SD ratio. He also has the highest value for his SDs amongst all English bowlers in Test cricket, which basically means not only did he produce the big-match performances most frequently but he was also consistent in all the series he registered an SD in.

Alec Bedser was a great bowler, with awe-inspiring consistency, but he did not have a single SD in his remarkable career, which is surprising, considering how many matches England won during his run. John Snow did not have any either. Jimmy Anderson is a modern-day hero with the most Test wickets by an Englishman. But he has just one SD in his career – in that too he needed the support of his batting.

England hadn't had a great run in Test cricket for two decades. At the end of the 1990s, they even lost to Sri Lanka and New Zealand at home, to complete a sorry picture that threatened a perpetual downhill slide. Gough was the man to change it.

Vs South Africa, 1998, Leeds: *The series was tantalizingly poised at 1–1. A memorable 116 from Mark Butcher helped the hosts post 230 after Mike Atherton elected to bat. Gough picked up 3 crucial wickets in the first innings to bowl out South Africa for 252. Pollock and Donald's fifers wrapped England up for 240 in the second, setting the visitors 219 for victory. But Gough ran through the top order reducing South Africa to 27 for 5 before Jonty Rhodes and Brian McMillan fought back with a century stand. Gough claimed the prized scalp of Rhodes – the highest scorer of the innings and the seventh wicket to fall, as South Africa fell short by 23 runs. Gough returned with figures of 6 for 42 off 23 overs in the second innings.*

England won 2–1. Gough registered his first SD.

Defeats in Australia and South Africa – both very strong sides, especially in their own backyards – set England back. But they bounced back.

Between May 2000 and March 2001, England won four series on the trot, including two significant away series, making a fair bit of history along the way.

It began at home with Zimbabwe, not a pushover side: if anything, it was the strongest Zimbabwe line-up in history. England won the two-Test series 1–0, with Gough as the second highest impact bowler in the series (after Ed Giddens).

Then came West Indies. England had not beaten them since 1969. In these thirty-one years, England had lost ten series against them and drawn three. A humiliating innings defeat began England's campaign that summer.

Vs West Indies, 2000, Lord's: *Things began badly in the second Test too. Even though England restricted West Indies to 267 in the first innings, with Gough picking up 4 wickets (including those of Lara, Chanderpaul and Adams), the hosts could only muster 134. Andy Caddick and Gough destroyed the West Indies top order between them and then Dominic Cork finished them off. West Indies were dismissed for 54 and the match turned on its head. England were set 188 for victory and when Gough came to the middle in his battle gear, they were 160 for 8. He made 4 off 19 balls in forty-four tense minutes, while Cork's 33 decided the issue, as their unbroken 31-run stand finished off the match.*

The momentum shift was palpable. After a hard-fought draw, the focus shifted to the penultimate Test.

Vs West Indies, 2000, Leeds: *Gough, Craig White and Cork bundled the West Indies out for 172 in the fourth Test. England then managed to take a 100-run first-innings lead. With everything to play for, Gough ran through the top order in the second innings, reducing West Indies to 21 for 4 (picking up all 4 wickets) before Caddick's fifer knocked them over for 61, giving England an innings victory and, with it, the series.*

This second batting humiliation in three Tests was too much for West Indies, and they capitulated in the last Test as well, giving England a historic 3–1 victory.

Darren Gough was the highest impact bowler (and player) of the series.

AC: We must remember that West Indies cricket was on a decline. Although Gough was absolutely sensational in this series, his ascendancy as a bowler perhaps came against a mediocre West Indies team. It was a historic win, sure, and taking nothing away from England's and Gough's performance, the fact is that it was achieved against a team which was not what it had once been.

Gough's propensity to help his team come back from behind would become a famous recurring theme that winter.

Vs Pakistan, 2000: *After being 0–1 down, England came back again to win the series 2–1. Graham Thorpe and Ashley Giles were the two big English stars of that series, but Gough, as the second highest impact bowler, was not far behind. England won after thirty-nine years in Pakistan – another historic moment.*

In February–March 2001, the season climaxed with the last away series in the set – perhaps the most challenging of all, in Sri Lanka. On cue, England lost the first Test by an innings.

Vs Sri Lanka 2001, Kandy: *Gough and Caddick picked up 4 wickets each in the second Test to bowl out Sri Lanka for 297. Led by captain Nasser Hussain's century, England went ahead. Gough, coming in at No. 11, remained unbeaten on 10 and spent fifty-seven minutes at the crease to put together a useful 41-run partnership with Robert Croft to help England post 387 in the first innings and take a lead that now looked substantial. And Gough was not done yet. He rattled the Sri Lankan top order, accounting for Marvan Atapattu and Aravinda de Silva, and later broke a threatening partnership between Chaminda Vaas and Kumar Dharmasena, dismissing the latter for 54, to restrict the hosts to 250. Chasing 161, England scraped through by 3 wickets.*

Gough was England's highest impact player. The series had been set up.

Gough again picked up crucial top-order wickets in the third and final Test in Colombo. England made heavy weather of a 74-run chase to eventually win by four wickets and thereby take the series 2–1. Gough was the highest impact bowler and the second highest impact English player of the series (after Thorpe).

AC: What is striking about Darren Gough is how un-English he was. Like all English bowlers, he could swing the ball – good outswing at a rapid pace – but what made him special was his ability to make the old ball talk. He could reverse-swing and bowl those lethal yorkers. His in-dippers would trap the opposition batsman stuck at the crease. Thus, his performances overseas, especially in the subcontinent were phenomenal.

> It was rare for an English bowler to be as effective with the old ball as he was with the new. Also, because of this gift of reversing the old ball, Gough was very good at polishing off the tail. He also had this ability to pick two or three quick wickets with his reverse swing and change the complexion of a match in a spell.
>
> **NN:** Only three English bowlers were better than him at finishing off the tail (minimum fifty matches): Alec Bedser, Fred Trueman and Graeme Swann.

Two of Gough's SDs were momentum-changing acts, a rarity in Test cricket history.

This period (May 2000 to March 2001), when Darren Gough was the highest impact pace bowler (minimum eight Tests) was clearly the foundation for the change that would come to English cricket in later years, and for that it is significant.

Apart from his big-match prowess, Gough also had two other qualities which make him such a high impact bowler.

Gough was a remarkably consistent wicket taker. In terms of only wicket taking, Gough is the fourth highest impact English bowler (minimum fifty Tests), after Bedser, Trueman and Swann.

This is apparent from Gough's conventionally calculated strike rate as well: he took a wicket every 51.6 balls. Fred Trueman is the only Englishman who has a higher strike rate than him (49.4). In those 139 years of Test cricket, only nine bowlers around the world have a better strike rate.

For such a wicket-taking bowler, a failure rate of 25 per cent is remarkable. It means that, in forty-four of the fifty-eight Tests he played, he at least did the job of roughly one player in the side. In fact, for a minimum of fifty Tests and 100 Test wickets, Gough is the fourth most consistent bowler for England – behind only Alec Bedser, Fred Trueman and Bob Willis (Jim Laker and John Snow were very consistent too, though they just missed playing fifty Tests).

When it comes right down to it, it is the edge Gough brought to an English side that began its famous ascendancy that is his biggest contribution to English cricket.

Apart from being the highest impact English bowler (minimum forty Tests) during the time his career ran (1994–2003), Gough was also the third highest impact pace bowler in the world in that period, after McGrath and Donald. Muralitharan, Kumble and Warne were the only bowlers higher impact than them then.

AC: He was also a hit-the-deck-hard type of a bowler, so I am not surprised that he has a good record in Australia on those hard pitches where he averages around 27 per wicket. I remember the famous hat-trick he took in Sydney in 1999.

NN: His impact in Australia is also amongst the best for an English bowler. And this despite the fact that England, during his career time frame, did not win a single Test series in Australia (in fact, they won just three out of the fifteen Test matches they played).

Gough was never a part of an Ashes win, which may be part of the reason he is not remembered as he deserves to be. His 'outgoing personality' too did not endear him to observers who prefer a certain reserve in their heroes. Perhaps he is too recent a figure in England's cricket history to be seen as a legend among the traditionalists.

But Gough's contribution to English cricket at a crucial time of its history cannot be underestimated.

AC: Gough came across as a hard-working bowler – someone whom the captain could go to when the team needed a wicket or an inspiring short spell to lift the morale of the team. He came through. This was a special quality: Gough did not bowl long spells but gave it his all in the 4 or 5 overs he bowled at a stretch.

He was a batsman's nightmare – Gough bowled a fuller length with the new ball and made it swing, he was equally effective with the old ball and made it reverse. Gough was a wicket taker who bowled with intensity and passion – a great competitor on the field.

NN/JV

13

THE MAN MOST RESPONSIBLE FOR SOUTH AFRICA'S DOMINANT OVERSEAS RECORD: DALE STEYN

Between 2006 and 2015, South Africa were unbeaten away from home in thirteen series – the second-best run for any team in Test cricket after the legendary West Indian team which went unbeaten for sixteen years and seventeen series (1980–96).

Seven of these thirteen series (which exclude a one-off Test with Zimbabwe and a washed-out series against Bangladesh) were in the subcontinent and West Asia – normally considered unconquerable territories for touring teams, especially ones from South Africa, Australia and England. It was a challenge on these 'spinner-friendly' and placid tracks to take 20 wickets. One man led from the front and was instrumental in South Africa's dominance in unfavourable conditions during this period: Dale Steyn.

AC: India's golden run in the early 2000s was on the back of some sterling batting performances, but South Africa's nine-year 'unbeaten' period was courtesy their superior bowling. Like South Africa, Australia also had a dominant phase and they too had a superior bowling attack, but theirs wasn't a one-man bowling unit. At any given time, they had at least two or even three bowlers who were match winners in their own right. While South Africa also had a formidable bowling unit, Steyn's impact on their side's fortunes was much more than all the rest put together. South Africa's performances hinged on one man's form.

Here is a list of the thirteen away series from South Africa's context:

Vs Pakistan, 2007: Steyn was the second highest impact bowler after Paul Harris.

Vs Bangladesh, 2008: Steyn was the highest impact bowler.

Vs India, 2008: Steyn was the highest impact bowler.

Vs England, 2008: Steyn was the second highest impact bowler after Makhaya Ntini.

Vs Australia, 2008–09: Steyn was the highest impact bowler.

Vs India, 2010: Steyn was the highest impact bowler.

Vs West Indies, 2010: Steyn was the highest impact bowler.

Vs Pakistan, 2010: Steyn was the second highest impact bowler after Harris.

Vs New Zealand, 2012: Steyn was the second highest impact bowler after Vernon Philander and produced a series-defining performance.

Vs England, 2012: Steyn was the second highest impact bowler after Philander.

Vs Australia, 2012: Steyn was the highest impact bowler.

Vs Pakistan, 2013: Steyn was the second highest impact bowler after Imran Tahir.

Vs Sri Lanka, 2014: Steyn was the highest impact bowler and produced an SD.

So, in these thirteen series, Steyn was either the highest impact or the second highest impact bowler for South Africa. The only series he did not play due to injury was a series against India in 2015, and which South Africa went on to lose. This is not a coincidence.

Now, this may just be one of our less contentious findings. It is the common consensus that he is the greatest fast bowler of the new millennium. But what about his overall standing, his legacy in Test history? How does he compare to, say, a Malcolm Marshall or a Glenn McGrath? This might be a tricky terrain, because cricket historians, perhaps more than chroniclers of other sports, suffer from acute nostalgia.

Conventionally, Steyn is the eleventh highest wicket taker in Test history, second highest for a South African pacer after Shaun Pollock. If we take bowling averages, he is at sixth position in history and holds the best average for any South African pacer. In terms of strike rate, Steyn's is the best in Test cricket history (minimum fifty Tests).

All solid numbers. But when assessing players across decades, there is the problem of how conditions of play change, which plain old numbers can never truly account for. For example, the difference between Fred Trueman and Dale Steyn's bowling average is one run in favour of Trueman. But part of Trueman's career (1952–65) was during the lowest run-scoring decade in Test history after the First World War, whereas Steyn's performances have come at a time when the batters have had more than a fair say. As such, these situational differences need to be accounted for. At Impact Index, therefore, we look at the match context of a performance and condense all the bowling parameters into one number to determine the true worth and legacy of a bowler.

AC: Batting averages have been growing steadily in the last three decades. The best way to ascertain this is to look at the top batsman in every decade and that's enough to show that the batting average of 60 is the new late 40s. Since that's the case, it's only natural that the bowling averages would change too.

Let's take a look at the premier fast bowlers of his era.

Jimmy Anderson: 463 wickets at 28.28 (strike rate 56.9 balls per wicket)

Stuart Broad: 360 wickets at 28.48 (56.8)

Zaheer Khan: 311 wickets at 32.94 (60.4)

Brett Lee: 310 wickets at 30.81 (53.3)

And then,

Dale Steyn: 416 wickets at 22.24 (41.3)

The difference is stark in conventional figures as well.

For a minimum of fifty matches in Test history, Dale Steyn emerges as the sixth highest impact bowler in the world after Muttiah

Muralitharan, Dennis Lillee, Malcolm Marshall, Shane Warne and Richard Hadlee. He is also the fourth highest impact pacer ever after Lillee, Marshall and Hadlee.

For a bowler of his pace and aggression, Steyn's consistency is phenomenal. His failure rate of 17 per cent so far in his career is the third best for any pacer after Joel Garner and Dennis Lillee (minimum fifty Tests).

> **AC:** Steyn has two uncanny abilities. One, to crank up the pace the moment he senses an opportunity or feels that the team needs a wicket. With the new ball, he bowls only at 80 per cent of his capacity and swings the ball prodigiously. Once the ball gets old, he beats batsmen for pace. Two, he bowls at the same pace throughout a Test match (in the first and the last spell of the day) and is too hot to handle for the batsman who has just walked in – the hallmark of a top bowler. That's how you pick wickets in lots of twos and threes and not a wicket here and a wicket there.

Vs Australia, Perth, 2012. *With the series at 0–0 and going into the final Test, South Africa get bowled out for only 225 in their first innings. Australia in their reply are dealt a blow as Steyn prises out Ed Cowan, David Warner and nightwatchman Nathan Lyon to leave them reeling at 35 for 4. Steyn adds Clarke's wicket to his tally to finish with 4–40 as Australia manage only 163. Within the context of the first innings of the match, Steyn hands South Africa a distinct advantage. Amla and de Villiers pulverize the Australian bowling in the second innings and set them an improbable target of 632 runs. Steyn takes 3–72 as Australia finish with 322. South Africa stamp their authority as the number one Test team.*

Serial series winner

Dale Steyn has produced seven SDs in eighty-four Tests – the most by any South African bowler. In fact, apart from Steyn, only one pacer in the history of Test cricket have produced seven SD performances: Hadlee (seven in eighty-six Tests). Steyn's SD-producing frequency is also the best among all Test bowlers. His ability to produce high impact performances in matches that would decide the fate of a series is a major reason for his country's success in Test cricket in the new millennium.

Vs Sri Lanka, Galle, 2014. *South Africa hadn't won a Test series in Sri Lanka for twenty-one years. In the first Test in Galle, South Africa, riding on Dean Elgar and JP Duminy's centuries posted 455 in their first innings. Sri Lanka, in their reply, folded for 292 as Steyn accounted for four top/middle order batsmen to finish with 5–54. In Sri Lanka's second innings, Steyn took four more wickets to finish with match figures of 9–99 as South Africa won by 153 runs. This was the only result Test of the series, giving Steyn's performance a series-defining status.*

During his career, Steyn emerges as the highest impact pacer in the world – 29 per cent ahead of the next best pacer, Mitchell Johnson. Steyn's seven SDs in this time-frame is the best for any bowler. He is also the most consistent bowler in this period, ahead of the likes of Muralitharan and Kumble.

South Africa attained their number one status in 2009 and held it for three months. They got it back again in mid-2012 and relinquished it only once for a three-month period before losing it after a drubbing against India away from home in 2015. Steyn has much to do with this dominance, not least because bowlers have more of a say in winning Test matches than batsmen. Besides, although the South African batting unit boasted the likes of A.B. de Villiers, Graeme Smith, Jacques Kallis, Hashim Amla and later Faf du Plessis – each capable of producing a match-winning innings on their own – Steyn was the bedrock of the bowling department. While Morne Morkel was an excellent support bowler, he was not a match-winning one. And Vernon Philander started off impressively but faltered since late 2013.

During this period of domination, Steyn's bowling impact was 45 per cent higher than Philander's and 128 per cent higher than Morkel's – such is the influence he had.

Of a total of fourteen SDs delivered by seven South African

bowlers during Steyn's career, Steyn produced seven of them alone. The next best is Shaun Pollock with two such performances. Morkel and Philander combined have given only two SDs during this period.

Dale Steyn breathed new life into the art of fast, controlled swing bowling at a time when it was dying in world cricket. There's always an element of romanticism associated with pace bowling but, in Steyn's case, his contribution to South Africa's Test cricket legacy made sure it's not only that.

AC: Unfortunately, he is the last bowler in today's era who makes you go wow. Even as the bat kept dominating the ball a little more every year, Steyn stood tall among his peers. There's a no-conditions-apply factor to his game. He's as lethal in seamer-friendly conditions as he is in spinner-friendly pitches in the subcontinent. He, quite literally, took the pitch out of the equation, and that's the most important reason for his success – conditions just didn't matter to him.

SS

14

A.B. DE VILLIERS IS THE MOST DOMINATING BATSMAN OF THE MODERN ERA

Considered a modern-day genius, A.B. de Villiers is the best contemporary batsman across all formats – his unconventional and aggressive stroke play adding to the aura around him. His 8,074 runs in 106 Tests at a batting average of 50.46 confirms his place amongst the post-millennium greats.

But what about his standing when compared with the all-time great Test batsmen?

The answer is staggering. Even with 25 batsmen who have a higher batting average and 26 batsmen ahead on aggregate runs, de Villiers emerges as the eighth highest impact batsman in the history of Test cricket, only behind Don Bradman, Peter May, Younis Khan, Greg Chappell, Brian Lara, Jack Hobbs and Inzamam-ul-Haq (minimum fifty Tests; till 5 November 2016).

If this sounds excessive, let's examine why de Villiers deserves this place in Test cricket history.

A big-match player

With six SDs in 106 Tests (second highest amongst South African batsmen after Kallis and Smith who had seven each in 166 and 117 Tests respectively), he has the sixth best matches to SD ratio for any batsman in the history of Test cricket after Don Bradman, Inzamam-ul-Haq, Hansie Cronje, Graeme Smith and Azhar Ali.

He achieved this as part of a formidable South African unit – thereby having shared impact with the likes of Graeme Smith, Jacques Kallis and Hashim Amla among others.

What makes de Villiers' big-match temperament doubly dangerous is his consistency. Given his attacking and innovative style of batting, a failure rate of 41 per cent is a phenomenal achievement. Just for perspective, he is more consistent than the likes of Inzamam-ul-Haq, Michael Hussey, Kumar Sangakkara and Sachin Tendulkar.

AC: A.B. de Villiers is a special player. He is a multidimensional batsman. Not only is he redefining the art of batting with his innovative stroke play but also challenging the conventional school of batting with his unique style in defence. He not only scores at a very fast clip which completely unsettles opposition bowlers but is also very unorthodox in his style and shot making, which makes it impossible for an opposition captain to set fields for him. And then he has this ability to call on his 'B-game' when required – that is, to drop anchor, change gears and defend and occupy the crease for long hours and grind the opposition bowlers down, something he displayed in South Africa's famous blockathon in India in 2015. This is really a remarkable quality in a batsman not usually associated with being technically correct.

It is also what makes him a genius. De Villiers has the ability to hit a perfectly good ball for a six. But, if the situation demands, can also block a half-volley. This is rare. Very few batsmen can do this. I remember Sachin Tendulkar cut down on his cover drive but that was out of desperation as he was going through a bad patch. De Villiers can call upon this dual skill set at will, and consistently. For him, it's not the method which counts but the final outcome.

But de Villiers wasn't an overnight wonder boy. In fact his transformation, which came well into the second half of his ongoing career (in both Tests and ODIs), is nothing short of sensational.

A mediocre beginning

For the first seven years of his career (December 2004 to December 2011) – a period in which he played sixty-eight Tests, de Villiers was not even among the twenty highest impact batsmen in the world. Although four of his five highest impact batting performances came in this period, none of them was definitive in deciding the fate of a series for South Africa, that is, he had no SDs in this period.

For South Africa, he was only the fourth highest impact batsman after Smith, Kallis and Ashwell Prince. And the least consistent amongst all the recognized ones with a failure rate of 47 per cent.

His batting average of 47.4 in this period was also somewhat skewed due to a few big innings. Kallis (59.5), Amla (48.3) and Smith (48.3) all averaged more than de Villiers in this period.

Then it all changed.

Dominating world cricket

Vs Sri Lanka, Cape Town, 2012. *The series was tied at 1–1 with all to play for in the decider third Test at Newlands. South Africa recovered after a couple of early setbacks with Alviro Petersen and Jacques Kallis putting together a double-century stand for the third wicket. De Villiers joined Kallis at 261 for 3 and the pair added 192 before the latter was dismissed for 224. The hosts posted a massive 580 in the first innings with De Villiers remaining unbeaten on an attacking 160 (off just 205 deliveries). Dale Steyn and company dismissed Sri Lanka for 239 in their first innings. Following on, the visitors fared better and posted 342 but were still comprehensively beaten by 10 wickets.*

De Villiers registered the first SD of his career. With significant contributions in the first two Tests, he was the highest impact batsman and player of the series.

This series marked a turning point in de Villiers's career. It brought out the big-match player in him, transforming a good batsman to an all-time great.

De Villiers has not only been the highest impact batsman but also the second highest impact player (after R. Ashwin) in the world (minimum twenty-five Tests) since December 2011. His batting impact in this period increased by a monumental 154 per cent – it is 37 per cent higher than the second highest impact batsman, Younis Khan.

Such domination has seldom been seen in the 139 years of Test cricket history. The percentage difference between the highest (de Villiers) and the second highest impact batsman (Misbah-ul-Haq) between 1 January 2011 and 1 February 2015 (de Villiers' period of dominance) is 55 per cent. If we look at the respective best period for the ten highest impact batsmen in Test history, only Peter May (66 per cent higher impact than the second highest impact batsman, Colin Cowdrey during 1954–57) and Greg Chappell (96 per cent higher impact than Vivian Richards during 1974–77) have enjoyed a greater supremacy than de Villiers.

But the duration of de Villiers's domination exceeds May's and Chappell's.

De Villiers has produced his six SDs in just thirty-three Tests – that is an SD almost every five Tests – nothing short of miraculous.

> **AC:** De Villiers is a global player. He has been successful all over the world because he is not only an excellent batsman of pace but of spin bowling too. He is quick on his feet and has great hands – this is a rare mix. And above all, he has a brilliant mind. He has this ability to detach himself from his own reputation (of being an aggressive stroke maker) and play according to the situation. It requires immense concentration – really staying in the moment. This is the main reason he has produced so many series-defining performances.

South Africa played twelve Test series in this period of dominance. They won nine, drew two and lost just one series in this period.

Vs New Zealand, Hamilton, 2012. *New Zealand are bowled out for 185 in the first innings. In the second Test, South Africa are in trouble at 69 for 4 when de Villiers joined Petersen at the crease. Wickets continued to tumble at the other end but de Villiers counter-attacked and, with the* *lower order, took South Africa to 253. He top-scored with a fine 83. New Zealand were skittled for 168 in the second innings. South Africa chased down their target of 101 with 9 wickets to spare.*

This was the only result Test of the series. De Villiers produced his second SD in consecutive series.

Vs Pakistan, 2013. *First Test, Johannesburg: A.B. de Villiers 31 and 103. South Africa won by 211 runs. Second Test, Cape Town: 61 (from 102 for 4) and 36 (from 88 for 3) chasing 182. South Africa won by four wickets. Third Test, Centurion: 121 (from 107 for 3). South Africa won by an innings and 18 runs.*

> **AC:** Batting in South Africa is the toughest. The bouncy, seaming and fast tracks there are treacherous for batsmen, no matter where they are from. Even South African batsmen, by and large, average less and have a lesser impact at home than overseas. Most modern-day greats who have done brilliantly all over the world have struggled in South Africa (Kumar Sangakkara, Matthew Hayden, Dravid are a few prime examples). It is then to de Villiers's credit that he has been hugely successful at home too.

Vs Pakistan, Dubai, 2013. *De Villiers (164) and Graeme Smith (234) are involved in a triple-century stand for the 5th wicket as South Africa amass 517 after demolishing Pakistan for 99 in the second test. The hosts fare better in the second innings but still go down by an innings.*

South Africa level the two-match series at 1–1. De Villiers again produces an SD in consecutive series.

He went on to produce two more SDs – against India in Durban in December 2013 (74 in the first innings in a 10-wicket win for South Africa) and against West Indies in 2014–15 (152 in an innings victory at Centurion and 148 in the first innings of an 8-wicket win in Cape Town).

> **AC:** All modern-day batsmen have at least one flaw in their batting. In contemporary cricket, for example, Kohli has had a problem outside the off stump with the swinging ball, Amla has trouble

with the incoming delivery while Steven Smith moves across his stumps too frequently, making him an lbw candidate – this is a T20 fallout. But de Villiers, despite being immensely successful in all three formats, including T20 cricket, has no such apparent weakness. De Villiers, in this respect, is flawless.

South Africa became the number one Test team in the world in August 2009 and for most of the period since then maintained their position at the top.

However, their recent form has been rather poor. They failed to win a Test match in Bangladesh and played out two draws. That was followed by a drubbing in India and a series loss at home against England. With other teams doing well in this period, South Africa has slipped to seventh in the ICC Test rankings. Not surprisingly, de Villiers has not produced a high impact performance in his last seven Tests (two series against India and England).

But seldom has a batsman established such supremacy over his contemporaries and sustained it for such a length in time. And what is truly mind-boggling is that his ODI career has followed a similar pattern and he has achieved the same dominance there too. In fact, if we consider both Tests and ODIs together, A.B. de Villiers is the highest impact batsman in history.

His eight SDs in ODIs make it a total of fourteen SD performances in international cricket in less than five years.

That is, dare we say it, Bradmanesque.

AC: There's this old tweet of mine that seems apt to quote here: 'I demand a DNA test of A.B. de Villiers. This game is only for humans.'

NN

15

KANE WILLIAMSON IS THE HIGHEST IMPACT BATSMAN IN NEW ZEALAND'S TEST CRICKET HISTORY

Who is the best batsman New Zealand has produced in Test cricket? Popular wisdom puts Martin Crowe right on top. Glenn Turner, Stephen Fleming, Ross Taylor and Nathan Astle usually follow.

When seen through the Impact Index sieve, though, it is twenty-six-year-old Kane Williamson who emerges as the highest impact batsman in New Zealand's eighty-six years of Test history (minimum forty Tests).

Just for perspective, Lara became the highest impact batsman in his country's history (crossing Sobers) only in 1998 at the age of twenty-nine, Dravid did it at twenty-eight, Sangakkara at thirty-three and A.B. de Villiers at thirty. Williamson reached this pedestal a year ago, at the age of twenty-five.

Williamson's completeness as a batsman is evident in his dominance in almost all of the individual impact batting parameters for New Zealand.

He has scored the maximum proportion of runs (Runs Tally Impact), absorbed the maximum pressure of falling wickets (Pressure Impact) and displayed the best ability to build partnerships (Partnership Building Impact).

He also has the second highest New Ball Impact (ability to face the new ball and score runs) after John Wright and, with a failure rate of

36 per cent, is the second most consistent batsman for New Zealand after Glenn Turner.

Even conventionally, Williamson's batting average of 50.31 is the highest for any New Zealand batsman (minimum forty Tests).

AC: Amongst this generation of Test batsmen who are billed to be future greats, four names stand out: Williamson, Steven Smith, Virat Kohli and Joe Root. Williamson is certainly at the top in this pack and, in all probability, will finish at the top too. This, despite being a No. 3 batsman, which is historically a much more difficult batting position than No. 4 (in terms of average runs scored per dismissal), where interestingly all the other three mentioned above bat too.

NN: It is interesting that you say so, given where he stands on impact as compared to his contemporaries. It is actually Williamson, the least fancied of the lot (probably because he is from New Zealand and not from the big three cricket-playing nations), who has the highest impact amongst the four. He has a 13 per cent higher impact than Root, 27 per cent higher than Smith and 36 per cent higher impact than Kohli.

AC: Also, we must keep in mind that New Zealand never get to play a four- or five-Test series unlike the big three – India, Australia and England. They mostly get two or three Tests in a series at home and away. This puts Williamson at a disadvantage when compared to the others. Unlike them, he does not get a second chance or enough opportunities to make a comeback in a series. He hardly gets time to acclimatize to the conditions and has to be at his best from the word go. Thus, for Williamson to have a higher impact than the other three is truly incredible.

Only two contemporary batsmen have a higher impact than Williamson.

For a minimum of fifty Tests, Williamson has the third highest impact amongst contemporary batsmen – after Younis Khan and A.B. de Villiers.

He is the thirteenth highest impact batsman in the history of Test cricket.

Williamson's is an ongoing career and he may well find it difficult to maintain the high standards he has set so early in his career. At the same time, if he manages to do so, he may well end up amongst the five highest impact batsmen in Test cricket history.

But sustained success did not come instantly to Williamson. Though he scored a century on debut against India in Ahmedabad, he did not actually produce the high impact performances early in his career. In fact, he was not even amongst the thirty highest impact batsman in the world (in eleven Tests since debut) till the home series against South Africa in 2012.

Williamson has been amongst the five highest impact batsmen in the world during the last four years.

Vs South Africa, Third Test, Wellington, 2012. *South Africa post 474 in the first innings. New Zealand reply with 275. Williamson contributes 39. The visitors declare at 189 for 3 in the second innings, setting the home team a target of 389. New Zealand are in early trouble at 1 for 2 when Williamson walks out to bat. It soon worsens to 32 for 3. Williamson holds one end up even as wickets continue to fall at the other. He remains unbeaten on a match-saving 102 off 228 deliveries. He occupies the crease for almost five-and-a-half hours – practically an entire day of Test cricket. New Zealand play out the 80-odd overs and earn a commendable draw.*

This performance marked a transformation in Williamson's career. He has been the fifth highest impact batsman in the world (after de Villiers, Younis Khan, Sangakkara and Misbah-ul-Haq; minimum twenty-five Tests) in the forty-two Tests he has played thereafter.

Williamson's temperament as a batsman and his ability to score tough runs under pressure stand out.

Soon he added another quality to his batting – the ability to rise to the occasion and deliver in the big matches.

Williamson has three series-defining performances in fifty-four Tests which makes his frequency of producing an SD performance amongst the best ever in Test cricket history.

Vs Sri Lanka, Second Test, Colombo, 2012. *New Zealand are 4 for 1 when Williamson walks out to the middle. Soon it is 14 for 2. Williamson and Taylor then put together a 262-run stand for the third wicket before* *being dismissed in quick succession for 135 and 142 respectively. New Zealand post 412 in the first innings. Tim Southee and Trent Boult restrict Sri Lanka to 244. The visitors declare their second innings at 194 for 9 (Williamson 18) setting Sri Lanka a target of 363. The New Zealand pacers dislodge the home team for just 195.*

It is New Zealand's first Test win in Sri Lanka in three tours. They come back after defeat in the opening Test to level the series. Williamson gets his first SD.

Vs West Indies, Third Test, Barbados, 2014. *The series is tied at 1–1 with all to play for in the decider. New Zealand, electing to bat, are in early trouble. Williamson comes out at 17 for 1 which worsens to 28 for 2. He resurrects the innings with a solid 43. New Zealand manage to post 293. West Indies reply with 317. Williamson then hammers 161 (from 1 for 1, 56 for 2, 68 for 3) in the second innings and takes the match away from the West Indies. New Zealand declare at 331 for 7. West Indies, set 308, are bowled out for 254.*

It's a rare series win for New Zealand in the Caribbean (their second in six attempts). Williamson gets his second SD.

Vs Pakistan, Third Test, Sharjah, 2014. *Pakistan had hammered the visitors in Abu Dhabi while the Dubai Test ended in a draw. In the third and final Test in Sharjah, Pakistan, batting first, post 351. New Zealand reply with a colossal 690, courtesy a 297-run partnership for the 3rd wicket between Williamson (192) and McCullum (202). Pakistan are bowled out for 259 in the second innings, handing New Zealand a massive innings victory.*

It was only their second drawn away series against Pakistan (they had previously lost six, won one and drawn one). Williamson earned his second SD in consecutive series for helping New Zealand come back from a Test down and level the series at 1–1.

That all his SDs were registered away from home is remarkable – and two of these were in Asia against excellent spin attacks.

AC: Williamson is a complete batsman. Not only has he scored big in seaming conditions at home, but also shown an excellent ability to play spin overseas. This is highly commendable for a batsman from New Zealand who has been bred on green tops and hardly gets to face quality spin bowling. This dual quality of being an exceptional player of both spin and pace is what separates him from the rest. Kohli has struggled against the moving ball in England, Smith is yet to score big in India and Root is yet to be tested in subcontinental conditions.

Playing the new ball

Williamson's ability to face the new ball, occupy the crease and score runs is the best in the history of Test cricket for any non-opener.

His ability to absorb the pressure of falling wickets is again amongst the best in Test cricket (only Mansur Ali Khan Pataudi, Peter May, Andy Flower and Angelo Mathews absorbed more pressure for their teams).

AC: Two things need to be factored in when we talk about Kane Williamson's sensational rise in such a short period of time. Firstly, conditions in New Zealand (along with South Africa) are the toughest for batsmen in world cricket – the red kookaburra ball does a lot after pitching (courtesy the green tops). Also, with Boult and Southee in the mix, there's been a concerted effort to prepare greener pitches to yield results. This is where he has played most of his cricket and achieved phenomenal success. If he had played a substantial part of his cricket in easier conditions, his batting average of 50 could easily have been 57 or 58.

Secondly, his side has never had a stable opening pair as such. Williamson, in that respect, has been as good as an opener for New Zealand – with the added pressure of knowing that his side has lost an early wicket.

The rise of New Zealand

The period between December 2013 and December 2015 was one of the best for New Zealand in their Test cricket history (1980–86 being their best ever in Test cricket). During these two years, New Zealand played seven series, won four, drew two (against Pakistan in UAE and

England away – in both cases coming back from behind to level the series) and lost just one (an away series in Australia).

Williamson was not only the highest impact batsman for New Zealand but in the world during this period.

He also achieved similar success in limited-overs cricket. In fact, Williamson is also the highest impact batsman for New Zealand in their ODI cricket history.

Interestingly, three other batsmen in history, A.B. de Villiers, Kumar Sangakkara and Andy Flower have been the highest impact batsmen for their countries in both Tests and ODIs.

AC: One thing which goes in Williamson's favour is that he is a decent T20 batsman, but not a great one. This means his focus is on Test cricket. Thus his priorities are not compromised and he does not need to modify his batting to suit the demands of T20 cricket. He will focus on Tests and ODIs, which will keep him ahead of the pack.

Here I will stick my neck out and say that Williamson will finish as the best Test batsman from this generation. He will be the first one from the current crop to find his name in the elite 10,000-club in Test cricket.

NN

16

DESPITE AN AVERAGE OF ONLY 36, ANDREW JONES IS THE SECOND HIGHEST IMPACT BATSMAN IN NEW ZEALAND'S ODI HISTORY

Andrew Jones played for New Zealand between 1987 and 1995. In that period, he played 39 Tests and 87 ODIs. Today, he is only remembered as a Test player because he averaged 44 in the longer format and 36 in ODIs.

Jones had a mediocre strike rate of 58 and did not score a single century in his ODI career.

Yet, till Kane Williamson burst on to the scene, Jones was the highest impact batsman in New Zealand's ODI history. Martin Crowe, who averaged 39 in ODIs, ranks below Jones on an Impact list for New Zealand ODI batsmen.

The reason is straightforward: He was a big match player.

Seven New Zealand batsmen have three or more series-defining batting performances in their careers: Stephen Fleming, Chris Cairns, Nathan Astle, Adam Parore, Martin Guptill, Brendon McCullum and Andrew Jones. No one else crossed two, not even Martin Crowe, widely considered the greatest Kiwi batsman. Fleming, Cairns, McCullum, Parore, Guptill and Astle all played over 125 ODI matches. Jones played eighty-seven.

No one in New Zealand, therefore, had anything near as good an SD to match ratio as Jones.

These were his series-defining performances:

Vs England, Auckland, 1988. *New Zealand 1–2 behind, with one match to go. England bat first, make a hard-fought 208 in 50 overs. Andrew Jones immaculately anchors the chase for New Zealand, is sixth out just 10 runs away from the target, for a 126-ball 90, as New Zealand win with 4 balls to spare, squaring the series.*

Vs Pakistan, Christchurch/Hamilton, 1989. *Against the second best ODI side of its time, New Zealand beat Imran Khan's side 3–1 in a home series. In the first and the fourth matches, both of which were low-scoring contests, Andrew Jones was the top scorer with 62 and 63 respectively.*

Vs England, Auckland, 1991. *Series even with one match to go. Jones comes out to bat at 7 for 1, crossing star batsman and captain Crowe on the way in. He bats for more than two hours and is out for 64 off 84 balls, destined to be the highest score of the match. A 30-ball 51 from wicketkeeper Ian Smith takes New Zealand to 224. A star-studded English line-up comprising Graham Gooch, Michael Atherton, David Gower, Allan Lamb, Robin Smith, Alec Stewart and Phil DeFreitas, 170 for 3 at one stage with 10 overs to go, fail to take England home as the three Kiwi Chrises (Pringle, Cairns and Harris) finish England off. New Zealand win by 7 runs and the series 2–1.*

The significance of SD performances comes from the place of those series in that country's cricket history. Above, for example, are the only three ODI series New Zealand did not lose between March 1987 and December 1992 against major countries (there were won series against Sri Lanka and Zimbabwe, neither of whom were strong teams then, especially away). They lost thirteen series in that period. This context lends Andrew Jones's role higher value.

Riding high on most batting parameters

When it came to proportion of runs scored (Runs Tally Impact), Jones is the third highest impact batsman for New Zealand, after Crowe and Williamson.

However, when it came to building partnerships, he is right up there in New Zealand's ODI history, ahead of even Williamson and Crowe.

In terms of consistency, while Jones was not at the top, he is high enough. His 47 per cent failure rate made him the seventh most consistent New Zealander ever, after Crowe, Williamson, Bruce Edgar, Jeremy Coney, Roger Twose and Martin Guptill.

When it comes to chasing down targets, Andrew Jones is the highest impact Kiwi batsman.

High impact in the 1992 World Cup

Andrew Jones was a key member of the famous New Zealand squad in 1992. He played at the crucial No. 3 position and was the second highest scorer for New Zealand in the tournament after Martin Crowe. Interestingly, he was the third highest impact Kiwi batsman, after Martin Crowe and Mark Greatbatch.

His sequence of scores in the tournament were 4, 49, 34*, 57, 10, 67*, 78, 2 and 21.

Vs England, Wellington, 1992. *Against eventual finalists, in reply to England's 200, Jones came out to bat at 5 for 1. While Greatbatch attacked at the other end, as planned, Jones kept his end up. Greatbatch left with the score at 64 after making 35 and captain Crowe and Jones controlled the game thereafter. Jones was eventually dismissed for 78, which got him the Man of the Match award. This win helped New Zealand top their group and eventually set them for their classic heartbreaking semi-final clash against Pakistan.*

Andrew Jones was twenty-eight when he began his international career in 1988. He was almost thirty-two when the 1992 World Cup ended. There was little chance that he would last until the next World Cup. Sadly, almost immediately after the tournament, Jones hit a bad spot of form and never really got out of it. He went twenty-three matches without hitting a 50, when he finally ended his ODI career in January 1995. This long rope is actually indicative of how valuable he had been to his team.

The lack of fanfare near the end also robbed him of a more meaningful assessment of his contribution to New Zealand ODI cricket.

AC: Another brilliant Impact Index finding, for the average of 36 is simply not good enough to take notice. But when you consider his form in the last twenty-three games (in which he averaged 16), his average was 44 before that, and that's a very good ODI average even today. Besides, the significance of his contributions in key matches must not be overlooked, for what's the point of bilateral series if the result is immaterial? World Cup 1992 was the first that I followed closely (was only fifteen at the time), and while I distinctly remember Greatbatch's heroics at the top, Crowe's brilliance in the middle with the bat and leadership and Deepak Patel's opening spell, I have no recollection of Jones's consistent presence. Once again, the orthodox statistics have failed to highlight a good cricketing story.

JV: Curiously, his average of 44.27 in 39 Tests is the sixth best in New Zealand cricket history (minimum thirty Tests), but he is the fourteenth highest impact batsman. All thirteen in front of him have SDs; he has none in Test cricket.

17

INDIA'S HIGHEST IMPACT BATSMAN DURING THE 1983 WORLD CUP WAS SANDEEP PATIL

There were many heroes when India won the Prudential World Cup in 1983.

Mohinder Amarnath, for winning the Man of the Match award in the semi-final and the final.

Kapil Dev, for his remarkable consistency with the ball and that classic innings under tremendous pressure (an unbeaten 175 against Zimbabwe after his team had been reduced to 17 for 5; in a league match they won by 31 runs).

Yashpal Sharma's valuable and gritty contributions with the bat.

Madan Lal's and Roger Binny's hugely effective seam bowling.

Then, there are one-off moments. Kirti Azad's bowling spell in the semi-final. K. Srikkanth's explosive knock in the final. Balwinder Sandhu's ball to dismiss Gordon Greenidge. Kapil Dev's running catch to finish off a rampaging Viv Richards.

No one really brings up Sandeep Patil. Sure, sometimes his innings in the semi-final is remembered, but more as a finishing touch than a leading role.

Yet, Patil was the highest impact Indian batsman in the tournament. Thirty-three years later, this is a story worth retelling.

AC: Recently I quizzed Kapil Dev about Sandeep Patil's contribution in the World Cup. His response was that he did 'all right'. The only person that he remembered doing exceedingly well was Roger Binny. If the captain didn't remember the impact, it's highly unlikely that we would.

Sandeep Patil made 216 runs in eight matches in the 1983 Prudential World Cup at an average of about 31. His highest score was 51.

He was sixteenth on the runs tally list for the tournament. And thirty-third when it came to batting averages.

Amongst Indians, Kapil Dev, Yashpal Sharma and Mohinder Amarnath all scored more runs than him.

AC: The failure of conventional numbers is that they don't take into account the context of a performance and, more importantly, its influence on the result. On the day, a quick-fire 25 that wins the match would receive the deserved recognition. Ten years down the line it's completely forgotten because the knock didn't register anywhere. On the other hand, the man who scored a 70 in that game would have that score register on his average much more over time. Numbers don't lie but they don't tell the entire story either.

Accounting for strike rate

Even though these were 60-over matches, scoring at a relatively quicker rate could still provide an advantage for the team. It often took the pressure away from other batsmen and sometimes changed the momentum of the game completely.

Right through the tournament, Patil played at a breakneck speed. For someone who had hit Bob Willis for six fours in an over the previous summer in a Test match, this was probably not surprising.

Here, it made him the joint-highest Strike Rate Impact batsman (strike rate as a ratio against the average strike rate of each match) in the tournament alongwith Kapil Dev, even higher impact than Viv Richards in this aspect.

AC: Strike rate in ODIs is always an important factor but it's even more relevant in a low-scoring game, as most matches were in that World Cup. Every team had three or four seriously good bowlers who could bowl 12 overs each and therefore there were longer periods of sustained pressure from both ends. If better bowlers bowl more overs, the chances of taking wickets increase manifold, and that makes overs from lesser bowlers less relevant. Also, there weren't many quick scorers in those times. The tendency was to wait for mistakes to happen; so captains had fielders in attacking positions for longer. Now, Sandeep Patil challenged that by being ultra-aggressive, and most opponents weren't ready for it. Before they could take corrective measures, the match had slipped from their grip.

Consistent performances

With a 25 per cent failure rate, Patil was India's most consistent batsman in the tournament.

Patil began with 36 off 52 balls in India's opening match against West Indies, which India won to set the tone. He had come in at 46 for 2 and finished as the second highest scorer in the match for India (after Yashpal Sharma, who made 89).

Next, against Zimbabwe, he came in at 32 for 2 as India chased down 155 and top-scored with 50 off 54 balls to make it a relatively easy match for India. It is worth remembering that this was against a side that had just upset Australia and from a situation where nothing could be taken for granted.

Then, in the crucial last group must-win game against Australia, he came in at 65 for 3 and produced 30 off 25 balls (second highest scorer) as India made 247 and eventually won comfortably.

Vs England in the semi-final

India chased 213. Despite being 50 for 2, they stabilized well and Mohinder Amarnath and Yashpal Sharma took them to calmer territories with a 92-run partnership. But when Amarnath was run out with the score at 142 for 3, and Patil came out, the calm was misleading.

One didn't even have to look at cricket played on any other day. In that same match, England, batting first, were 141 for 3 at one stage, before they folded for 213. Even more curiously, in the other semi-final between West Indies and Pakistan being played simultaneously, Pakistan had been 139 for 3 at one stage, and then folded for 184. West Indies won easily.

Both these collapses had happened while batting first; the pressure was considerably more when chasing. By no means was India out of the woods, despite the sense of security the Amarnath–Sharma partnership had brought. And this was a World Cup semi-final after all.

What followed was the stuff of legend. With 72 runs to make, Patil didn't waste any time. Sharma and he added 63 in just 9 overs – an unthinkable scoring rate in that era. Within fifty minutes, the match was over. Patil scored 51 not out off 32 balls with eight boundaries. His rapid pace of scoring just did not give any space to England to even comprehend some kind of a comeback into the match.

Vs West Indies, in the final

He almost did the same thing in the final against West Indies. Batting first, India had done well to overcome tough conditions through Srikkanth (38) and Amarnath (26). When the latter was dismissed, it was 90 for 3 as Patil walked in. Almost immediately, it was 92 for 4 as Yashpal Sharma went. Kapil Dev came in, hit three boundaries and promptly vanished; 110 for 5. Kirti Azad lasted three balls; 111 for 6.

It was all coming apart, so Patil decided to counter-attack. He made 27 off 29 balls but was the eighth wicket to fall at 153, critical runs at a crucial stage. As he walked back to the pavilion, he had no way of knowing that India had already scored 13 runs more than what West Indies would manage. His contribution at this juncture, in a manner of speaking, would eventually separate the sides.

Of course, it can be argued that Amarnath's innings was more crucial, as he kept the lethal West Indian pacers at bay early on, and prevented a collapse, as Srikkanth cut loose at the other end for a while. But it is equally true that during Amarnath's stay at the crease, India lost one wicket for 88 runs and during Patil's stay, India lost four wickets for 63.

Then, some gutsy batting from Madan Lal, Syed Kirmani and Balwinder Sandhu helped India reach 183, which would go a long way to add to their scoreboard pressure, of course. The rest, inevitably, is history.

So, in two of the biggest cricket matches in the 1983 World Cup, Patil was the second highest scorer for India, both innings coming at a breakneck speed, one while chasing.

This big-match play, coupled with his consistency, comfortably made him India's highest impact batsman. And the second highest impact batsman in the tournament, after Viv Richards.

Special place in Indian ODI history

Incidentally, Patil had a series-defining performance the year before too. In 1982, he had produced a 64 off 55 balls against England as India won the series 2–1. It was the only ODI series India had ever won before the 1983 World Cup against a major side (Sri Lanka in 1982 excluded).

Patil's batting average of 25 in 45 ODIs with a highest score of 84 belies his importance to Indian ODI cricket, as does his disappointingly high failure rate of 55 per cent.

But if we take thirty matches as the minimum, he is actually the third highest impact ODI batsman for India ever, after Sachin Tendulkar and Virat Kohli. Patil's big-match performances added that X-factor element to his impact at a time when India hardly won anything in this format.

Patil also has the highest Strike Rate Impact in Indian ODI history, even ahead of Kapil Dev (though his conventional strike rate was higher; it means when you take match strike rates into account as well, Patil was actually better). You'd never get this from examining plain strike rates (Patil's conventional strike rate was 82), as standards have changed so much in thirty years.

Patil was a high impact Test player as well, though there is no doubt he underachieved in the twenty-nine Tests he played. His failure rate of 59 per cent is very disappointing there too, given how unambiguously brilliant he was at his best (and in all conditions too, as his performances in Australia and England demonstrated). But here too he registered as India's second highest Strike Rate Impact batsman after Sehwag. He garnered one SD against Australia in their backyard (in 1981), in a dream series for him – and one of only three times till date India have managed to not lose a series there.

Sandeep Patil's ODI contributions are historically even more significant. It's time they were recognized more.

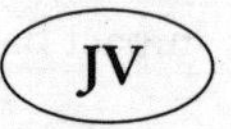

18

THE BATSMAN TO ABSORB THE MOST PRESSURE FOR INDIA IN THE 2011 WORLD CUP: VIRAT KOHLI

Virat Kohli was twenty-two when the 2011 World Cup began. He had played forty-five ODIs for India and his average of 46 suggested a talented player with a promising career ahead. He was slotted into the team at No. 4 amidst heavyweights Tendulkar, Sehwag, Gambhir, Yuvraj and Dhoni.

As it happened, Tendulkar made the most runs for India in the tournament and registered the highest impact (primarily because of his runs tally) and Yuvraj Singh had the highest batting average. The unsung hero for India was Virat Kohli, who went virtually unnoticed for his 282 runs at an average of 35.

He did something, though, that no one outside the team is likely to remember later. He absorbed the most pressure (of falling wickets) right through the tournament. He came under pressure thrice and all three times, he absorbed it and stabilized his side.

Vs Ireland: No ordinary minnow, this. Ireland had beaten England at the same venue just four days earlier and after scoring 207, had India at 21 for 2 when Virat Kohli walked in. With his hero Tendulkar, Kohli stabilized the Indian innings with a 34 off 53 balls, which allowed the batsmen who followed to finish off the match comfortably.

Vs West Indies: Two weeks later, with Sehwag missing, he walked out at 8 for 1 as India batted first, with Tendulkar dismissed. It became 51 for 2, when Yuvraj came out. Together, they took India to safety, adding 122 runs, before Kohli fell for 59 off 76 balls. It would be the second highest score of the innings, after Yuvraj's 113. India eventually won comfortably.

Vs Sri Lanka: Two weeks later, Kohli was playing the World Cup final. In reply to Sri Lanka's 274, India were 31 for 2 when Kohli walked out as Tendulkar walked back. The match was squarely in the balance. He batted for over an hour with Gambhir, during which he faced 49 balls and scored 35; Kohli's dismay was apparent to everyone when he gave Dilshan a return catch. Still, he had helped take the score to 114, and set the foundation for a special innings by M.S. Dhoni.

No big score, no eye-catching performance, but Virat Kohli had already shown resolve and calm in the middle when India was in trouble, twice while chasing.

Less than a year later, he would establish himself as the best chaser in the history of the ODI game, and gradually make his way towards being an all-time great ODI batsman as well.

But at World Cup 2011, he was just twenty-two – the youngest member of a triumphant team was actually doing a veteran's job.

AC: That's what happens with the absence of big scores in a big tournament. This ability to absorb pressure was evident early on in Kohli's career. He knew how to stabilize the ship, and the best part about his stay in the middle is his ability to keep the scoreboard ticking. Sometimes when wickets fall, you drop anchor and, while you absorb pressure of falling wickets, you don't take the game forward – that could cost you the game in the end. But that's never been the case with Kohli. He dissects the chase like a surgeon. What we saw in 2011 were just glimpses of what he would become one day – the greatest of all time in run chases.

JV

19

DURING THE 2011 WORLD CUP FINAL, AT 31 FOR 2, THE BATSMEN MOST LIKELY TO TAKE INDIA HOME HAD NOT BEEN DISMISSED

The 2011 World Cup final in Mumbai. No team had ever won the World Cup in front of their home crowd.

Thanks to a classy innings by Mahela Jayawardene (103 off 88 balls) and a late blitz from Thisara Perera (22 off 9 balls), Sri Lanka had reached a competitive 274 off their 50 overs.

The last 9 balls of the innings had yielded 24 runs. The atmosphere in the stadium was tense.

India came out of a shortened dinner break and immediately lost Sehwag. Gambhir joined Tendulkar at 0 for 1 to nervous cheers. As Tendulkar began to settle down, he also produced two vintage boundaries off Nuwan Kulasekara, which raised the hopes of an expectant Mumbai crowd.

With the score at 31 for 1, the first ball of the seventh over by Lasith Malinga got Tendulkar to edge to Sangakkara, who accepted it gleefully behind the wicket. Silence enveloped that ground, and indeed the country.

The curious thing was this – given that India were chasing under pressure in a big final, and given that 31 for 2 meant mathematical pressure as well – if India had to choose five batsmen from the top seven to win the game for them that day, Sehwag and Tendulkar are the ones they would leave out.

Here's a table of India's top seven, until that day (2 April 2011).

India's Top 7 Till the Final

Batsman	*Matches*	*Pressure Impact*	*Chasing Impact*	*Total*	*Career Batting Impact*
Virat Kohli	53	100	100	**100**	72
Yuvraj Singh	270	85	50	**68**	72
Gautam Gambhir	113	62	67	**64**	55
Suresh Raina	114	77	50	**64**	55
MS Dhoni	182	62	58	**60**	75
Sachin Tendulkar	452	54	42	**48**	100
Virender Sehwag	225	54	33	**44**	69

All numbers in percentages vis-à-vis the highest impact batsman in that particular parameter.

The above table compares the Pressure Impact and Chasing Impact of the top seven Indian batsmen who played the World Cup final.

It is curious that both Tendulkar and Sehwag were the least likely to deliver in these circumstances here. Their relatively low Pressure Impact was partly due to them opening the innings. But that's not why their Chasing Impact was also relatively lower; it had nothing to do with staying not out but just performing in chasing innings. (Curiously, only Pakistan had a similar batting structure when it came to combining Pressure and Chasing Impact; no other team in that tournament was skewed thus.)

Interestingly, Virat Kohli and Gautam Gambhir were ace chasers – even at that time, they had the highest Chasing Impact in Indian ODI history. In fact, despite playing just fifty-three ODIs, Virat Kohli was already the highest Chasing Impact batsman in the history of ODI cricket at that time.

Since then, Kohli has only cemented this quality – he remains the highest impact chasing batsman ever in ODI cricket history by a huge distance (he is ahead of the next best – Graham Thorpe – by an unbelievable 30 per cent).

Gambhir too remains the fifth highest impact chaser of all time in ODI cricket after Kohli, Thorpe, A.B. de Villiers and Vivian Richards.

And they were not the only chasing stars in that team. Out of India's ten highest impact chasers in ODI history till then, six were in that team. A staggering fact, really.

When it came to absorbing pressure too, Virat Kohli had already shown signs of being outstanding; in fact, he absorbed the highest pressure for India in that 2011 World Cup – a significant role he played without getting much attention for it.

Yuvraj and Raina had just come out of leading India to a famous chasing win against defending champions Australia just two matches back. Kohli and Dhoni had been highest impact batsmen chasing under pressure in the previous two years. And Gambhir was India's second highest impact chasing batsman in the last two years (after Kohli).

Kohli's brilliance would flower even more emphatically after this tournament, while Dhoni and Raina would justify their billing from the Twenty20 format in the fifty-over format too. Man of the Tournament, Yuvraj, and the highest impact batsman of the World Cup final, Gambhir, would gradually fade out, though.

That night, however, it had all been perfectly set up.

AC: The stars had aligned in India's favour. Firstly, despite the late flourish, Sri Lanka's score was not daunting in a 50-over game. Yes, you can add a few runs to the final total as scoreboard pressure in a big final, but you could also take away a few for the dew that was likely to – and eventually did – play a significant role.

There were two other factors that went in India's favour that night: no team had played Malinga as well as India (Kohli and Dhoni being the key batsmen in this regard) and even Muralitharan wasn't as big a force against this Indian team, and they were the two best Sri Lankan bowlers. Add to that, after the initial burst, Malinga had a very average day (I don't remember him being off the mark by so much and so often till then) and the improper utilization of resources by Sangakarra (Muralitharan not only didn't finish his quota of overs despite going at just 4.87 runs per over (RPO) but also bowled in non-key phases of the innings). On the contrary, Kulasekara, the most expensive Sri Lankan bowler that night bowled more than the offie. It was odd.

JV: The selection for that Sri Lankan XI itself had been odd. Herath being left out made little sense.

AC: Coming back to the chasing ability of some of the Indians batsmen – Kohli and Dhoni have been two of the finest chasers in the history of world cricket. I've never seen someone breaking down the chase as meticulously as these two; they would know exactly how much they needed to do at every stage. If a boundary wasn't needed, they would keep pushing ones and twos. Apart from the ability to hit boundary shots at will, they have the unique ability to get 6 runs an over without taking risks. So, for a sub-300 total, they don't even need to break a sweat.

As for Gambhir, he's always been someone who did best when there was a target in front of him, whether he was playing for Delhi or for India. In fact, his best scores in the longer format of the game are also in the second or third innings. On that night though, he was my Man of the Match, and not Dhoni. In my book, he absorbed more pressure and brought India to a stage where a win was within reach.

JV: You're right about Gambhir's innings having higher impact, but only just. His innings had a 4 per cent higher impact than Dhoni's. While he definitely absorbed more pressure (at 31 for 2), Dhoni's pace of scoring cannot be underestimated here. He came in to bat at 114 for 3, so the match was wide open then. Also, Dhoni's role as captain and wicketkeeper took him ahead, so he was comfortably the highest impact player, even if Gambhir was the highest impact batsman.

AC: That is an interesting note about keeping and captaincy. While we give him more weightage, do we deduct anything in case of dropped catches or stumpings? Or like in Sangakkara's case, poor captaincy? Just because he's squatting 300 times, he shouldn't be given extra credit.

JV: But they are crucial concrete roles – one expending physical energy the other mental energy. Wicketkeeping deserves a flat value (where we also calibrate the advantage he gets of being able to take catches, and also deduct byes from his value), and a captain gets captaincy value only when his team wins. We think Dhoni deserved this one.

JV/SS

20

MITCHELL STARC WAS NOT THE HIGHEST IMPACT BOWLER IN THE 2015 WORLD CUP

In the 2015 World Cup, Mitchell Starc got the Man of the Tournament award for his undeniably lethal bowling. It was not surprising: his bowling was photogenic; he was the joint highest wicket taker with Trent Boult; and Australia won the tournament.

Yet, he was not even the highest impact bowler of the tournament, let alone player.

In none of Australia's three knockout games was Starc the highest impact bowler for his team. Against Pakistan in the quarter-final, it was Josh Hazelwood (4–35 in 10 overs); against India in the semi-final, it was Mitchell Johnson (2–50 in 10 overs); and against New Zealand in the final, it was James Faulkner (3–36 in 9 overs). Twice in these matches, Starc was the second highest impact bowler for Australia and once the third highest.

Therefore, Starc shared impact with the other three Aussie bowlers, and ended up being a support actor rather than the lead actor in the most crucial games – even though it felt different, just watching him bowl (like when he took a crucial wicket like McCullum's in the final). In strong bowling sides, registering impact is sometimes about plain luck, but here, there is another curious reason too.

Starc was the joint highest wicket taker of the tournament (with Trent Boult), but 8 of his 22 wickets were lower-order batsmen (Nos.

9–11). Boult, meanwhile, took only 2 of those in his 22. Since Impact Index gives a lower value to these wickets, for obvious reasons, Starc went down in impact compared to Boult despite a superior Economy Impact.

Now, Starc easily had the best economy rate in the tournament (3.50). Boult (4.36) was considerably behind him in terms of conventional numbers, but on the Economy Impact, Boult was only marginally behind him as more runs were scored per over in New Zealand than Australia (since grounds are smaller in New Zealand).

James Faulkner turned out to be the highest impact bowler in the tournament. But Starc did register very high impact on some individual bowling parameters. Besides the highest Economy Impact, he had the highest lower-order (9–11) Wickets Impact in the tournament. Also, he did not fail even in one match (failure rate 0 per cent).

Still, the Man of the Tournament should rightfully have gone to Steve Smith. He was the sixth highest scorer in the tournament, but in each of the three knockout games (the most significant matches in any tournament), Smith contributed prominently: 65 (off 69) against Pakistan out of 216 for 4, 105 (off 93) against India out of 328 and 56 not out (off 71) after being 2 for 1 against New Zealand. Any one of these performances would have individually got him a tournament-defining performance for his batting alone; no batsman in World Cup history has been this consistent (only Aravinda de Silva in 1996 comes close) in knockout games.

None of this is to take credit away from Starc's magnificent bowling in the tournament, but Steve Smith was the highest impact player, and was the best choice for the Man of the Tournament award. Frankly, you could not give Starc the award on logic, but emotion.

AC: We all tend to ignore the fact that a bowler bowling well from one end allows the other one to be more successful. Starc was definitely the standout performer for the simple reason that he was putting immense pressure on the opposition to go after others. It was a given that you would not be able to get him away, so what option do you have but to go after the other bowlers? For example, in the final, New Zealand went after

James Faulkner because they knew that, in the last ten overs, there will be Starc bowling again. So, in the powerplay overs, Faulkner came and took three wickets. And before that, Starc had taken the McCullum wicket, which was huge, a serious body blow – New Zealand's belief was sucked out with that wicket.

JV: Yes, McCullum's wicket was huge, but New Zealand had recovered; they were actually 150 for 3 after 35 overs, with Ross Taylor and Grant Elliot set. It was actually quite ominous for Australia. But Faulkner came in and got Taylor and the dangerous Corey Anderson and a little later, even Elliot. He changed the match for Australia.

AC: That's there. Starc, however, cleaned up the tail right through the tournament at important times.

JV: But Trent Boult got more top- and middle-order wickets than Starc in the tournament. Surely that's a bigger contribution?

AC: Yes, but Boult bowled in New Zealand where the ball was darting around more, while Starc bowled on flatter pitches in Australia. Also, Boult would bowl much longer spells (as McCullum played with three or so specialist bowlers). So, for both those reasons, he got more of those wickets. But Starc's economy was a huge factor and he also bowled at the death, which was very significant. For me, he was the best bowler of the tournament.

In a tournament which was dominated by the bat, and given that Australia played on flat pitches in Australia, this may be an emotional reason to see a bowler get that award.

JV/SS

21

INDIA'S SECOND HIGHEST IMPACT ONE-DAY BOWLER: MADAN LAL

Madan Lal took 73 wickets in sixty-seven ODI matches for India at an average of 29 and an economy rate of 4.05. Nothing special on any count here. He had a 41 per cent failure rate as an ODI bowler, which is unimpressive as well.

Yet, he comes up second highest when it comes to the Bowling Impact charts for India after Anil Kumble (we have taken a minimum sixty ODIs, which is the average number of matches a player takes to get a series or tournament-defining performances in ODI cricket).

There are two special attributes that make him stand out in the history of Indian cricket.

Master restrictor

After Kapil Dev, Madan Lal is the second highest Economy Impact pacer in Indian ODI cricket history.

Kapil Dev's greatest asset in this format was his Economy Impact (which measures the economy rate of a bowler in a match relative to the economy rate of every match he has played).

AC: Hasn't the economy rate increased for bowlers over the last twenty years? An RPO of 4 in the 1980s is equivalent to one of 5.5 today. So, how's it fair to compare? Are you comparing

Madan Lal's economy rates with the bowlers of that era? And does he stand out there too?

JV: On Impact Index, it is all taken care of simply because it measures every performance relatively in the same match. So, the standards of its time are built into every reading.

After Kapil Dev, the highest impact bowlers till date (minimum sixty ODIs) in this aspect for India are Harbhajan Singh, R. Ashwin, Anil Kumble and Ravindra Jadeja – all spinners. Javagal Srinath and Manoj Prabhakar are the pacers who come after Madan Lal on this chart.

However, it is curious that Madan Lal's two most notable triumphs in ODI cricket had nothing to do with his restrictive ability. Those two performances came in crucial knockout games for India in the two historic wins India had in that period: the 1983 World Cup and the 1985 World Championship of Cricket.

This is the other notable reason why he is of so high impact; Madan Lal had two tournament-defining performances in just sixty-three completed matches.

Vs Australia and West Indies, Prudential World Cup, England, 1983. Madan Lal failed with the ball just twice in the eight games he played in the 1983 World Cup and was at his best at some of its most important moments. In the match against Australia, which was practically a quarter-final, Madan Lal helped defend a decent Indian total of 247 by supporting the initial breakthroughs from Roger Binny with 4 for 20 in 8.2 overs, which routed Australia for 129.

His most notable moment came in the final when India played West Indies. After India managed to reach 183 (to which Madan Lal contributed a precious 17), West Indies were 50 for 1 in no time and the match looked gone. Then, Madan Lal got Haynes spooning a good-length ball to cover, which seemed a minor blip at the time. Seven runs later, Viv Richards, batting like he was in a school game, savagely pulled Madan Lal to midwicket and Kapil Dev ran back to take a famous catch. Richards walked back for 33 off 28 balls. The first sign of unrest in the West Indian ranks was followed by a serious moment of doubt very soon when Larry Gomes edged Madan Lal to slip. Within 16 runs, Madan Lal had taken 3 wickets as the situation completely transformed from certain defeat to a possible sensational upset.

> **AC:** While there are 100 (120 back then) overs bowled in an ODI, only a couple turn the course of a match. That was indeed the case with the ball that dismissed Viv Richards. I was only six at that time, but the image of Kapil Dev running backwards to take that lovely catch is still fresh in my mind. Richards not only had the ability to take the match away in a few overs but also was in sublime form, and that's why the importance of that wicket can never be overstated. In fact, that dismissal can be viewed as one of the most important events in the history of Indian cricket.

Eventually, because of the timing of his best performances, Madan Lal emerged as the highest impact bowler of the tournament. Interestingly, his highest impact in the tournament came for a quality not usually associated with him: his 17 wickets tally was the joint second highest in the tournament.

Vs New Zealand, World Championship of Cricket, Australia, 1985. As compelling a tournament as any World Cup, this one-off tournament showcased some outstanding cricket, particularly from an inspired Indian team that won even more convincingly than in 1983.

Madan Lal had a poor tournament overall but came good in the semi-final against New Zealand, who batted first. He got Martin Crowe before he had settled down and later got 3 more wickets as New Zealand tried for quicker runs. His 4 for 37 off 8 overs played a big role in restricting them to 209. India went on to win that game and the tournament.

> **AC:** Madan Lal came across as a hard-working bowler ... someone you could throw the ball to at any stage of the game with the guarantee that he'd run in hard and give his 100 per cent. His biggest strength was his deception; he didn't look, and, to

> be fair, wasn't, as penetrative as Kapil or Hadlee, but had the uncanny ability to surprise the batsman with sharp off-cutters. With an action that suited outswing bowling, he could bowl a sharp off-cutter without much change in action, and that deceived some of the best.

An impact summation

Madan Lal played seven ODIs for India between 1974 and 1976 and was then dropped, only to make a comeback against England in 1981. He was a regular feature in the team till 1985, then sat out for a period of nearly a year, and came back in 1986 to play seventeen more ODIs.

In that main period between 25 November 1981 to 29 March 1985, Madan Lal played forty-one ODIs and was the third highest impact bowler in the world after Joel Garner and Michael Holding ahead of the likes of Kapil Dev, Malcolm Marshall, Geoff Lawson, Richard Hadlee and Imran Khan.

During that period, he was the second highest impact player for India after Kapil Dev, and the fifth highest impact player in the world after Kapil Dev, Viv Richards, Joel Garner and Michael Holding.

These two tournaments remain the highlight of Madan Lal's ODI career. The three highest impact performances of his ODI career came in the World Cup (against Australia, Zimbabwe and West Indies), and the fourth was in the semi-final at the World Championship of Cricket.

India's two biggest wins after these tournaments were the 2011 World Cup and 2013 Champions Trophy. No player had a tournament-defining performance in both.

It is his performance in those two big moments that define Madan Lal's place in Indian cricket history.

JV/SS

22

THE SECOND HIGHEST IMPACT PLAYER IN WEST INDIES' ODI CRICKET HISTORY: CARL HOOPER

Bio profiles of Carl Hooper always harp on the assumption that he could have done so much more with his obvious talent, the ostensible equal of Brian Lara's. They usually look at his Test performances and occasionally his ODI numbers, but eventually dismiss both as mediocre going purely on his averages (around 35 in both formats).

Admittedly, a batting average of 35 in ODIs at a strike rate of 77 with just 7 centuries does not suggest anything extraordinary. Lara averages 40, for example, at a strike rate of 80 with 19 centuries. While Hooper additionally also has 193 wickets in his 227 matches, his average of 36 apiece clearly gets him pronounced a part-time bowler.

Impact Index finds an entirely different story.

When we look at a list of the highest impact West Indian ODI players of all time, Carl Hooper comes up as the second highest impact player (and all-rounder) after Viv Richards. Given that Richards is the highest impact ODI player ever, from any country, this seems even more surprising.

West Indian cricket has not produced many genuine all-rounders, besides Hooper and Garry Sobers. Even in ODI cricket, Viv Richards and Chris Gayle marginally make it as batting all-rounders. Dwayne Bravo, Phil Simmons, Darren Sammy and Kieron Pollard are lower impact, both as batsmen and bowlers compared to Hooper, as are Larry Gomes and Keith Arthurton.

On an international stage, Carl Hooper comes up as the sixteenth highest impact player of all time (minimum sixty matches) – he is certainly a part of an elite group. The (bowling/batting) all-rounders ahead of him are Viv Richards, Imran Khan, Andrew Flintoff, Shane Watson, Greg Chappell, Wasim Akram, Kapil Dev, Jacques Kallis and Shaun Pollock.

The ones with less impact than him in ODI cricket include Hansie Cronje, Ian Botham, Shakib Al Hasan, Irfan Pathan, Andrew Symonds, Sanath Jayasuriya, Richard Hadlee, Shahid Afridi, Chris Cairns, Lance Klusener and Mohammad Hafeez.

Vs England, December 1997. *In the third match of the four-nation tournament at Sharjah, it is 50 for 3 when Hooper comes out to bat. In one of his finest innings, he makes 100 not out off 135 balls in a team total of 197. But England eventually win by 4 wickets (Hooper gets 1–22 in 8 overs); they would go on to beat West Indies in the final too a week later and win a rare multi-nation event.*

Hooper was also a big match player. Only Viv Richards (8) had more series-defining performances than him (5) amongst West Indians in ODI cricket.

Hooper, the batsman, is higher impact than the likes of Gayle and Samuels

Contrary to popular assumption, Lara is not up there when it comes to ODI batting impact for West Indies. Viv Richards, Clive Lloyd, Gordon Greenidge and Desmond Haynes are all higher impact than Lara. Then, Ramnaresh Sarwan and Shivnarine Chanderpaul come between Lara and Hooper on that chart. This makes Hooper the eighth highest impact batsman in West Indies' ODI cricket history.

After Hooper, come the likes of Chris Gayle and Gus Logie and Marlon Samuels.

AC: No. 5 or 6 is the toughest position to bat at in ODI cricket because of how little time you get, and this has never changed. You tend to play the situation a lot more in those positions. Hooper batted there for about two-thirds of his career, and so you have to look at his batting average of 35 from that angle.

Vs Australia, January 1996. *28 for 3 when Hooper walked out to bat. Soon, it was 54 for 5. Fellow-spinner Roger Harper stayed with him for a bit, but no one else did. West Indies got to 172 for 9 in the allotted forty-three overs, Hooper 93 not out in 96 balls. Australia, despite being 74 for 7 at one stage, went on to win by one wicket, thanks to Michael Bevan's famous 78 not out.*

Still, at the time, Hooper was deemed inconsistent for often giving his wicket away after being set. His batting failure rate of 46 per cent supports this notion, but does not prove it conclusively. Lara's failure rate was 43 per cent, Chanderpaul's 45 per cent. Were they really that much more consistent? Gayle's has been 48 per cent but do people consider him that much of an underachiever?

It did not prevent him from being a big match player though. Hooper's two batting series-defining performances are equal in number to Lara's in 72 lesser (completed) matches.

Vs Pakistan, October 1988. *In the final at Sharjah, twenty-one-year-old Hooper comes out to bat at 89 for 2 and top-scores with 62 off 71 balls, seeing off Wasim Akram and Abdul Qadir at their best. Defending 235, led by Ambrose, West Indies dismiss Pakistan 11 short. (Hooper also takes 1–35 in 7 overs.) This was Hooper's first SD.*

Hooper is the third highest impact spinner for West Indies in ODI cricket

This is surprising, isn't it, until you think about it a bit more? Hooper's 193 ODI wickets came in 227 matches at an economy of 4.36 in 1,600-odd overs. This is a lot of work, not the sort you would associate with a part-time bowler.

AC: West Indies had a good fast-bowling attack during the period he played, so he was always a marginal, rather than the key, bowler, where restricting the opposition was most often the objective. Given that, his economy rate of 4.36 in ODIs is very good, especially because batsmen try to go after relief bowlers.

But should he be compared to specialist bowlers? He is the fourteenth highest impact West Indian bowler in ODIs (minimum sixty matches) – higher impact when it came to just economy, and sometimes he took important wickets too.

Vs South Africa, January 1999. *On a bouncy Durban pitch, Hooper takes 4–52 in 10 overs – the wickets of Gibbs, Klusener, Kallis and Boucher, as South Africa make 274 for 9. But West Indies cannot handle the South African pacemen and are all out for 219.*

Two aspects of Hooper the bowler stand out through Impact Index. First, he is the third highest impact West Indian spinner ever in ODIs, behind Sunil Narine and Roger Harper (minimum sixty matches).

Second, Hooper is the seventh highest impact partnership-breaking bowler in West Indian ODI history, after Chris Gayle, Dwayne Bravo, Phil Simmons, Roger Harper, Jerome Taylor and Sunil Narine.

With a 45 per cent failure rate, Hooper was more consistent with the ball than Harper and much more than all-rounders like Darren Sammy, Dwayne Bravo, Marlon Samuels, Chris Gayle or Kieron Pollard.

Hooper actually started out higher impact than Lara in ODIs and stayed so for almost half his career

During Hooper's ODI playing years (March 1987 to March 2003), he was the tenth highest impact player in the world (minimum fifty ODIs) and the highest impact West Indian player by a distance.

In fact, if we just take the six years from January 1988 to December

1993, Hooper, who played exactly 100 matches in that period, comes up as the fifth highest impact ODI player in the world after Imran Khan, Dean Jones (a single-skill player having a legendary run), Curtly Ambrose (remarkable for a bowler to be so high impact in ODIs given that they get limited overs to bowl) and Mark Waugh.

Curiously, in the last four years of his career (1999–2003), Hooper was the second highest impact West Indian ODI player after Chris Gayle. His failure rate as a player was still remarkably at 25 per cent.

And he was still higher impact than Lara. Of course, Lara was a single-skill player, but still, the idea that Hooper was more valuable to his side than Lara, boggles the mind a little bit, doesn't it?

Hooper was closest to a batting all-rounder for West Indies in Test cricket, only after the great Garry Sobers and Frank Worrell

Hooper scored 5,762 runs in 102 Tests at an average of about 36.5 with 13 centuries. He took 114 wickets at an average of almost 50 apiece and five wickets in an innings four times in about 2,300 overs in his Test career. That is not the work of a part-time bowler.

Hooper comes up as the fourteenth highest impact West Indian player then, ahead of the likes of Gordon Greenidge, Desmond Haynes, Rohan Kanhai, Ramnaresh Sarwan, Shivnarine Chanderpaul and Chris Gayle.

But are we comparing apples and oranges here? Are we comparing single-skill players with Hooper, who was a genuine all-rounder in ODIs, and in Tests was almost 75 per cent there?

The conclusion is even more fascinating then. There is only one batting all-rounder – the superhuman to dwarf all others, much like Bradman was as a batsman. But there is only one Garry Sobers in cricket history.

The only other West Indian player who comes close to being a batting all-rounder is Frank Worrell, who was a lot else besides. He was Royalty, much like Sir Garry himself. He comes in third on a list of batting all-rounders and near-batting all-rounders in Test cricket.

And then, there is Carl Hooper, at seventh position.

Consistency – yes, that's worth bringing up here. Hooper's 24 per cent failure rate as a player then made him more consistent (albeit with two skills) than Richardson (29 per cent), Lara (30 per cent), Lloyd (33 per cent), Chanderpaul (37 per cent) and the big one – Viv Richards (36 per cent).

In conclusion, Hooper was an emphatic two-skill player

The energy a player has to play with is finite, no matter how prodigious the talent. This is why even the greatest all-rounders are not expected to deliver consistent performances in any one discipline, even though they may be capable of it talent-wise.

However, it appears to have been expected of Carl Hooper. Could this additional pressure be what prevented him from expressing his true potential?

If he had been seen as a dual-skill player, would he have got the space to bat with the same freedom as the other high impact all-rounders got in ODI history? Would that space to fail have made him an even better player?

One thing is for sure – his place in cricket history would be more correctly defined then.

AC: The first thought I have of Carl Hooper is someone who can hit the long ball, a batsman playing in a nice maroon floppy hat who could hit towering sixes. I was in a team that played against him, and I remember he was sending the ball to the roof of the Chinnaswamy stadium. He was just toying with our spinners.

All of us thought he could bowl a bit, but when you go through these numbers and delve a little deeper, you realize that perception is so much stronger than the truth sometimes.

Cold stats, or conventional statistics, just don't do justice to some players.

JV

23

THE FOURTH HIGHEST IMPACT PLAYER IN ODI HISTORY: ANDREW FLINTOFF

In ODI cricket, the highest impact players are typically the great all-rounders, courtesy their dual skills (as opposed to bowlers in Test cricket). Usually, they are batting all-rounders, which is also because of the limited bowling one gets to do in this format.

Not surprisingly then, three of the five highest impact players in ODI history are all-rounders (minimum sixty matches).

And Andrew Flintoff is right up there.

He is the fourth highest impact player in one-day cricket ever (minimum sixty matches), after Viv Richards, Dennis Lillee and Adam Gilchrist.

That makes him the highest impact bowling all-rounder in ODI history.

The main reason for Flintoff's high impact is his big-match prowess.

Flintoff is amongst the biggest big-match players in ODI history

Flintoff's tally of seven series-defining performances in 141 ODIs (135 completed matches) is the highest by an Englishman. Two of those came from all-round performances, four as a pure bowler and one as a pure batsman.

But the more startling fact is this. Flintoff's match to SD ratio is the highest for any player in ODI history. He is followed by Dennis Lillee, Glenn Maxwell, Adam Gilchrist and Quinton de Kock.

Clearly, Flintoff was given to rising to the occasion.

Vs India, 2002. *ODI series in India at 2–3. After a decent start, England are 173 for 5 when Flintoff comes in to bat in the 28th over, which soon becomes 174 for 7, thanks to a relentless Harbhajan Singh. Flintoff holds the rest of the innings together and is only out in the last over, for 40 off 50 balls, which has taken England to a respectable 255. India, cruising at 155 for 2 at one point, are still favourites at 205 for 4 in the fortieth over, when Flintoff gets Kaif. He bowls tightly and finishes with 3–38 in 9.5 overs as India lose by 5 runs. Series ends at 3–3.*

Impact Index also identifies series-defining performances (SDs) based on consistency in series where the series scoreline does not take teams to the brink. If a player gets an impact of 5 twice in a series, he gets an SD.

Astoundingly, in an ODI series against South Africa in 2008 – a five-match series in England (one abandoned due to rain) – he registered an impact of 5 four times in a row. Entirely inevitably, England won 4–0.

Vs West Indies, 2009. *ODI series tied at 2–2. In the deciding game affected by rain, England make 172 for 5 in 29 overs. Flintoff knocks over Simmons and Sarwan, as West Indies are 45 for 3. But they recover through Bravo and Pollard, and at 140 for 6 in the 27th over, the game is still alive. Then Flintoff takes a hat-trick – Ramdin, Rampaul and Benn knocked over in successive balls – and the fight leaves West Indies. England win the series 3–2.*

Although he got 5–19, this was Flintoff's last ODI game. He got an SD in his last game, which is very rare.

Flintoff is the highest impact bowler for England in ODI cricket

Flintoff is ahead of Darren Gough and James Anderson who follow him on this list.

Among English bowlers, Flintoff has the fifth highest Wickets Impact (proportion of wickets taken in matches played) after Steven Finn, Stuart Broad, Darren Gough and James Anderson.

He has the second highest Economy Impact for any English bowler after Bob Willis.

He has the second highest Partnership Breaking Impact for any English bowler after Graeme Swann.

AC: The strange thing about one-day cricket is that most of the time, except for the first few overs when the ball may be swinging, no one appears to be trying to get you out till the fiftieth over. Flintoff was a serious exception. He was a wicket-taking bowler in this format and could get well-set batsmen out. He had intent as well as execution.

JV: The best partnership-breaking bowlers are curiously the less accomplished bowlers a lot of the time because they are often change bowlers. That Flintoff and Swann are on this list is very revealing, as they were topline bowlers as well.

AC: Flintoff also bowled that 'heavy ball', which hit the bat hard. And he was a good exponent of reverse swing as well, so he could bowl at the tail end of an innings and stop runs. This is why he was worth his weight in gold.

Only Jos Buttler and Ian Botham have a better Strike Rate Impact than Flintoff

The explosive nature of his batting is well reflected in his status as the third highest Strike Rate Impact batsman for England in ODI history, after Jos Buttler and Ian Botham.

Vs Sri Lanka, ICC Champions Trophy, 2004. *England play Sri Lanka and are struggling at 70 for 3 after nineteen overs, when Flintoff comes out to bat. In the next two hours, he turns the match on its head, with a scintillating 104 off 91 balls, with 9 fours and 3 sixes and is out at the very end of the innings. It gives England a big advantage as the rain-shortened match on an otherwise sluggish wicket destroys Sri Lanka's hopes.*

Flintoff was the highest impact player in the world during his career

Between April 1999 and April 2009, the period during which Flintoff's ODI career of 141 matches ran, he was the highest impact bowler for England, the seventh highest impact bowler in the world and the fifth highest impact batsman for England . All this also made him the highest impact ODI player in the world during that period.

England won sixty-nine out of the 135 completed matches Flintoff played in. He averaged 46 in those with the bat and 18 with the ball.

Of the forty-four series or tournaments England played in during that period, England won just eleven. They did not reach the semi-finals in any of the World Cups during Flintoff's career, which further accentuates his importance to his team and to ODI cricket in general. That he was the highest impact ODI player in the world – despite England's mediocrity in ODI cricket at the time – suggests that he was a true legend.

> **AC:** He was one of the true mavericks of the game. Seriously, he could do everything. He could walk into any side as a bowler and he was more than a handy batsman as well. There have hardly been any hitters in the English ODI set-up. Flintoff was unlike an English cricketer – flamboyant and ahead of his time. English one-day cricket has always been somewhat behind the curve, not him, though. Unsurprisingly, he was compared to Ian Botham.

24

THE HIGHEST IMPACT PLAYER IN TEST HISTORY: ALAN DAVIDSON

Don Bradman is the highest impact batsman and player in the history of Test cricket when you consider a minimum of fifty Tests – no surprises there. But if we take forty Tests as minimum, it would shock many that the Australian southpaw all-rounder Alan Davidson actually comes up as the highest impact player of all time.

Yes, higher impact (as a player with two skills – batting and bowling) than Bradman, who is next on the list. This is shocking because Bradman, on conventional averages, is much higher than anyone who has played a substantial number of matches; the gap between him and the next best is not replicated anywhere else.

Davidson is also higher impact than Garry Sobers, normally considered the greatest Test player after Bradman.

The reason is straightforward: high-calibre bowlers have a higher impact than batsmen of a similar standard; that is simply the nature of Test cricket ('bowlers win matches' and all that). It follows then that the bowling all-rounder is higher impact than the batting all-rounder. Sobers is the highest impact batting all-rounder of all time, but there are four bowling all-rounders with higher impact than him (minimum forty Tests) – Davidson, Trevor Goddard, Imran Khan and Richie Benaud. (R. Ashwin is likely to join them, indeed better them, as a later story in the book elaborates on).

Davidson played for Australia between 1953 and 1963, and averaged 24.59 with the bat in forty-four Tests, and 20.53 with the ball while taking 186 wickets. Those averages suggest that he was an outstanding bowler, but he was considerably more than just a bowler. His batting average camouflages the fact that he batted in one of the lowest scoring decades in Test history.

In fact, Davidson is the second highest impact bowler in Australian Test history, after only Dennis Lillee. Despite being very good on every bowling parameter, Davidson's impact is also this high because of his four SDs as a bowler, and one as an all-rounder. These performances came at a crucial time in Australian Test history.

After the exit of Bradman in 1948, despite a brief stay as the best team in the world, Australia lost Test supremacy to England in 1953, as Len Hutton and then Peter May led England to their most prolific phase in their Test history. Between 1951 and 1958, England did not lose a single one of their fourteen Test series; this also included three Ashes triumphs. It was only in the 1958–59 Ashes that Australia regained their top status again, with a resounding 4–0 victory in Australia. Alan Davidson, with very high impact performances in the first two Tests, led the way.

Vs England, Brisbane, 1958. *In a low-scoring opening Test, Davidson first took 3 wickets as England managed 134, and then scored 25 in Australia's hard-fought 186. England struggled to score runs in the third innings, primarily because of Davidson's 28-12-30-2. None of these figures appear to stand out on their own, but taken together, they are substantial: Davidson was Australia's highest impact player in the match.*

Vs England, Melbourne, 1958–59. *In the next Test, Davidson took 6–64 as England made 259. Neil Harvey's stunning 167 took Australia to 308; Davidson contributed 24. Ian Meckiff destroyed England in the second innings with 6–38, and Davidson chipped in with 3–41 as well. Australia took a 2–0 lead and this time, Davidson was Australia's second highest impact player, but only just.*

This was the second time Davidson had produced two high impact performances in a series as Australia dominated. He had done it against South Africa just before this in what had turned out to be a landmark series for him.

Davidson's beginnings had been dismal with a failure rate of 75 per cent as a bowler (and the same as a batsman) during his first four-and-a-half years, during which he played twelve Tests, and did not justify his place in the team. Still, the team persisted with him and he came good in South Africa.

Finally, with Benaud as newly appointed captain, Davidson flowered. Australia did not lose a Test series for as long as Benaud and Davidson played together. Davidson was the world's highest impact player from then till the end of his career, and Benaud the second highest. Those were heady times for Australia.

Vs West Indies, Brisbane, 1960. *Still among the most memorable Test matches ever played, it also had Davidson's highest impact performance. West Indies 453, Davidson 5–135. Australia 505, Davidson 44. West Indies 284, Davidson 6–87. Chasing 233, Davidson came out to bat at 57 for 5. First with Ken Mackay, then with Benaud, Davidson made valuable runs, finally dismissed for 80 after more than three hours of batting. A collapse ensued and four wickets fell within six runs to give Test cricket its first tied Test.*

In the very next Test, Davidson scored 35 out of Australia's 348 but more importantly took 6–53 in the first innings to give his team a lead that eventually led to a comfortable seven-wicket win. Davidson delivered in every single match of the series, which Australia narrowly won 2–1, thanks to a tense two-wicket win in the final Test.

Strangely, for someone capable of producing outstanding batting performances, Davidson had a high failure rate of 75 per cent with the bat. It is the timing of his two highest impact batting performances that really qualified him as an all-rounder.

Vs England, Manchester, 1961. *The old enemy again, series at 1–1, fourth Test. Australia 190, Davidson 0. England 367, Davidson 3–70.*

Australia 296 for 6 when Davidson walked out, just 119 ahead. An innings of 77 not out with ten boundaries and two sixes helped put Australia 255 ahead. Davidson then took 2–50 as a famous collapse from 150 for 1 was prompted by Benaud (6–70) and Australia won by 54 runs. The last Test was drawn and the series stayed at 2–1.

Overall, Davidson's five SDs in forty-four Tests is the best SD to match ratio in Test history (minimum forty Tests) – even better than Bradman who had five SDs in fifty-two Tests. And after you realize that these five SDs came in his last thirty Tests, you might want to look for your jaw on the floor.

When it comes to consistency as well, only two batting/bowling all-rounders (excluding wicketkeeping all-rounders) were more consistent than him – both South African – Trevor Goddard and Shaun Pollock.

It was the timing of Davidson's finest performances that lifted their worth beyond the numerical value of the wickets he scalped and the runs he garnered.

As a post-Bradman Australia asserted themselves to emphatically become the world's best Test team, it was Alan Davidson who let out the loudest war cry.

AC: When we look back at that era, we rarely take into account that they played very little cricket. Davidson played forty-four Tests in ten years. And in the first 25 per cent of his career, he really didn't contribute much. Generally when you start out so poorly, it is very rare that you go on to become the mainstay of a team. I can't think of another instance. So, the second coming of Davidson is just phenomenal. The turnaround can happen for a period of six months or a year but to do it for as long as Davidson did it for (about five years) is just remarkable.

25

THE MOST UNDERRATED TEST PLAYER OF ALL TIME: TREVOR GODDARD

About 2,500 runs in forty-one Tests for South Africa at an average of 34.46 with just one Test century. And 123 wickets at an average of 26.22. Now what about those decent numbers would suggest such a radical claim?

Useful all-rounder (left-arm medium pace and opening bat), no doubt. But great? Here's what emerges on closer scrutiny.

Trevor Goddard always chipped away, he invariably contributed. His failure rate of 7 per cent is the fourth-lowest in Test history (minimum forty Tests) after M.S. Dhoni, Adam Gilchrist, both of whom also kept wickets, and Jim Laker. Goddard kept contributing and often it wouldn't even be noticed, let alone remembered.

Vs England, Port Elizabeth, 1957. *South Africa are trailing 1–2 when the last Test begins. South Africa 164 all out. England, the best team in the world then, 110 all out. Goddard 2–13 in 13 overs. South Africa 134 all out, Goddard 30. England 130 all out, 58 runs short. Goddard 2–12 in sixteen overs. Note not just the wickets but the restrictive role. How much of this would stand out in memory, or even on a scorecard later?*

The above was one of three series-defining performances in Goddard's career. The other two were:

Vs Australia, Adelaide, 1964. *Series at 0–1. Australia make 345, Goddard 5–60 in 25 overs (8-ball overs) – producing the most restrictive spells in the game, besides also taking wickets. South Africa make 595 – Goddard contributing 34 at the top, before Eddie Barlow and Graeme Pollock dominate. He makes an unbeaten 34 in the second innings as South Africa win easily. With two catches and his captaincy contribution, it's a significant impact again, and the series scoreline remains at 1–1. Goddard dominated in two other Tests as well in the series, the last one securing a draw to keep the series scoreline intact.*

Vs Australia, South Africa, 1966. *A 3–1 series for South Africa. Goddard dominating in three Tests with more than useful contributions with both bat and ball in the other two games.*

As a bowler, Goddard's hallmark was not taking wickets but his ability to restrict the opposition. He was more than 50 per cent better at it than South Africa's next best bowler in this aspect, the more celebrated Shaun Pollock. Unsurprisingly, he is among the world's best in Test history as well; the fourth highest Economy Impact bowler of all time, after Lance Gibbs, Glenn McGrath and Muttiah Muralitharan.

He was a captain too in thirteen Tests – three series – and lost just one to England; the other two were drawn. Curiously, he had much higher impact as a batsman than as a bowler in these matches.

In the eleven Test series Goddard played (1955–70), South Africa lost four, drew four and won three (their last three before the apartheid ban). During this period, Trevor Goddard was the most consistent and the third highest impact player in the world after Alan Davidson and Richie Benaud.

His name should be taken with the greatest all-rounders and players of the game. In fact, he is the third highest impact player of all time (minimum forty Tests) after Alan Davidson and Don Bradman.

AC: Trevor Goddard who? Well, I won't be the only one with that expression for a very simple reason – he's never been a part of any cricketing discussion that I've seen or heard. In any case, there's limited information about South African cricket before the apartheid era and whatever little is there, it's about Graeme Pollock or Barry Richards, and how they would've ended as all-time greats if they continued to play top-flight cricket for longer. It's a travesty that we don't know more such stories, so thank you, Impact Index. The world is poorer that we did not see more of Pollock and Richards (for very good political, if not cricketing, reasons), but the world is also poorer not to acknowledge the stories that still exist.

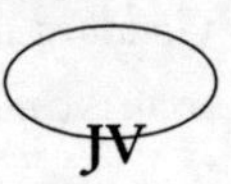

26

THE MOST RESPECTED TELEVISION COMMENTATOR OF ALL TIME IS ACTUALLY AUSTRALIA'S THIRD HIGHEST IMPACT PLAYER EVER

Richie Benaud's influence went way beyond the middle. His statesman-like presence gave legitimacy to Kerry Packer's World Series Cricket in 1977, which went on to change world cricket. Thereafter, given the place of television rights in the game, it can be said that Benaud is the most significant commentator in cricket history, and widely acknowledged as being among the very best qualitatively too.

Curiously, his enormous success as a media personality took away a lot from what he had accomplished on the field. He is a legend of proportions that the modern generation is just not aware of.

Benaud is the third highest impact Australian Test cricketer of all time (minimum forty Tests) after Alan Davidson and Don Bradman (which means the second highest impact after Bradman, if we take fifty Tests as minimum). And the sixth highest impact player of all time, after Alan Davidson, Don Bradman, Trevor Goddard, Muttiah Muralitharan and Imran Khan. Benaud is then followed by Malcolm Marshall, Garry Sobers and Richard Hadlee.

To date, Benaud is Austalia's second most consistent all-rounder ever (non-wicketkeeper) after Davidson, and their second most successful as well. And also the second highest impact spinner in

Australian Test history after Shane Warne (again, minimum forty Tests).

Even though he is supposed to have begun slowly in his first twenty-seven Tests (or rather, his first seven series), he actually did well as a bowler – even registering a series-defining performance in the tour to India in 1956, with two big performances that helped Australia win 2–0.

Vs India, Chennai/Kolkata, 1956. *On the first day of the series, Benaud's 7–72 finished off India for 161, and pretty much the match with it, as Australia batted well and took a big lead. In the third Test, Benaud made 24 out of Australia's 177, then 6–52 to still get his team a 41-run lead. Then he made 21 out of Australia's 189–9 declared, following up immaculately with 5–53, as India lost by 94 runs. Australia won the series 2–0.*

He became even more consistent with bat and ball from the 1956–57 tour of South Africa, and was the highest impact spinner in the world from then till the end of his career (February 1964). And the second highest impact Test cricketer in the world after teammate Alan Davidson. No wonder Australia dominated that era.

Vs South Africa, Cape Town/Johannesburg, 1958. *In the second Test, Benaud made just 33 in Australia's substantial 449, but then led the way with the ball – 4–95 to dismiss South Africa for 209 – and then opening the bowling and garnering 5–49, as they were blown away for just 99. In the fourth Test, Benaud top-scored with 100 in Australia's 401, then followed up with 4–0 and 5–84. Australia won by 10 wickets, and eventually went on to win the series 3–0.*

Benaud was also a highly respected captain, whose team did not lose a single series under him. As a player too, he flourished under the added responsibility.

Vs England, Adelaide/Melbourne, 1959. *With Australia 2–0 up – and set to dethrone England as the best Test team in the world by winning the Ashes after eight long years – captain Benaud made 49 out of Australia's 476. Then, with 5–91 in the first innings, and 4–82 in the second, the* *historic moment was ushered in. Lastly, with a 4–43 and a 64 in the final Test, as Australia won by 9 wickets, it became a thrashing, rather than just a victory.*

Once England's unbeaten reign as the world's best team was thwarted in the 1958–59 Ashes, it was Australia all the way for the next six years.

Australia played seven Test series after that as the world's best team; Benaud played in the first six. Australia won four of those and drew two.

Vs England, Manchester, 1961. *The Ashes were at 1–1 with two Tests to go. Benaud did not figure significantly in the first three innings of the fourth Test. Australia made 190 (Benaud 2), England 367 (Benaud 0–80) but Australia fought back with 432 (Benaud just 1) and then, when England needed 256 to win in 230 minutes on the final day (which meant 67 runs an hour), and were sauntering along at 150 for 1, the script changed dramatically. The Australian captain was suddenly and emphatically written in. England just 106 more to win with 9 wickets in hand. First, Benaud broke through, bowling into the rough, by getting Ted Dexter (who had been promoted to No. 3 from No. 6) for a superb swashbuckling 76 as he tried to cut but nicked. Two balls later, Benaud bowled the opposing captain Peter May behind his legs. And he got the next four wickets to fall in a space of 21 runs. The rest was a formality, as Australia won the Test by 54 runs, and led the series 2–1. This turned out to be the final series scoreline, because the next Test was drawn. Often considered to be the second greatest Test match after the tied Test (which happened barely six months before this one, at Brisbane), this one had a greater impact on the series scoreline, as it also came deep into the series.*

This was his fifth series-defining performance – a tremendous SD to match ratio, given that he played just sixty-three Tests.

Richie Benaud retired in 1964, at thirty-three as Australia's most significant post-war cricketer (in part due to his captaincy profile). Despite the dominance of Australia in later years, with many new legendary stars, given his long innings as a broadcaster, this is a status he never quite relinquished.

AC: I grew up listening to Richie Benaud, and it took me some time to figure out that he wasn't just a media personality but someone who bowled leg-spin and even led Australia. When you're so good at the thing you're currently doing, that transcends everything else that you've achieved in life.

When you talk of Australia, you talk about a pantheon of match winners and impact players – the list is endless, really. Just to see that Richie Benaud is of as high impact as this is simply shocking, especially given his conventional figures. Obviously, Davidson and he combined brilliantly together and won Australia a lot of series.

They also played in an era when batting was not glamorous (it was a low-scoring era, as mentioned earlier as well), and since batting stories didn't come out much, those ten or twelve years just seem to vanish from public memory and are hardy spoken of now. That era has not been documented as well as others have, and it is interesting to see how many stories in this book are from it. Maybe this is true for the entire cricket world and not just India – without batting stories from this period, we tend to just move on to the next best story, or the stories from the next generation, where batting stories became more prominent.

27

THE SECOND MOST CONSISTENT ALL-ROUNDER IN TEST HISTORY: TONY GREIG

Tony Greig is remembered today mostly for his charming and infectious brand of commentary. Or for his association with the Kerry Packer rebel league and his infamous 'grovel' interview. You would imagine that a character so colourful would have got his fair due for his showing on the field. That isn't the case, though.

For a minimum of fifty Tests, Greig emerges as the second most consistent all-rounder in the history of Test cricket after Shaun Pollock. A Test batting average of 40 and a bowling average of 32 in fifty-eight Tests suggests something special anyway, but his failure rate is what separates him from the greatest players to grace the field. Greig's failure rate of only 12 per cent was better than the likes of Imran Khan, Garry Sobers, Ian Botham, Kapil Dev and Jacques Kallis – all legends of the game.

When it came to influencing series scorelines by providing series-defining performances, Tony Greig wasn't as instrumental as Ian Botham (six SDs in 102 Tests), Imran Khan (six in eighty-five Tests) or Wasim Akram (eight in 101 Tests).

Greig had only two SDs to his name in fifty-eight Tests, but – and this is important – he only ever failed in seven Tests. Only seven Tests out of fifty-eight! Stunningly, Greig didn't fail in a single Test match between mid-1973 and mid-1976, a twenty-six-Test streak over a duration of three years. In this period, he was the second highest impact player after Greg Chappell and the most consistent player in the world.

Apart from being highly consistent, Greig also produced some high impact performances. Here are some of them:

Vs India, Kolkata, 1973. *India, batting first, managed only 210 runs as Greig chipped in with the wicket of Salim Durani. England, in their reply, were 56 for 4 when Greig walked in to bat, but his 29 wasn't enough as England fell short of the Indian total by 36 runs. India, in their second innings, fared even worse as they scored only 155 with Greig triggering a collapse after they were 112 for 3 at one point of time. Greig finished with 5 for 24. Chasing 192 on a pitch where only two batsmen had managed to score 50-plus runs, England were in disarray at 17 for 4 when Greig and Mike Denness initiated a fightback. Out of their 97-run partnership, Greig scored 67 before perishing to Chandrasekhar. His dismissal saw the next four wickets falling for 24 runs as England fell short by 28 runs. The next highest scorer was Denness with 32 runs. India levelled the series 1–1 and would go on to win it 2–1. Although it came in a losing cause, Greig's all-round display was the highest impact performance of his career.*

Vs West Indies, Port-of-Spain, 1974. *Trailing 0–1, going into the fifth and final Test, England opted to bat first and were bowled out for 267. West Indies, in reply, were cruising at 224 for 2 when Greig turned the match on its head. In a space of 20 balls, Greig sent back 4 West Indian batsmen for just six runs. He went on to pick up the remaining four wickets to end with figures of 8–86 as West Indies managed to have a lead of only 38 runs. England, riding on Boycott's 112, posted 263. Chasing 224, West Indies again succumbed to Greig's off breaks as he accounted for Alvin Kallicharran, Clive Lloyd and Rohan Kanhai to finish with 5 for 70. West Indies fell short by 26 runs and England managed to level the series 1–1. This was the first series-defining performance of Greig's career.*

Vs New Zealand, Auckland, 1975. *England, after opting to bat first, declared at 593. Greig chipped in with 51. New Zealand, in reply were going strong at 125 for 1 when Greig broke the partnership by removing*

John Morrison. Greig went on to pick 4 more wickets to finish with 5–98 in the first innings. New Zealand, after being asked to follow on, were again ravaged by Greig as he picked up 5–51 to finish with 10 wickets in the match. This Test influenced the series result as the next and last Test ended in a draw. Even though Greig produced an SD performance, his contribution is mostly mentioned as a footnote because the match became infamous for Ewen Chatfield collapsing on the field from a Peter Lever bouncer.

Vs India, Kolkata, 1976. *After a surprise English win in the first Test, Bob Willis set the tempo in the second by picking 5–57 to bundle India out for 155. England, in their reply, were struggling at 90 for 4. Greig and Roger Tolchard then built a partnership of 142 runs. Tolchard scored 67 while Greig contributed 103. That England scored 321 in 178-odd overs signified their toil on a tricky pitch. India managed only 181 in their second innings as Greig chipped in with the wickets of Anshuman Gaekwad and Gundappa Viswanath. England won the match by 10 wickets, and held their advantage over India in the series for what would turn out to be a rare series win in the subcontinent.*

As a batsman, Greig's hallmark was to absorb pressure. He actually emerges as the sixth highest Pressure Impact batsman for England in their Test history after Peter May, Robin Smith, Graham Thorpe, David Gower and Ken Barrington (Minimum: 50 Tests). As a batsman, his consistency was better than specialist batsmen such as Michael Vaughan, Dennis Amiss, Allan Lamb, Nasser Hussain and Ian Bell.

As a bowler, Greig' consistency is better than specialist bowlers such as Phil Edmonds, John Emburey, Wilfred Rhodes, Ray Illingworth and Ashley Giles.

Greig's fielding acumen is as underrated as the rest of his career. He is amongst the ten highest impact fielders in the history of Test cricket and the second highest impact fielder for England after Paul Collingwood in Tests. His presence at forward short leg is perhaps remembered more now for the chatter than the work he did there.

He was an all-rounder in the truest sense, with a remarkable level of consistency in Test history, and the fifth highest impact English Test cricketer ever, after Ian Botham, Wally Hammond, Graeme Swann and Fred Trueman (minimum fifty Tests).

Most of the chapters in this book celebrate cricketers who have not got their due. This one is about a player who is celebrated but not necessarily for the right reason.

AC: It's quite incredible how excellence in one profession overshadows achievements elsewhere. Just like Richie Benaud, Tony Greig will be always be alive in our memories for his unique style of commentary. In fact, he's one of the role models for us New Age commentators – bringing pictures to life and turning a match into a must-watch event to remember. But his numbers as a player are incredible too. Something that would've gone unnoticed by today's generation (because of the lack of television coverage during the era he played in). Not failing even once in twenty-six Tests is a superhuman effort. That's the real value of a true all-rounder – doing something worthwhile in almost every game if not every innings. We must remember that he was an off-spinner playing most of his cricket in England and that, perhaps, explains the average of 38 there as a bowler. But even then, his propensity to break partnerships and convert a good day into a great day was remarkable.

SS

28

THE HIGHEST IMPACT PACE BOWLER IN THE HISTORY OF TEST CRICKET IS DENNIS LILLEE

Dennis Lillee's bowling greatness is hardly a hidden fact. But, given the number of worthy contenders there are for the title of 'The greatest fast bowler in Test history', he doesn't exactly get up there automatically.

Ordinarily, one would have to choose from among Richard Hadlee, Malcolm Marshall, Courtney Walsh, Curtly Ambrose, Imran Khan, Wasim Akram, Waqar Younis, Alec Bedser, Fred Trueman, Dennis Lillee, Glenn McGrath, Shaun Pollock, Allan Donald and Dale Steyn (minimum fifty Tests). The primary names from here are perhaps those of Hadlee, Marshall, Imran, Steyn, McGrath and Lillee.

Through Impact Index, though, Dennis Lillee comes up as the highest impact pace bowler ever (minimum fifty Tests), ahead of all these other luminaries. (And the second highest impact bowler of all time, after Muttiah Muralitharan.)

This may seem outlandish, because purely on wickets tally, Lillee is sixteenth in Test history in a list of pace bowlers. When it comes to bowling averages, Lillee is sixteenth again (minimum fifty Tests). When it comes to strike rate (balls per wicket), Lillee is twelfth.

In the past, we have identified many high impact players with *relatively* low conventional numbers on the basis of their big match performances or series-defining performances. Although Lillee has five SDs in just seventy Tests, Hadlee and Steyn (seven SDs each) and

Number	Name	Matches	Bowling Impact	SDs	Top/Middle-Order Wickets Tally Impact	Lower-Order Wickets Tally Impact	Economy Impact	Failure Rate (per cent)
1	Dennis Lillee	70	**100**	5	100	92	36	14
2	Malcolm Marshall	81	**98**	6	90	73	30	23
3	Richard Hadlee	86	**92**	7	89	92	27	20
4	Dale Steyn	85	**90**	7	90	100	27	17
5	Imran Khan	88	**86**	5	80	73	41	21
6	Glenn McGrath	124	**83**	4	90	68	100	18
7	Craig McDermott	71	**80**	4	82	59	9	24
8	Allan Donald	72	**79**	3	92	73	25	20
9	Jeff Thomson	51	**76**	3	83	51	5	22
10	Michael Holding	60	**76**	3	79	68	27	28

Minimum Test matches: 50.

All numbers (except for failure rate and SDs) in percentages vis-à-vis the highest impact pacer in that particular parameter.

SDs: Series-defining performances.

Impact numbers of only Tests with two completed innings included.

Marshall (six SDs) fare marginally better, not only on count but also on the frequency of producing an SD performance.

So, the reasons that Dennis Lillee registers a higher impact than the other legends go beyond the usual. Let's take a look at them.

The table on p. 154 is a list of the ten highest impact pacers in the history of Test cricket (minimum fifty Tests).

Lillee has taken the highest proportion of top/middle-order wickets in Test cricket, among fast bowlers

Even in conventional terms, Lillee took 5.07 wickets per match (355 wickets in seventy Tests). In all of Test history, only Muralitharan is ahead of Lillee in this respect.

Amongst the ten highest impact pace bowlers, only Steyn is active in world cricket and he takes 4.91 wickets per match, despite having the best strike rate in Test history. But Lillee goes ahead of Steyn in terms of impact because of a simple reason – he took more top- or middle-order wickets than lower-order. An impressive 73 per cent of Lillee's wickets were either from the top- or middle-order (Nos 1–7) whereas, in Steyn's case, it is 68 per cent.

Fellow legend Greg Chappell, whose career ran simultaneously with Lillee's, and who also captained him later, says that Lillee sought nicks rather than dismissals that involved being lbw or bowled. This entirely explains why he had a higher percentage of dismissals involving catches than any other premier bowler, including Glenn McGrath. And also why he had such a high proportion of top-order wickets.

AC: Australia tends to produce bowlers who hit the deck hard and make the ball do something off the pitch. To have the discipline to bowl a steady line for someone as rapid as he is, shows what a shrewd operator he was. Lillee had a very good bouncer; so obviously, he used intimidation too as a bowler, and for someone like that to also bowl the off stump channel consistently – that's a rare combination. The thing is, in Australia, due to the bouncy conditions you don't get too many leg-before or bowled dismissals, so the most effective bowlers bowl that line outside off which induces a lot of edges. He did

> both very well. Behind that intimidating, aggressive façade, there was a very shrewd cricketing brain in operation.

Chappell felt that Lillee was too good for the tail, or perhaps that those batsmen weren't good enough to nick them. Again, this explains his higher proportion of top/middle-order wickets. Despite this, curiously, as far as proportion of lower-order (Nos. 8–11) wickets go, Lillee is fifth in that too in Test history, after Muttiah Muralitharan, Shane Warne, Dale Steyn and Anil Kumble.

Clearly, wicket taking was second nature to Lillee.

The Ashes, The Oval, 1972. *Australia 1–2 behind when the last Test commences. Lillee takes 5–58 as England are dismissed for 284. Australia get a 111-run lead, but England fight back and make 356; Lillee 5–123. Led by Keith Stackpole (79) at first, then Paul Sheahan (44 not out) and Rod Marsh (43 not out), Australia win memorably by 5 wickets.*

Lillee is the highest impact player in the match that draws the series 2–2.

At the age of twenty-three, Lillee had an SD performance in just his second Test series. It was a sign of things to come.

Lillee was a better bowler after his injury setback

Lillee had fearsome pace in those early days, and, as a direct consequence, a recurring back injury took him out of the game barely six months later. He underwent intensive rehabilitation and lost nineteen months of international cricket.

> AC: Very few fast bowlers come back stronger after such career-threatening injuries. It seems he came back sharper and wiser, mastering the art of cranking it up when it was really needed. You'll find the same quality in Dale Steyn, if you were to compare these two bowlers from different eras.

Greg Chappell remembers how Lillee still had good pace, but chose to bowl slightly within himself, bowling the quicker ball when it was needed. He adds that he has never seen a better bowler to good batsmen than Lillee because he bowled very few loose deliveries, and it demanded enormous discipline to deal with his good balls. Even now, Chappell feels, he can think of no one who bowled a higher percentage of good balls as consistently as Lillee did.

This totally harmonizes with what Impact Index next found.

Only one bowler in Test cricket history was more consistent than Lillee

By Impact Index measures, only one bowler, spinner or pacer, in Test history has been more consistent than Dennis Lillee (minimum fifty Tests). Lillee's failure rate (the occasions when he did not register an impact of even 1 in a match) of 14 per cent is jaw-dropping, especially given the injury that threatened to end his career so early on.

Only Joel Garner had a lower failure rate (of 12 per cent) in his fifty-eight-Test career, though his overall impact is lower than many others, primarily because he took fewer top- and middle-order wickets.

The likes of Muralitharan (16 per cent failure rate), Steyn (17 per cent), McGrath (18 per cent), Hadlee (20 per cent), Imran (21 per cent), Warne (23 per cent), Marshall (23 per cent) and Ambrose (27 per cent) are all below them in this respect.

Lillee is also the most consistent player (after Jim Laker, who never failed in 15 Ashes Tests) in Ashes history (minimum fifteen Tests), with a failure rate of just 4 per cent. This is remarkable, given that he is more consistent than all the wicketkeeper-batsmen as well (whose specialist wicketkeeping functions register flat Impact values, based on historical evaluation). This consistency went some way in his being the third highest impact pace bowler in Ashes history till date after Craig McDermott and Sydney Barnes.

The Ashes, Edgbaston, 1975. *In the opening Test of the series, Australia begin well by putting up 359. Lillee and Max Walker demolish England thereafter, for a paltry 101, which pretty much decides the match. Lillee's figures were 5–15 in 15 overs. Jeff Thomson finds his length in the second innings and Australia win by an innings. This would be the only result Test of the series.*

Lillee registers his second SD.

Lillee was also a very high impact ODI bowler

Even though he played just sixty-three matches, Lillee is also the highest impact ODI bowler of all time (minimum sixty ODIs).

His Top- and Middle-Order Wickets Impact is the highest ever. But here, as happens in the limited-overs format with many great bowlers, he was also hard to get away. To date, Lillee is the second highest Economy Impact Australian bowler after Glenn McGrath.

His high ODI impact is also due to his three SDs, series in which he was very consistent right through. Not bad for a bowler who did not consider this format his natural habitat.

Lillee was the highest impact player in the world during one of Australia's most dominating periods in Test cricket

That Test team was the best in the world for a while (1972–77) and is still amongst the greatest sides in Test history.

Led by the dynamic Ian Chappell, Lillee was also fortunate to have Jeff Thomson as a fearsome opening partner (which, however, also means he shared impact with him) and a formidable batting line-up, with Greg Chappell leading the way.

Lillee was the highest impact player in the world in that period (he played thirty Tests then) and his was the biggest contribution towards making Australia the unbeatable side they were. This, despite Jeff Thomson being the second highest impact bowler after him and the Chappell brothers being the highest impact batsmen in the world, with Ian Redpath not far behind. The adage 'bowlers win matches' was demonstrated by him better than anyone else in that period.

Three of Lillee's five SDs came in this period, more than any other bowler in the world.

Vs New Zealand, Auckland, 1977. *Series at 0–0, final Test. New Zealand 63 for 1, despite best batsman Glenn Turner's loss. But all out for 229, Lillee 5–51. Australia get a big lead, and Lillee gets leeway to bowl flat out, resulting in 6–72 for him, as Australia win the Test by 10 wickets and series by 1–0.*

This is Lillee's third SD.

Lillee's great run continued till his retirement

His success continued beyond the dominant period. In fact, he was the second highest impact bowler (minimum twenty Tests) in the world after Imran Khan from 1978 till he retired in early 1984.

He registered two more SDs in this period – first against New Zealand in 1980 and then against Pakistan in the following summer in 1981 – both for producing two high impact performances which helped Australia win the series.

Vs New Zealand, Brisbane, 1980. *In the series opener, Australia electing to field, restrict New Zealand to 225. Lillee keeps it tight and picks up two wickets in the first innings. Australia reply with 305. Lillee then runs through the New Zealand top and middle order in the second innings (6–53; which included 5 top- and middle-order wickets). The visitors are routed for 142. Australia win by 10 wickets.*

Lillee continues to torment New Zealand in the second Test.

Vs New Zealand, Perth, 1980. *Lillee's 5–63 keeps New Zealand down to 196. Australia take the lead and post 265. Lillee picks up 2 wickets in the second innings but more importantly is highly restrictive as he chokes the New Zealand batsmen with a miserly spell (14 runs in 15.1 overs). New Zealand are dismissed for 121. Australia chase down their target of 53 with 8 wickets to spare.*

Vs Pakistan, Perth, 1981. *Australia, inserted in the series opener, are bowled out for 180. But they fight back in style with Lillee leading the way. His 5–18 with support from Terry Alderman skittles Pakistan for 62. Australia amass 424 in the second innings and set Pakistan 543. The visitors are bundled out for 256 with Bruce Yardley picking up 6 wickets.*

Vs Pakistan, Brisbane, 1981. *After winning the first Test, Australia combats a formidable batting line-up of Mudassar Nazar, Mohsin Khan, Majid Khan, Javed Miandad, Zaheer Abbas, Wasim Raja and Imran Khan by dismissing them for 291 on a decent pitch, with Lillee taking 5 of the top 6 wickets. He finishes with match figures of 9–132 as Australia win the match, and series, easily. Australia would lose the next Test by an innings, but win the series 2–1.*

When he retired in January 1984, Lillee held the world record for most Test wickets – 355 of them. Pertinently, he was also the highest impact Test bowler of all time (minimum fifty Tests).

Lillee was, by far, the highest impact bowler during his career

If we just consider the period when Lillee's career ran (1971–84), he comes up as the highest impact bowler in the world (minimum forty Tests). Michael Holding, with the next highest impact, is a fair distance away.

When it came to Wickets Impact, Lillee was right on top, but even in terms of restrictive ability, he was up there (third highest Economy Impact pacer after Imran Khan and Sarfraz Nawaz).

As captain, Greg Chappell always felt that Lillee was the most likely bowler to make the breakthrough when the team really needed a wicket. This explains why Lillee also has the third highest Partnership Breaking Impact after Derek Underwood and Bishan Singh Bedi in that period of Test cricket. It is rare for a strike bowler to also regularly break set partnerships as well.

Lillee was also the best pressure building bowler (taking wickets in quick succession to put pressure on the batting team). Needless to say, he was also the most consistent bowler in the world. Inevitably, Greg Chappell says, in a big game, or on a big occasion, Lillee was the one who delivered the big performance.

The Centenary Test, Melbourne, 1977. *Australia are dismissed for a paltry 138 but then England are blown away for 95 by a fearsome Lillee, at his peak then. He takes 6–26 then and later, 5–139 as England, on a pitch that has eased up considerably, chase 463 to win. Eerily, Australia win by exactly the same margin as they had in the very first Test match a hundred years before – 45 runs. The match is remembered today for many things – Rick McCosker batting with a broken jaw, David Hookes's exuberant innings during which he struck five fours in a Tony Greig over, Rod Marsh's unbeaten century, and most memorably, Derek Randall's 174 in a big fourth innings case (for which he got the Man of the Match* *award) but the highest impact performer in the match was Dennis Lillee by a big distance. Just take a look at the scorecard and it will become clear why.*

Not surprisingly, Chappell remembers no other player fitter than Lillee in his era or too many fitter players even since then.

Consider the substantial amount of Test cricket Lillee played, despite that debilitating injury early in his career, and also the consistency that never dropped.

If there has been a more complete fast bowler in the history of Test cricket, he has been well hidden.

AC: It is curious that sixty of his seventy Tests were in Australia and England, which provide favourable conditions to fast bowlers. He was an outstanding bowler, no doubt about it, but it is interesting that he took just 3 wickets in three Tests in Pakistan (with an average of 101) and did not play a Test in India. And in the 32 overs he bowled in West Indies, his figures were 0–132. He didn't really play enough in these conditions for us to make a judgement call on this, unfortunately.

JV: The Packer controversy prevented that as it was an Australian second XI that came to India in 1979 – the only Australian tour of India during Lillee's career. Australia did go to Pakistan twice during his career, and the second time it was similarly Packer. But the first series, in 1980, was very odd. Pakistan prepared a low-scoring track to aid spinners in the first Test, which they won, and then rank featherbeds to hold on to that series scoreline. Imran did better than Lillee then, but it was the spinners who decided the series. And when it came to West Indies, there were two tours. In the first tour, he just played in the first Test, which was a draw on a featherbed. And the second series was Packer-affected. So, you can't really hold it against him; he didn't cherry-pick his series.

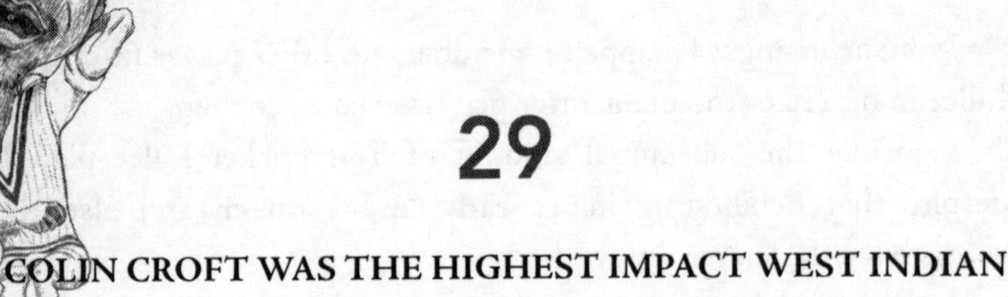

29

COLIN CROFT WAS THE HIGHEST IMPACT WEST INDIAN BOWLER DURING HIS CAREER

Colin Croft played just twenty-seven Tests for West Indies, all between 1977 and 1982. He played alongside Andy Roberts, Michael Holding and Joel Garner primarily – part of the fearsome foursome that set the foundation for the world domination Clive Lloyd's West Indies team was to accomplish.

Croft took 125 wickets at an average of 23.30 during this period – the most in his team. Only Garner played more Tests than him in that time (just one more), which also suggests something about Croft's consistency. Both Garner and Holding, however, had better bowling averages while Roberts was somewhat on the decline, relatively speaking.

Despite this, Croft is remembered largely as the fourth best bowler in this lot and more for his propensity to bowl the short ball dangerously than for being a match and series winner for his team.

Impact Index finds that he was actually West Indies' highest impact bowler in that period, remarkable given that a team with such a high-class attack always tends to share impact. Significantly, he was the second highest impact bowler in the world too just then, after Dennis Lillee – who was at his peak and on his way to being the highest impact bowler in Test history at the time.

Croft was the only West Indian to have two series-defining

performances, besides Viv Richards, and was higher impact overall than even Richards (high impact bowlers tend to be the highest impact players in Tests). All of this marks out his contribution to West Indies' world domination as legendary – not quite the status Croft enjoys.

This is why he should.

Vs Pakistan, Kingston, 1977. *In his debut Test series, the series scoreline against a spirited and talented Pakistan side was 1–1 after four Tests. Croft had taken 8–29 in the first innings of the second Test (his second Test too), which had gone some way in keeping the series alive for the hosts. Now, at crunch time, he was the leading bowler again, as he took 4–49 to help dismiss Pakistan for 198 and then took the first three wickets before Pakistan had touched 35, as they chased 442 in the fourth innings. That was a blow from which Pakistan, despite showing enormous fight, never quite recovered. West Indies won 2–1, largely due to a fearsome debutant amidst them, who had registered an SD in his first showing.*

Croft went on to do well in his tours of Australia, New Zealand, Pakistan and England too. And then, England came to the West Indies.

Vs England, Port-of-Spain/Barbados, 1981. *West Indies won the series 2–0 and in both the result Tests, Croft led the way. First, his 5–40 decimated England for 178 as they tried to reply to 426 – the match largely decided there itself. Then, in the next Test, he took 4–39 and 3–65 as West Indies took an unassailable 2–0 lead in the series, which would eventually be the series scoreline.*

This was the second of his two SDs. Bizarrely, he would play just one more Test series, in Australia, which was drawn 1–1. He took 7 wickets in three Tests in that series and never played for West Indies again.

Whether it was his reported indiscipline that ended his career prematurely (he was barely twenty-nine) or the emergence of a certain Malcolm Marshall, or the infamous Rebel Tour to South Africa in 1983 for which he was banned along with seventeen others, there is no doubt that Croft made an impact for an all-time great West Indian team for which he doesn't get credit today. He was the leading bowler for Clive Lloyd's team during those crucial early years.

In fact, if we take twenty-five Tests as the minimum (which we never do normally because it is just not enough of a sample size), Colin Croft comes up as the highest impact West Indian bowler of all time. And no, it is not just because of his SDs. He also took the highest proportion of top- and middle-order wickets than any West Indian bowler in Test history. In proportion to his matches, he broke the most partnerships in West Indian Test history, along with Colly Collymore (who otherwise had about half the impact of Croft). He inflicted the most pressure on the opposition with his bowling in Caribbean Test history, again in proportion to the number of Tests he played. And he was the most consistent West Indies bowler of all time, with a failure rate of 11 per cent.

The endings of some stories just do not make sense.

AC: It is incredible that even in the presence of Garner, Holding and Roberts, Croft managed to slip in two SDs, and this in spite of impact being shared by the fearsome foursome. Also, if you aren't seen as the best amongst the lot, you won't even be bowling with the new ball and in the right phases of the game, i.e. the wicket-taking phases. Anyone who's played cricket knows that there are certain phases in the game when the probability of taking wickets is higher and then there are phases when you know that it's all hard work as wickets are unlikely to fall. And that's where the captain uses his resources carefully – get the workhorse for the second phase and the premier bowler for the former. While Croft's name might not be taken in the same breath as some of the fast bowling greats of all time, the batsmen who played against him respected him immensely. That's the one certificate that really means something to a player.

JV

30

AUSTRALIA'S HIGHEST IMPACT PLAYER IN THEIR LEAD-UP TO WORLD DOMINANCE: CRAIG MCDERMOTT

Craig McDermott's relevance as his country's highest impact bowler in two distinct phases of its Test cricket history is his true legacy.

He is the fourth highest impact bowler after Dennis Lillee, Shane Warne and Glenn McGrath in Australia's Test cricket history – in spite of being the sixth highest in terms of wicket aggregate – 291 wickets in seventy-one Tests and holds the eleventh position with a bowling average of 28.63 in an all-time Australian list.

The rebuilding phase

Australian cricket was going through a major transformation after the retirement of Lillee, Jeff Thomson and Greg Chappell in the mid-1980s. They had won just seven out of the thirty-eight Tests played in this period.

It is in this period that a young McDermott was unearthed during the Frank Worrell Trophy in 1984. Despite a terrific Ashes series in 1985, his form dwindled thereafter and he barely got a consistent run through most of the latter half of the decade.

Although he was the highest impact bowler in Australia's victorious 1987 World Cup campaign and in the subsequent home series against New Zealand (their solitary Test series win in this period), a string of poor performances followed and he was dropped from the national side for two years.

This, despite being the highest impact bowler and also the highest impact player for Australia in this time frame (minimum twenty Tests).

Most pundits wrote him off. His career was under threat.

A great return

McDermott was recalled for the last two Ashes Tests in 1991. By this time, Australia were well on the surge.

The Ashes, 1991. *Fourth Test at Adelaide. McDermott walks out to bat at 298 for 7 and scores 42. Australia extend their total to 386. He then picks up 5–97 as England are dismissed for 229. Australia set the visitors 472 in the fourth innings. England manage to play out the 96 overs bowled by McDermott (2–106) and company to earn a respectable draw.*

In the fifth Test at Perth, McDermott returns 8–97 and 3–60. Australia win by 9 wickets.

Australia win the five-match series 3–0. McDermott registers his first series-defining performance for these two high impact performances.

It is a dream comeback.

As Australia found its winning ways, this big-match temperament became McDermott's defining quality for the rest of his career.

Vs India, Australia, 1991–92. *Australia win the five-match series 4–0. McDermott registers his second SD, again for his high standards throughout the series. In the first Test at Brisbane, he takes 5–54 and 4–47. Australia win by 10 wickets. In the fourth Test at Adelaide, McDermott picks up 5–76 and 5–92. Australia win by 38 runs.*

Vs South Africa, Adelaide, 1994. *In the third Test, McDermott records 3–49 and 4–33 (all top- and middle-order wickets). Australia win by 191 runs.*

McDermott registers his third SD as Australia draw level from behind.

AC: His teammate Dean Jones told me that McDermott would invariably have a health issue on the morning of a big game.

So much so that David Boon and others started making fun of him. But in spite of that nervousness before the start of the big game, he would invariably deliver big.

The Ashes, 1994–95. *At the first Test at Brisbane, McDermott returns 6–53 and 2–90. Australia win by 184 runs. Again, in the second Test at Melbourne, he registers 3–72 and 5–42. Australia win by 295 runs.*

Australia win the series 3–1. McDermott has his fourth SD.

McDermott was the second highest impact bowler in the world (minimum thirty Tests) from his comeback till his retirement (1991–96) after Wasim Akram.

He was also the most consistent bowler in the world in this time frame with a remarkably low failure rate of just 19 per cent.

McDermott played a pivotal role as Australia's leading strike bowler in that period, as they became the second best Test team in the world, playing sixteen series, winning ten and losing just three.

Despite missing most of the Ashes (1993) and not being a part of the side that won the historical Frank Worrell Trophy in 1995, which saw the end of the great West Indian domination, it is remarkable that McDermott emerged as the second highest impact bowler in the world for two-thirds of his career. The main reason for this was his four SDs in just forty-seven Tests in this period. It also means that he has the fourth best matches to SD ratio for an Australian bowler after Lillee (five SDs in seventy Tests), Richie Benaud (four SDs in sixty-three Tests) and Jeff Thomson (three in fifty-one).

It is also worth noting that his four SDs all came in Australia.

AC: A thing that goes against him is that his Ashes record in England (average of over 34 per wicket) wasn't great and most Australians players are judged on that one facet more than everything else put together.

Home Test bowling legend

McDermott is the highest impact pace bowler in home conditions in the history of Test cricket, primarily because he registered all his four SDs in Australia. In fact, he has the third highest impact at home for any bowler in Test cricket history after Muttiah Muralitharan and Anil Kumble. This means McDermott had a higher impact with the ball in Australia than Malcolm Marshall in the Caribbean, Allan Donald in South Africa, Imran Khan in Pakistan and Richard Hadlee in New Zealand – a phenomenal achievement.

Overall, McDermott is the tenth highest impact bowler in the history of Test cricket.

He was the second highest impact bowler and player for Australia (after Shane Warne, minimum forty Tests) during his career (1984–96), by the end of which Australia were well on their way to dominating world cricket for the next twelve years.

AC: My memories of watching him play are of a bowler who was bowling big outswingers on one tour and would bowl equally effective inswingers on the following tour. He was like any other Australian fast bowler when it came to the art of intimidation (wore zinc cream on his lips and nose and, yes, it was considered to be quite an act those days), but was very un-Australian as a bowler, for he was a swing bowler. Most successful Australian fast bowlers have been seam bowlers who master the craft of hitting the deck hard and getting some lateral movement off it, but McDermott was a genuine swing bowler. He bowled a lot fuller than the other fast bowlers from Australia and also mastered the art of using the crease intelligently. The thing with bowling fuller is that you bring two more modes of dismissals into play – lbw and bowled. He did trap a lot of batsmen in front of the stumps, and if the pad wasn't in the way, bowled many too.

NN

31

TERRY ALDERMAN – A HIGHER IMPACT BOWLER THAN MICHAEL HOLDING, WASIM AKRAM AND FRED TRUEMAN

Terry Alderman picked up 170 Test wickets for Australia – which places him only at the nineteenth position on his country's wickets-tally list.

He has a bowling average of 27 in forty-one Tests. Ten Australian bowlers have a better average in Test history (minimum forty Tests).

Through Impact Index, however, Alderman emerges as the seventh highest impact bowler (minimum forty Tests) in Australian Test cricket history, after only Dennis Lillee, Alan Davidson, Shane Warne, Glenn McGrath, Craig McDermott and Richie Benaud.

He also manifests as the sixteenth highest impact bowler (minimum forty Tests) in the history of Test cricket, above legends like Michael Holding, Curtly Ambrose, Wasim Akram and Fred Trueman. It's an interesting story.

Alderman had an inconsistent first half despite a great start

The Ashes, Nottingham, 1981. *In the opening Test, England, put in, were skittled out for a paltry 185. Dennis Lillee led the destruction. But he did not do it alone. He was supported splendidly by a debutant – a right-arm swing bowler from Perth. Terry Alderman returned with 4–68* *in 24 overs. Australia, however, were bowled out for 179. But that did not deter Alderman as he tormented the English batsmen again in the second innings (5–62 in 19 overs) – not overawed by the occasion or overwhelmed by senior partner Lillee, who took the other 5 wickets. The duo routed England for 125. Australia stumbled a bit, but chased down 132 with 4 wickets in hand.*

This was the only Test Australia won that summer. In the absence of Jeff Thomson, they had discovered a new star.

Alderman was the highest impact bowler of the series. It was a debut series that promised much.

> **AC:** Imagine this – in six Test matches, England could've possibly batted twelve times, which means 120 English wickets to be taken over the entire series (that is if they got bowled out every time). Out of which 81 wickets were taken by these two – i.e., Alderman and Lillee. Now, that's a stat that rarely appears in today's age.

However, Alderman failed to replicate the success of his sensational debut. A string of failures followed by a major shoulder injury forced him out for sixteen months (November 1982–March 1984).

He was then banned for three years from international cricket after he signed up for twin Rebel tours to South Africa in 1985–86 and 1986–87. He did not play Test cricket for four years (December 1984–December 1988).

He failed to make any further sustained impact in the first half of his career. In twenty-two Tests, his failure rate was an unacceptably high 45 per cent.

Alderman was the highest impact Test bowler in the world after his comeback

Alderman returned to Test cricket after four years in the third Test of the Frank Worrell Trophy in Melbourne in December 1988. He captured 4–68 and 3–78 in the two innings and was the highest impact bowler of the match, even though Australia went down by 285 runs.

His career took off from this Test.

Alderman was the highest impact bowler in the world from December 1988 till he retired in May 1991 – for a period of two-and-a-half years (minimum ten Tests) – truly remarkable for someone coming back from two major setbacks.

His Bowling Impact in these nineteen Tests was a whopping 148 per cent higher than his impact with the ball in the first half of his career.

Both his series-defining performances came in this period.

Alderman was an Ashes great

England had won five out of the six Ashes series between 1977 and 1986. But the Australian renaissance, via captain Allan Border and coach Bob Simpson, famously began when the team won the Reliance World Cup in 1987. The upward trend would climax two years later.

The Ashes, 1989

First Test, Leeds: Alderman 5–107 and 5–44. Australia won by 210 runs.

Second Test, Lord's: Alderman 3–60 and 6–128. Australia won by 6 wickets.

Fifth Test, Nottingham: Alderman 5–69 and 2–32. Australia won by an innings and 180 runs.

Australia won the six-match series 4–0. Alderman picked up 41 wickets in six Tests at 17 runs apiece.

He was the highest impact bowler and player of the series.

Alderman earned his first SD for consistently producing high impact performances in the series.

The series marked a change in Ashes history. Australia won the next seven Ashes till the urn returned to England in the 2005 classic.

Alderman played seventeen Ashes Tests in his career (four series). Using a filter of fifteen Ashes Tests, he emerges as the fourth highest impact fast bowler in Ashes history, after Craig McDermott, Sydney Barnes and Dennis Lillee.

In the final analysis, two things made Alderman such a high impact bowler.

One, his wicket-taking propensity. In Australia's illustrious Test history, only four bowlers had a higher impact than him when it came to taking wickets (minimum forty Tests) – Dennis Lillee, Glenn McGrath, Shane Warne and Mitchell Johnson.

Two, his performance during big occasions – his two SDs in just forty-one Tests and their historic significance. The 1989 Ashes win began a sixteen-year winning streak for Australia. Beating Pakistan meant vanquishing the second best Test team of that era (after West Indies).

Seldom do cricketers, and rarely fast bowlers, have the mental strength and the physical ability to come back from a major setback and leave a mark. Alderman came back from two and emphatically reached the pinnacle.

AC: Top-class bowlers are blessed with two things – one, they seldom get injured and miss matches due to that, and two, they rarely lose form badly enough to spend years in exile. Still, while one successful comeback is not hard to imagine, to make two is stretching the envelope a little and, therefore, Alderman's performances were nothing less than spectacular. Another interesting Impact Index insight.

NN: A bit surprising given that he was an Ashes great, and history tends to be kinder to those people ...

AC: For Australians and Englishmen, well, the Ashes has been the be-all and end-all of their existence, right? And since these two countries started playing cricket before anyone else did, what they thought meant a lot to the cricketing world. Also, the early cricket observers and writers came only from these two countries and, therefore, most stories told are from their perspective, and invariably from that of the Ashes.

NN

32

THE SECOND HIGHEST IMPACT BATSMAN IN THE HISTORY OF ODI CRICKET: DEAN JONES

Dean Jones averaged about 45 in one-day cricket in 164 matches at a strike rate of 73. There are thirteen batsmen ahead of him on averages (minimum sixty ODIs): A.B. de Villiers, Michael Bevan, Virat Kohli, Hashim Amla, Jonathan Trott, M.S. Dhoni, Michael Hussey, Zaheer Abbas, Viv Richards, Kane Williamson, Joe Root, Gordon Greenidge and Sachin Tendulkar.

However, when it comes to impact, there is only one batsman ahead of him – Viv Richards.

The main reason for Jones being the second highest impact ODI batsman of all time is his six series/tournament-defining (SDs/TDs) performances. And because Jones also has the best SD/TD to matches ratio in ODI history after, predictably, Viv Richards.

Dean Jones and Viv Richards are in a somewhat rarefied zone when it comes to ODI batsmen – they were emphatic match and series winners for their respective teams.

However, while Richards gave SD/TD performances all around the world, most of Jones's SD/TDs came in the Benson & Hedges triangular series in Australia. Interestingly, seventeen of his twenty highest impact batting performances in ODI history came in matches where Benson & Hedges were sponsors in home games.

The best ODI batsman in the world

Jones's peak period came after Richards's. From January 1988 to April 1994, when Jones retired, he was, by a distance, the best ODI batsman in the world. He was followed by Geoff Marsh, Mark Waugh, Brian Lara and Andrew Jones (minimum sixty matches).

Besides having the highest Runs Tally Impact, he also absorbed the third highest pressure of falling wickets in ODI cricket at that time, after Javed Miandad and Imran Khan.

He was also the most consistent batsman in ODI cricket at the time, with a failure rate of just 34 per cent in 110 completed matches.

All his six SD/TDs came in this period – no one else got more than three then.

In the 1987 World Cup, before his purple patch began, he had been the most consistent Australian batsman, though having only the fourth highest impact. It is a pity for him that Australia did not do well in the 1992 World Cup because he was the second highest impact batsman for Australia then, only after David Boon. Sadly, he did not play the next World Cup in 1996, and thus perhaps missed an opportunity to accentuate his position in Australian ODI history.

The six series/tournament-defining performances

Vs Pakistan, 1990. *9 for 1 as Jones walks in, facing Imran, Waqar and Wasim at their best. Which is soon 23 for 2 as Australia chase 162 in the first final. An unbeaten 83 by him sees Australia home by 6 wickets. He produces a busy 46 in the second final that Australia win by 69 runs.*

Vs New Zealand, 1990. *13 for 1 as Jones walks in to chase New Zealand's 163 in bowling-friendly conditions in Auckland in the final of the Rothman's Cup. A little over two hours later, Dean Jones emerges with an unbeaten 102 off 91 balls, the second highest score 24, Border not out with him for 19 off 66 balls, as Australia win by 8 wickets.*

Vs New Zealand, 1991. *49 to help Australia score 202 and win by six wickets in the first final. Walking in at 0 for 1 in the next final, scoring 76 to take Australia through to a target of 206 in the second final.*

Vs West Indies, 1991. *Out of Australia's 172, Jones top-scores with 64 against Ambrose and Marshall. It proves sufficient on a difficult pitch as McDermott and Whitney give it back to the West Indies in their backyard, to give Australia a 2–0 lead in the bilateral series. Jones had top-scored with an unbeaten 88 in the match before. Australia would eventually win the series 4–1. Jones gets an SD for his high impact performances in the first two ODIs which helps Australia set the tone for the rest of the series. This is the only SD performance of Jones's career in a bilateral series.*

Vs India, 1992. *73 out of Australia's 233 in the first final to see Australia comfortably through as India collapse in bowler-friendly conditions.*

Vs South Africa, 1994. *Producing a 79 at 35 for 2 out of a team total of 247 to help Australia win the second final. And a 25 in the next match, which is won by Australia as well.*

Other notable performances

Vs England, 1985. *Chasing 214 in the World Championship of Cricket, Australia lose three wickets for 1 run at 58. Twenty-three-year-old Jones produces a 78 off 94 balls, and along with Robbie Kerr steers Australia home.*

Vs Pakistan, 1987. *121 off 113 balls against Imran and Wasim out of Australia's 273. Pakistan wins by 1 wicket though, thanks to Asif Mujtaba's heroics in the end.*

Vs England, 1990. *145 out of Australia's 283 off 136 balls with twelve fours and four sixes. His team wins by 37 runs.*

Vs West Indies, 1989. *Jones unbeaten on 93 out of Australia's 226 for 4 in 38 overs in a rain-shortened match. West Indies wins comfortably though.*

Despite a 42 and 67 in his last ODI series in South Africa, he departed from the scene, perhaps a trifle too soon.

Dean Jones produced some memorable Test innings for Australia too – a 48 in his debut Test on a difficult pitch in West Indies and a famous 210 in India in only his third Test being just two of those highlights. But Jones felt ODI cricket led to a more cutting-edge existence for cricketers as players tend to be 'found out' quicker in that format, according to him.

His contribution to Australian ODI cricket is immense. He was the main force behind Australia being almost unbeatable at home (though, sadly, not in the 1992 World Cup) and as a significant ODI team just before complete world domination beckoned.

Just like Allan Border's contribution to setting a foundation that led to that domination, Dean Jones's contribution with the bat in ODIs has its own place.

AC: He was ahead of his times and understood the one-day game differently from others. In his era, Test cricketers and one-day cricketers were not different, so there was a similar kind of mindset in both formats. And Dean Jones defied that. He was focusing on things like rotating the strike and running hard between the stumps – facets that had not been explored thus far. The way he made sure to touch down, crouching low, holding the bat right at the top, making full use of the length of the bat and the arm stretch, nobody else had done that before him. He was a pioneer in that sense.

He was so astute in his preparation that he told his coach Bob Simpson to calculate the time it took for the ball to travel to long on and back, and then calculate the time he took to return for two runs. He realized that if he turned for the second from a particular area, he would make it back nine out of ten times. And he did. He revolutionalized running between the wickets.

Viv Richards and Gordon Greenidge were really the only high impact batsmen before him. Richards still remains the highest impact ODI batsman ever, and his dominance was built around big shots. But Dean Jones wasn't that kind of a batsman. Also, he understood the dynamics of the Australian grounds he was playing in. He knew attempting sixes and fours wasn't the way to win games there, so it isn't surprising that the vast majority of his high-impact performances came at home. Perhaps it was his template that Michael Bevan adopted later.

JV

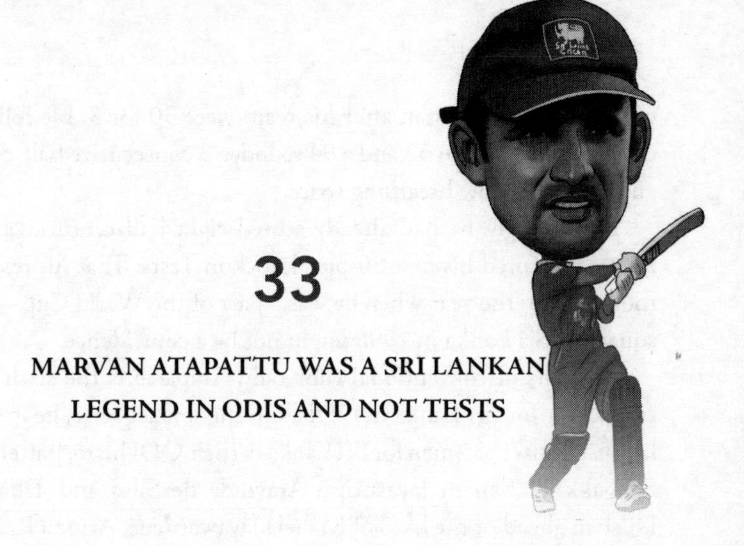

33

MARVAN ATAPATTU WAS A SRI LANKAN LEGEND IN ODIS AND NOT TESTS

The string of scores didn't have the monstrosity of 0, 0, 0, 1, 0, 0 but 8, 0, 4, 19, 5, 3, 4, 10 wasn't a straight ride to any hall of fame either.

Sri Lankan right-handed batsman, Marvan Atapattu, very famously started his Test career with five ducks in his first six Test innings but the struggle didn't pertain to only Tests as he scored only 53 runs in his first eight ODI innings over a span of six years.

Atapattu was well and truly baptized by fire during his introduction to international cricket.

ODIs to the rescue

Apart from his five ducks at the start, the only other thing Atapattu is remembered for in world cricket are his six double centuries in Tests. Given his style of play and his inability to score runs at a quick pace, his batting was classically suited to the longer format.

The shocker? Atapattu's Batting Impact was 68 per cent more in ODIs than in Tests.

The season of 1996–97 was his fourth stint and third comeback in Tests whereas in ODIs it was his third stint and second comeback. Moreover, it was in an ODI that he produced his first significant performance as a Sri Lankan batsman: 58 off 100 balls in a team total of 189 against Pakistan after his team were 30 for 3. He followed it up with an unbeaten 52 and a 94 to lodge 3 consecutive half-centuries and buy him some breathing space.

Interestingly, he had already scored eight half-centuries in ODIs before he scored his first 50-plus knock in Tests. That his resurgence took place in the year when he was a part of the World Cup–winning squad for Sri Lanka in 1996 might not be a coincidence.

In terms of conventional runs tally, Atapattu is the sixth highest run-scorer for Sri Lanka in ODIs. On the impact scale, he is the fifth highest impact batsman for Sri Lanka in their ODI history after Kumar Sangakkara, Sanath Jayasuriya, Aravinda de Silva and Tillakaratne Dilshan ahead of the likes of Mahela Jayawardene, Arjuna Ranatunga and Angelo Mathews.

Big-match temperament

Atapattu produced six series-defining performances as a batsman in his 268-match ODI career holding the third position among all Sri Lankan batsmen after Jayasuriya (11) and Sangakkara (7). Dilshan and de Silva also have six each but in more matches. When it comes to matches to SD ratio, Atapattu is second after Jayasuriya. Atapattu produced an SD in approximately every 45 ODIs, Jayasuriya in every 40 ODIs. Sangakkara in comparison has a matches to SD ratio of 57. Jayawardene produced one in every 107 ODIs, whereas de Silva produced an SD in approximately every 51 ODIs.

Interestingly, five of Atapattu's SDs came in the finals of a triangular series or a multi-nation tournament that included two Asia Cup triumphs. Another interesting facet is that four of his six SDs came away from home.

They also helped affirm Sri Lanka's ability to win tournaments away from home.

Vs England, Lord's, 1998. *An opening stand of 132 between Nick Knight and Michael Atherton propelled England to a total of 256 batting first in the final match. Sri Lanka, in reply were jolted hard with Sanath Jayasuriya perishing off the second ball for a duck. Under pressure, Marvan*

Atapattu and Romesh Kaluwitharana built a 138-run partnership before the dismissal of the latter. At 210 for 2, Sri Lanka looked to be cruising before a mini-collapse saw them losing three wickets for 23 runs. Atapattu on the other end, though, was calm and composed and saw Sri Lanka home with five wickets and 17 balls to spare. Atapattu scored an unbeaten 132 off 151 balls and scored more than 50 per cent of Sri Lanka's total runs. This remains the highest impact innings of his career.

Even when it came to World Cups, Atapattu had a decent run for Sri Lanka. He was only the fourth highest impact batsman for Sri Lanka in their disastrous 1999 World Cup campaign but was their second highest impact batsman in the 2003 World Cup (after de Silva) where Sri Lanka made it to the semi-finals.

Almost an all-round batting package

Marvan Atapattu excelled in almost all the individual batting parameters. In terms of Runs Tally and Partnership Building Impact, he is second only to Sangakkara in Sri Lankan ODI history. In terms of Chasing Impact, he is second only to de Silva. When it comes to consistency, Atapattu has the fourth lowest failure rate of 46 per cent in Sri Lankan ODI history after Sangakkara, Ranatunga and Dilshan.

His batting in ODIs was an all-round package despite his inability to score runs quickly and it might be for this very reason that he is never considered an ODI great for Sri Lanka. Atapattu had a negative Strike-Rate Impact which means that he scored runs at a rate lower than the match norm but he more than made up for it with his other skills.

Given his stop–start career initially, and how he managed to revive it in what was likely to be his final chance for Sri Lanka, handling pressure was second nature to Atapattu. He is the second highest Pressure Impact batsman for Sri Lanka in their ODI history after Chamara Silva. The stunning part, though, is the fact that, amongst all openers and No. 3 batsmen in ODI history, Atapattu's Pressure Impact is third only to that of Andy Flower and Jacques Kallis.

Vs South Africa, World Cup, Durban, 2003. *The equation was simple, South Africa needed a win and Sri Lanka needed to avoid a defeat by a heavy margin to qualify for the next stage. Sri Lanka, after opting to bat first, were precariously poised at 90 for 3 after 22 overs when Marvan Atapattu and Aravinda de Silva joined hands to build a counter-attacking partnership of 152 runs in only 136 balls. Atapattu scored 124 off 129 and de Silva 73 off 78; the next highest score was 16 as Sri Lanka finished with 268. South Africa's chase was truncated due to rain and a bizarre Duckworth-Lewis understanding on their part made them infamously tie the match which was good enough for Sri Lanka to move to the next stage.*

Inglorious ending

Atapattu's performances had dipped since 2005 in comparison to the rest of his career, but he still had higher impact in the two years leading up to the World Cup than the likes of Tillakaratne Dilshan, Russel Arnold and Upul Tharanga who all featured in Sri Lanka's 2007 World Cup campaign.

Atapattu was ingloriously benched throughout the duration of the tournament and he would never play an ODI for Sri Lanka again. It was only because of the request of the then Sri Lankan sports minister that Atapattu was drafted into the Test squad for the tour of Australia which Sri Lanka eventually went on to lose 0–2 and in which Atapattu was their third highest impact batsman after Sangakkara and Jayawardene. Sri Lanka's next home assignment was against England, and Atapattu expressed the desire to play in front of his home crowd. The selectors, though, indicated that they didn't want Atapattu in the team. Once he got a hint of his fate, he famously labelled the Sri Lankan selection council as 'a set of muppets headed by a joker'. Needless to say, the comment pretty much sealed any chance of a comeback to the national set-up, and Atapattu promptly retired from all formats at the end of the Australian tour.

Yet, in a comeback of sorts, Atapattu returned as the Sri Lankan batting coach in 2011 before being named head coach of Sri Lanka in 2014.

The first half of Atapattu's career fitted in neatly among the likes of Sanath Jayasuriya, Arjuna Ranatunga and Aravinda de Silva, and his next half among the likes of Kumar Sangakkara and Mahela Jayawardene.

Few would dare to put Atapattu with any of them on a Sri Lankan chart of batting greatness. Though, they would be right on the money if they did.

AC: This is a curious case. I would not have believed that he'd be a high impact ODI batsman – his 6 double centuries in Test cricket being a big reason, of course. His ODI numbers are curious too; there are oddities in his conventional numbers as well. He is averaging 48 in South Africa over twenty-four ODIs, which is fairly high and the third-best amongst all visiting batsmen in South Africa (after Ricky Ponting and Sourav Ganguly). In contrast, his average in India is only 28 in 29 ODIs. It's a discrepancy worth questioning, but, perhaps, the answer is pretty simple. This piece talks about his low Strike Rate Impact, which suggests that he was a Test batsman who fitted the bill in ODIs because he was right at the top, opening the innings, and the low strike rate actually allowed him to survive in South Africa where the ball darts around and the par score used to be around 220 to 240. So, you want a batsman like Atapattu with proper technique who could blunt the new ball and score runs. No surprises then that he scored runs in South Africa.

SS: Why hasn't he been successful in Tests in South Africa where he averages just 21 in fourteen innings?

AC: Nobody has. Tests are a completely different ball game in South Africa.

SS: Why hasn't he been as successful in Test cricket then? Atapattu has got a 68 per cent higher impact in ODIs. What is the reason? It is very interesting. You expect him to be a very good Test player but he wasn't.

AC: If you see his conventional numbers in Tests, he has done fairly well in tough assignments like Australia (average 41 in eight innings), England (average 50 in eight innings) and West Indies (average 46 in six innings), but has struggled in Pakistan (average 19 in fourteen innings) and hasn't been great in Sri Lanka (average 39 in seventy-eight innings) and even

India (average 37 in thirteen innings). As a result, his overall average fell.

SS: But, of course, you also have to see the context in which those runs came. Surprisingly, he doesn't have a single series-defining performance in Tests at a time when Sri Lanka were dominant at home.

AC: His conventional numbers in Sri Lanka aren't great and as a result I think he misses out on being a high impact Test batsman on that count. He did reasonably well in tough assignments, albeit the low sample size of matches, but Sri Lanka hardly won anything away from home. His poor numbers in the subcontinent also suggest that he was perhaps a better player of fast bowling than spin. But this is a bit of an eye-opener really, that he has been contributing heavily to Sri Lankan ODI cricket and has impacted the results more often than we give him credit for.

SS

34

NO BATSMAN IN THE HISTORY OF ODI CRICKET HAS ABSORBED MORE PRESSURE THAN ROGER TWOSE

In the territory of the Indian slogan '6+4=10dulkar' is this one from New Zealand: 'We need sixes, fours and Twose to win.'

Roger Twose played just eighty-seven ODIs for New Zealand between 1995 and 2001. He averaged 39 in them with just one century. However, except for Kane Williamson, Ross Taylor and Martin Guptill, no one is above him in even ODI batting averages (minimum sixty matches). With Impact Index, the story is even sharper.

The Impact view

Roger Twose is the seventh highest impact New Zealand batsman in ODI history after Kane Williamson, Andrew Jones, Martin Crowe, Ross Taylor, Martin Guptill and Nathan Astle.

To date, Twose is the fifth most consistent batsman ever for New Zealand, after Martin Crowe, Kane Williamson, Bruce Edgar and Jeremy Coney.

In terms of proportion of runs scored in all matches played (runs tally impact) by a New Zealander, Twose is number five after Crowe, Williamson, Jones and Taylor.

Most pertinently, when it comes to absorbing the pressure of falling wickets, Twose did it best. Not just among New Zealanders, but in all of ODI cricket history (with Michael Bevan, much more famous for this role, just marginally behind him).

Despite many other notable attributes, this is the quality that immortalizes Roger Twose in ODI cricket history.

Remarkably, in the fourteen highest impact innings in his career, every single one of them has him absorbing pressure. Every single one. This, despite batting at No. 4 or 5 most of the time for New Zealand, which also suggests how much he contributed in keeping his team in the game.

Vs South Africa, 1999*. Twose steps out at 11 for 2, which is soon 29 for 3. 78 off 123 to lead New Zealand to 220. South Africa win by 7 wickets.*

Vs South Africa, 1999. *New Zealand 44 for 3 when Twose walks in, which becomes 68 for 4. An unbeaten 79 off 77 balls takes his team to 191, but they lose a tight match in the end.*

Vs South Africa, 2000. *New Zealand 24 for 2 when Twose enters the stage. 39 for 3 when Chris Cairns enters, 189 for 4 when they are separated; 84 off 72 balls for Cairns. 238 for 6 when Twose is dismissed, for 103 off 115 balls, his only international century. But South Africa win by 3 wickets off the last ball.*

Vs West Indies, 2000. *Chasing 172, New Zealand are 23 for 2 when Twose joins Nathan Astle. An unbeaten 76 to Astle, 68 to Twose as New Zealand win by 8 wickets.*

Vs South Africa, 2000. *New Zealand 8 for 2 when Twose steps out. He top scores with 38 in a rain-affected match as New Zealand make 114 for 5 in 33 overs. South Africa win again.*

New Zealand lost quite a few of the above games. In fact, they did not win a single bilateral ODI series away from home during Twose's career. They were not a great side, it is clear, and this manifested in all the pressure Twose was subjected every time he came out to bat.

Yet, a couple of the most memorable triumphs in New Zealand cricket history happened then, and Twose played a big part in it.

ICC KnockOut (now called Champions Trophy), Kenya, 2000. *New Zealand met Pakistan in the semi-finals, the same team which had knocked them out of the World Cup semi-finals the year before in England, when the Kiwis had looked like they would go all the way. Like that time, Saeed Anwar got a crashing century here too, and Pakistan even got a little more than then, setting a target of 253. New Zealand were 15 for 2 when Twose walked in to bat. Even more than Akram, this looked like Azhar Mahmood's day. But Twose wouldn't let up. Primarily with Astle, he batted for over two hours and through thirty more overs, and made 87 off 101 balls, before being dismissed 86 from the target. New Zealand's strong middle- and lower-order took them home with one over and four wickets to spare.*

It took New Zealand to their first world event final.

There, against an inspired Indian team that was seeing the benefits of positive cricket under new captain Sourav Ganguly, he came out to bat with New Zealand reeling at 35 for 2, as they chased a formidable 265, and stabilized the innings somewhat, but was dismissed for 31 off 35 balls, the job a bit easier but incomplete at 109 for 4. Then, Chris Cairns played one of the great one-day innings –102 off 113 balls and New Zealand won their first major title.

It remains their only world cricket title till date. Twose got a tournament-defining performance for playing a leading role in getting his side through the semi-final. It was the also the only limited-overs event New Zealand ever won in away conditions during Twose's career.

Golden period followed by the end

Between January 1999 and December 2000, a period of two years, Twose was the fourth highest impact ODI batsman in the world, after Inzamam-ul-Haq, Michael Bevan and Adam Gilchrist. This must have been visible through his conventional numbers too, as Twose was ranked number two (after Bevan) in the ICC official ODI batting ratings at the end of 2000. Predictably, Twose also absorbed the most pressure by any batsman in the world in this period.

In the early 1990s, Twose had migrated to New Zealand from England with the hope of playing Test cricket. That particular dream did not work out too well for the Warwickshire pro, even though he did play sixteen Tests without great success. It was in the shorter format of the game that he made his mark.

Barely four months from reaching his peak as an ODI player, and after a spot of bad form in early 2001, Twose quit the sport to pursue a career in banking and management in England.

It brought the curtain down on a highly underrated career that really should have received much more attention at the time.

AC: The failure of conventional numbers to account for context is particularly significant in ODI cricket. In Test cricket, it is believed largely that bowlers win you matches and batsmen only set up matches, but in ODIs, there is no argument that batsmen often win you matches. And so the contribution of a batsman should be viewed from that frame of reference: how much he really contributed to his team's successes.

Twose features very high when you look at the circumstances he came out to bat in: walking in when the team is struggling, which is often in New Zealand conditions. The new ball is never easy to handle there. Of course, there is also the tournament-defining performance in what still remains New Zealand's only world title.

You can argue that Twose played only eighty-seven games and not the 200–250 matches so many play these days. But in the limited period he played, he obviously had a lot of impact. Conventional numbers will never identify that because we tend to look at number of runs scored in a career to distinguish players, and that can never be a fair indication. Twose's story is exactly the sort that would go missing without the Impact Index filters. But look through it and, suddenly, an important story emerges.

JV

35

NO BATSMAN IN TEST CRICKET HISTORY ABSORBED MORE PRESSURE THAN M.A.K. PATAUDI

The conventional view on Mansur Ali Khan Pataudi (or Nawab of Pataudi Jr) is that he was one of India's greatest captains and an unorthodox, fearless player who gave India a sense of belief. And that he was a very good batsman who would have touched greatness if he had not lost one eye in an accident six months before his Test debut.

All of this is true. But he was more than this – in deed, not just in potential.

In the history of Test cricket (minimum forty Tests), no batsman in the world has absorbed more pressure (of falling wickets) in his career than M.A.K. Pataudi. Those immediately below him include Peter May, Andy Flower, Angelo Mathews, Kane Williamson, Brian Lara, Warwick Armstrong, Younis Khan and Clem Hill (Williamson and Younis have ongoing careers, of course).

Perhaps, more than anything else, this demonstrates Pataudi's greatness. Losing one eye was not his only cricketing tragedy – he was also not part of a world-beating side. It would be entirely human to not be fully motivated in such circumstances but it did not stop him from repeatedly playing at his best when his team needed it the most.

His batting average of 35 in forty-six Tests (between 1961 and 1975) does not suggest that he was a world beater. However, in the five years when he was at his peak (1964–68), he averaged 56 in Australia (in three Tests), 45 in England (three Tests) and 43 overall in twenty-five Tests. Even this does not tell the real story, given how little success Indian teams had in those days, especially overseas, and how many players scored more runs and averaged more than him in world cricket.

Pataudi scored tough runs, more than anybody else in the world in that period. In fact, he was the second highest impact batsman in the world in this period (minimum twenty Tests), after Garry Sobers, partly because of his extremely high Pressure Impact. He also had one series-defining performance to his credit at a time when India hardly won any series.

Vs Australia, October 1964. *Australia are 1–0 ahead and in the second Test at Mumbai, India are 146 for 4 in response to Australia's 320 when Pataudi walks in. A three-and-a-half-hour 86 ends at 293 and India manage to match Australia's first innings. But Australia bat reasonably well, and India are set a highly competitive 254 in the fourth innings to win. Soon it is 4 for 1, then 71 for 3, 99 for 4, till Pataudi walks in to bat at 113 for 5, which soon becomes 123 for 6. Going by Indian cricket history till then, that was the end of the match, and the series, and the crowd of 42,000 was likely to go back disappointed but not surprised. However, Pataudi and Vijay Manjrekar (in the twilight of his career) change the match around in the next three hours, and even though both are dismissed with 30 runs still to make, a pulsating finish by Chandu Borde and K.S. Indrajitsinhji (Ranji's nephew) provide India one of its great Test wins. In the next Test, India manage their first drawn series against Australia. This would be the only SD of Pataudi's career. Even here, his quintessential quality of batting under pressure came to the fore.*

At twenty-one, Pataudi was also the youngest captain in world cricket. His record of nine wins in forty-one Tests was not great – the misfortune of not being in a world-beating side – but it was his unconventional thinking that moved India towards being one in just a few years' time. He was responsible for establishing the mindset of playing the best bowlers, even if they were predominantly spinners – and the all-time great trio of Bedi, Chandrasekhar and Prasanna (and

Venkataraghavan) responded magnificently to that. For this reason, he was considered India's finest captain for a long time.

In that 1964–68 period, India won two series, drew two and lost three (two of them away). It was India's best period thus far, and Pataudi played a big role in turning the tide.

Vs England, June 1967. *The opening Test at Leeds. England 550 for 4 declared. India 59 for 4 when Pataudi walks in, 164 all out, as he walks out with the highest score of 64, their match still in a shambles. Following on, Engineer and Wadekar show some fight (as they scintillatingly knock off 168 in two-and-a-half hours) but the team is still 158 behind England as Pataudi walks in at No. 6. He is in for almost six hours and ninth out at 506, with 148 of the most exemplary runs a captain can make, as India post their highest Test score against England. India still lose the match by six wickets and the series 0–3.*

> **AC:** It is remarkable though that he averaged 56 in Australia, in just three Tests. And 45 in England, again in just three Tests. He toured both countries just once each, and given this small sample size, you can't help feeling that his returns would have been much better if he had toured more. These are outstanding numbers in and of themselves.

Out of the 83 Test innings Pataudi played, he came under pressure fifty-six times – that means 67 per cent of his Test innings were played under pressure – a huge percentage. He overcame this pressure twenty-three times, or 41 per cent of the time, a remarkable conversion rate given the regularity with which he had to do it.

Vs West Indies, Bridgetown, 1962. *Walking in at 89 for 4, making 48 against Hall, Gibbs, Valentine and Sobers, helping his team reach 258.*

Vs Australia, Chennai, 1964. *Replying to Australia's 211, India are 56 for 4 when Pataudi walks in, then 76 for 5. An unbeaten 128 gives his team the first-innings lead.*

Vs Australia, Melbourne, 1967. *Pataudi walks in at 25 for 5. Ninth out at 162, highest scorer with 75.*

Vs Australia, Brisbane, 1968. *Australia 379. India 9 for 3 when Pataudi walks in. Out 128 runs later for 74.*

Vs New Zealand, Mumbai, 1969. *After conceding a first-innings lead of 73 to New Zealand, India are 105 for 3 when Pataudi comes in, soon 111 for 4, effectively 38 for 4. His 67 takes India to a respectable total from where they win the Test (but the series is later drawn 1–1).*

Vs Australia, Chennai, 1969. *Replying to Australia's 258, India are 40 for 4 when Pataudi steps in. And seventh out at 158, to give India some respectability, hopes to level the series 2–2 still alive (but thwarted later).*

In his career (1961–75), Pataudi played thirteen Test series; India won four, drew three and lost six. Historically, it was an upward swing, and he had a lot to do with it. Sadly, when Indian cricket turned a corner and won back-to-back Test series in West Indies and England (1971), he was not even in the team, having been dropped after two poor home series against New Zealand and Australia. He was there to complete India's hat-trick of series wins though, against England at home, after being dramatically recalled mid-series, post an eye-catching century for South Zone against the MCC.

Vs England, Chennai, 1973. *Series tied at 1–1. England make 242. India are 89 for 3 as Pataudi walks in, making a comeback after three years. He responds by attacking immediately, much to the delight of a rapturous crowd, who even get to see him hit two sixes. He reaches his 50 and then slows down considerably, clearly intent on playing a match-defining long innings. Unfortunately, his turn is cut short at 73 – he is fifth out at 220, still the highest scorer in an innings that sees the tail wag a bit (and cross 300). Bedi and Prasanna do their magic and India need just 86 to win. Ostensibly just 86. But soon it is 11 for 2, then 44 for 3. Pataudi walks in at 51 for 4, but when highest scorer Durrani goes at 67, there are serious jitters since Gavaskar is injured. But Pataudi keeps his calm and gathers the runs slowly. Then Eknath Solkar departs at 78 for 6, and a barely fit Gavaskar walks in and plays out 11 balls without scoring. Pataudi continues gathering the runs (14 not out off 41 balls) and India win by 4 wickets. India 2–1 in the series – which would be the final series* *scoreline as the next two Tests are drawn. Very close to being an SD for Pataudi and he has made a decisive comeback.*

Sadly, that would be Pataudi's last triumph (he averaged 15 in the next six Tests) and was dropped from the side in 1975.

Largely due to his remarkable Pressure Impact, if we keep forty Tests as the minimum, Pataudi comes up as the eighth highest impact Indian Test batsman after the obvious big three (Dravid, Tendulkar and Gavaskar, in this order), G.R. Viswanath, Virat Kohli, Murali Vijay (the last two have ongoing careers, of course) and then Navjot Sidhu (another interesting, and somewhat odd, story through Impact Index).

The temptation of imagining what a batsman like this could have done in a stronger side, like the ones the big three played for, is understandable but perhaps misplaced. For, in the end, the most revealing statistic in the context of his career is his failure rate – a neat 50 per cent, unacceptably high for a batsman of his obvious ability and class. This inconsistency was a problem right through his career – even during his 1964–68 peak, his failure rate was at 48 per cent (Sobers above him had a failure rate of 25 per cent, while Barrington, Cowdrey, Barlow and Simpson below him were at 30, 32, 40 and 33 per cent respectively).

With someone capable of making such tough runs, it was clearly not about ability. If anything, there was perhaps a lack of intensity or motivation to play with bloody-minded focus in both innings. The majority of his outstanding performances came when his side had its back to the wall, which clearly seemed to turn him on fully.

He was a nawab after all.

AC: Prima facie, it comes as a big surprise that he would be the man to absorb the most pressure in Test history. But when you dwell on it a bit, given the team he played for and the era he played in, the kind of teams he played against, it begins to make sense. When you're in a weak team, you don't get a good start and then the pressure is always telling. Nine out of ten times, your bowlers haven't put you in a strong position either, so whichever angle you look at it from, you're chasing your tail most of the time. Especially as a middle-order batsman, coming in at the fall of quick wickets.

Perhaps his persona was also such that people don't really talk about what a great leader he was. His captaincy numbers are not great, but given the side he had, he accomplished a great deal as captain. Cricket was an amateur sport in India at the time, and given that context, what M.A.K. Pataudi did was remarkable.

This piece is an eye-opener in that sense because there don't seem to be too many people left telling stories of that period. And that too by a man who batted with just one eye. It is hard enough to face international bowlers with two eyes, but to do it with one eye, that's like fighting a battle with one hand tied behind your back.

36

YOUNIS KHAN IS THE HIGHEST IMPACT ASIAN BATSMAN IN TEST HISTORY

Younis Khan's name rarely figures in lists of South Asian greats, which tend to feature Sachin Tendulkar, Kumar Sangakkara, Rahul Dravid, Sunil Gavaskar, Inzamam-ul-Haq, Virender Sehwag and V.V.S. Laxman. Even at the international level, Ricky Ponting, Jacques Kallis, Michael Clarke and Viv Richards are considered superior batsmen. It is not that conventional numbers do him any harm, for Younis's batting average is the second highest for any Asian batsman after Sangakkara and the tenth highest in Test history (minimum fifty Tests).

Given his relatively unattractive style of play though, he doesn't quite get the adulation that he deserves. Grafters rarely do.

Even amongst Pakistani batsmen, Younis doesn't quite get the adulation reserved for the technically gifted – Inzamam-ul-Haq, Javed Miandad and Mohammad Yousuf – despite being the highest run scorer in Pakistan Test history and the man with the best average.

Much like how Dravid was considered second fiddle to Tendulkar and Azharuddin in Tests, Younis was seen as a support act to Inzamam and Mohammad Yousuf. Dravid got due recognition in the latter part of his career once the 'big names' retired; Younis's story seems to be going along the same lines as well.

Conventional numbers establish Younis as one amongst many great

Asian Test batsmen. Through impact numbers, though, he transcends into another league.

Vs Zimbabwe, Harare, 2013. *Even though this performance came against a second-string Zimbabwean side, it is worth a mention, given that it saved Pakistan the blushes. After being asked to bat first, Pakistan managed 249 in their first innings as Zimbabwe responded with 327. Pakistan, in their second innings, were 23 for 3, still adrift of Zimbabwe's first innings score by 55 runs. Younis Khan scored a back-to-the-wall 200 as Pakistan finished with 419. Zimbabwe, chasing, fell short of their target by 221 runs as Pakistan gained a 1–0 lead in the series. This win for Pakistan would hold an even bigger significance given they went on to lose the next Test and draw the series 1–1.*

The Impact viewpoint

Younis Khan's high impact is the result of a combination of the number of series-defining performances he has delivered for Pakistan and his ability to absorb the pressure of falling wickets.

In his 110-match Test career so far, Younis has produced six SDs, his ratio of producing an SD every eighteen Tests is the second-best for any Asian batsman (minimum fifty Tests) after Inzamam (one SD in every fifteen Tests).

Younis's batting is generally identified with the amount of grit on display and it reflects in his Pressure Impact – the sixth highest in the history of Test cricket (minimum fifty Tests) after Peter May, Andy Flower, Angelo Mathews, Kane Williamson and Brian Lara, and the second highest for any Asian batsman. Younis's Runs Tally Impact is also the second highest for any Asian batsman after Saeed Anwar, identifying his propensity to score a large amount of runs in winning causes. Even conventional numbers support this claim – Younis Khan's batting average of 77 is the fourth best for any batsman in a winning cause in the history of Test cricket after Bradman, Inzamam and Garry Sobers (minimum thirty won Tests). Younis's penchant for scoring a significant amount of runs in the fourth innings is well documented, and it is no surprise that he is the highest impact fourth-innings batsman in the history of cricket as well. Even conventionally, his average of close to 57 in the fourth innings is the fourth best in Test history after Geoffrey Boycott, Sunil Gavaskar and Jack Hobbs (minimum twenty innings). Younis Khan's average of close to 142 in winning causes in the fourth innings is also the highest in Test history.

Vs India, Bengaluru, 2005. *Trailing 0–1 going into the final Test, Pakistan were 7 for 2 when Younis Khan and Inzamam-ul-Haq took guard. What followed was a masterclass in batting. Inzamam batted for six hours for his 184 as Younis batted eleven-and-a-half hours for his 267. Pakistan finished with 570. India, in reply, responded with 449. Pakistan, looking for a declaration, were helped by Younis's rapid unbeaten knock of 84 off 98 balls as India were asked to chase 383. India eventually fell 168 runs short. Pakistan drew the series 1–1 as Younis Khan produced his first SD performance with the highest impact batting performance of his career.*

AC: In Younis Khan's case it is easy to explain why he is not heralded as one of the best batsmen in the world. Pakistan do not tour away from home enough to be tested and respected in a global scenario. This is true of Sri Lankan players also. So, in Khan's case, he has played only twenty-five Tests out of his 110 in Australia, England, New Zealand and South Africa. If we were to break this down further, he has played only three Tests in Australia. Virat Kohli, in comparison, has already played eight Tests in Australia at the age of twenty-eight and his career is only forty-eight-Test old. Although, it must be said that Younis Khan has done well in the limited opportunities that he has got. Of course, the lack of away matches is not his fault when the team itself is not touring much, but it does take a little sheen away from his achievement, and he is likely to be known as a flat-track bully. But if a batsman has done it over a hundred Tests, he is definitely more than that. It's not just plundering runs at home.

Aesthetics too play a significant role in judging cricketing genius, and Younis's batting style would lie right at the bottom of this pack. While he's fairly rooted against spinners, he's rarely stable against pace and swing. In the last tour to England, his unique and rather jumpy style of batting invited a lot of snide remarks too – cat on a hot tin roof, etc. Not often do you find anyone in the pantheon of greats being described in this fashion.

A tumultuous career

Younis Khan has been mired in controversies and scraps with the Pakistan Cricket Board (PCB) for most of his career. The sustained high of his performances has not, therefore, been in an enabling environment.

Having made his Test debut in 2000, Younis was slowly beginning to come of age in the 2001–02 season when a bomb blast in Lahore put a question mark on Pakistan's hosting capabilities. In 2003 and 2004, Pakistan played a total of only five Tests, a period in which Younis could have stabilized the solid start to his Test career (after his debut and until the blasts in Lahore, he was the second highest impact batsman for Pakistan after Inzamam). Instead, he missed out on almost two years of Test cricket. Again, when Younis Khan looked to have hit his straps as an international batsman, Pakistan didn't play a single Test in 2008. A second terrorist attack in Pakistan, this time on the Sri Lankan team in 2009, made sure Younis would never play a home Test again.

If the domestic problems were not big enough, a spat with the PCB saw Younis sit out from an Australian tour and handed an indefinite ban (which threatened to become a life ban) from international cricket in 2010 on allegations of infighting within the dressing room. If he hadn't played any more Tests after that, Younis Khan would still have finished as the second highest impact batsman for Pakistan but would have only been the fifth highest impact Asian Test batsman. Thankfully, for Pakistan and himself, Younis did go on to play again, and play a decisive role in Pakistan's resurgence in world cricket.

Vs Sri Lanka, Pallekele, 2015. *With the series level 1–1 going into the final Test, Sri Lanka, riding on Dimuth Karunaratne's 130 posted 278. Pakistan, in their reply, managed only 215 as Younis Khan could manage only 3 runs before getting run out. Sri Lanka further consolidated their position by scoring 313 in their second innings. Pakistan, chasing 377, were*

13 for 2 when Younis walked in to bat. Along with Shan Masood (125), he revitalized the Pakistan innings with a stand of 242 runs for the third wicket. With 127 runs still needed to win, Younis and Misbah ensured Pakistan reached home without any more loss of wicket. Misbah finished on 59 as Younis batted seven hours for his 171. This was the highest fourth-innings chase in Pakistan's Test history and the sixth highest, overall, in Test history. The fact that it came in a series decider made it all the more special.

Pakistan's new triumvirate

At the start of Younis Khan's career, he was the less heralded one in the Inzamam–Yousuf–Younis triumvirate. Now, at the fag end of his career, he plays the leading role in the new triumvirate of Younis–Misbah–Azhar which has played a crucial role in Pakistan's resurgence in Test cricket.

Since 2011, Pakistan's win/loss ratio has been the second best for any team after South Africa and they haven't lost a single series in their adopted home in the UAE. In this period, Younis has been the third highest impact batsman in the world after A.B. de Villiers and Misbah-ul-Haq (minimum thirty Tests). Younis Khan's Pressure Impact in this time frame is also the third best in the world after Dinesh Chandimal and Angelo Mathews. It is interesting to note that each batsman in the Younis–Misbah–Azhar trio has a very high Pressure Impact which shows that they have taken responsibilities in different situations. This is even more fascinating given that Pakistan have been such a strong side in this period (a high Pressure Impact is easily explainable for someone like Angelo Mathews and Dinesh Chandimal who have had to shepherd a weak team in this period).

To cap Pakistan's glorious rise in Test cricket, one of Younis's biggest contributions to Pakistani cricket was his role in helping his country achieve the No. 1 ranking in Tests for the first time in their history.

Vs England, Kennington Oval, 2016. *Having been comprehensively overpowered in the last two Tests, Pakistan had the tough ask of levelling* *the series after falling behind 1–2 going into the final Test. A resolute English display of 328 runs in the first innings meant that Pakistan needed to score big to not face a nervy chase in the fourth innings. Younis Khan, having struggled woefully in the first three Tests, returning scores of 33, 25, 1, 28, 31 and 4, joined Asad Shafiq at 127 for 3 with the match hanging in perfect balance. Shafiq (109) and Younis combined for 150 runs before the former's departure led to a mini-slide with Pakistan losing three wickets for 43 runs. Younis had already crossed his century and given Pakistan a lead of 69 runs when Sarfraz, the last recognized batsman departed. Younis, though, had a supreme sense of understanding that the match and his job was far from done. After all, Pakistan had squandered a 103-run lead in their last Test to lose the match convincingly. In a superb display of batting with the tail, Younis added 134 runs for the eighth and the ninth wickets, himself scoring 90 of them before departing for a stellar 218. With a lead of 214 runs, Pakistan bowled out England for 253 before comfortably finishing the chase with 10 wickets to spare. Younis's knock of seven-and-a-half hours helped Pakistan level the series and gain the No. 1 ranking in Tests.*

It was Younis Khan's sixth Test SD, and the first by a Pakistani batsman in England since 1987. Incredibly, five of Younis Khan's six SDs have come overseas – the most (along with Rahul Dravid and Inzamam-ul-Haq) by any batsman away from home in the history of Test cricket.

Highest impact active Test batsman in the world

On a world stage, Younis Khan emerges as the third highest impact batsman in Test history (minimum fifty Tests) after Don Bradman and Peter May which makes him the highest impact Test batsman alive today.

The difference between Younis Khan and Peter May's batting impact is only 3 per-cent. Given Pakistan's dominant run in Tests in the past four years or so, there is a chance of Younis Khan eclipsing May to finish as the highest impact Test batsman of all time after Bradman.

An incredible turnaround for a man who hasn't played at home for the last seven years and was almost handed a life ban from the game in 2010.

AC: Over the last decade, Pakistan have not played at home. Sure, UAE has conditions similar to those back at home, but home conditions is more than just a pitch that is to your liking. There is no crowd support. Crowd plays a huge role in home conditions. I say this from personal experience. I have actually felt it twice playing for India. When I made my debut against New Zealand, in front of a full crowd, I hit Daniel Vettori for a four and the crowd was on its feet, chanting. I could feel the vibration while batting in the middle and I got carried away and played another shot and got out.

SS: So, it can go both ways?

AC: It can go both ways but once you get used to it, you use it to your own advantage. It was my debut Test, so I got carried away. But ten years later, if I was still playing, I would have used it to my advantage. If the crowd was having an effect on me, it was obviously having an effect on the opposition. So, if things are going wrong, it might deflate the opposition more easily. I felt that in the Boxing Day Test match when 70,000 people started chanting – one can feel intimidated just by that. The crowd does play a huge role, and Younis Khan played ten years of his cricket in empty stadiums. This could easily go unnoticed in Younis Khan's case, but any cricketer worth his salt will tell you that it does matter; it makes you do things you thought you couldn't do. Apart from this, what sets him apart are really his fourth-innings heroics. One has to remember that fourth innings is not easy in the subcontinent as pitches tend to deteriorate a lot and batting becomes tougher, and that is where, I think, Younis Khan has been exceptional. This ability puts him in the league of the legends of the game.

SS

37

THE HIGHEST IMPACT PAKISTANI TEST BATSMAN AFTER YOUNIS KHAN AND INZAMAM-UL-HAQ: MISBAH-UL-HAQ

He does not belong to the elite club of 50-plus batting average in Test cricket that three batsmen in his country's Test cricket history do – Younis Khan, Javed Miandad and Mohammad Yousuf. Six Pakistani batsmen have a higher runs aggregate and ten have scored more Test centuries: Younis has 33, Inzamam 25, Yousuf 24 and Miandad 23.

But when one critically analyses his performances and the pivotal role he has played in the middle order for Pakistan, it is Misbah-ul-Haq (with an average of 48.31 and just ten Test centuries) who emerges as the third highest impact batsman in Pakistan's Test cricket history, after only Younis Khan and Inzamam.

Misbah is not only a Pakistani great. He is the twelfth highest impact batsman (minimum fifty Tests) in the history of Test cricket. Just for perspective, he is higher impact than Garry Sobers, Jacques Kallis, Graeme Smith, Rahul Dravid, Sachin Tendulkar, Matthew Hayden and Vivian Richards.

AC: Well, while these numbers are great, they do not tell you the complete story. If we look at Misbah's career, we find that he has hardly played any matches outside Asia. In fact, out of a total career Tests of sixty-eight, Misbah has played only nineteen Tests outside Asia. If we delve further, we find that he has a poor record, both conventionally and impact-wise in the two Tests he has played in Australia (average 25) and the three in South Africa (average 22.5). He's played only once in England (and has done reasonably well) but unfortunately, he's unlikely to play there again. He hasn't toured Australia often enough either ...

Most of these batsmen (Tendulkar, Richards, Dravid, Smith, etc.), compared to whom Misbah has a higher batting impact, have tasted success all over the world in different conditions. So, taking nothing away from his phenomenal achievement at home (which in his case is the UAE, where he has played twenty-six of his thirty-one home Tests), questions will still be raised about his performances in challenging conditions overseas.

Critics would say he hasn't been tested enough – a stigma which Misbah will have to live with, and maybe rectify, to be truly remembered as an all-time great. Otherwise his career numbers will always be taken with a pinch of salt.

NN: Yes, while Misbah will have to prove his mettle overseas, aren't we biased when we judge batsmen from the subcontinent? Why is an Australian or an English batsman with a fantastic home record but poor overseas record still considered great, but the same yardstick not applied to Asian batsmen?

AC: Yes, there is a bias. And that is primarily because conditions in England and Australia (and South Africa and New Zealand) are generally considered tougher for all batsmen from all over the world as compared to batting conditions in the subcontinent.

But having said that, the modern history of cricket must factor in these anomalies. If an Australian has done nothing of note in the subcontinent, he should be at par with the Asian batsman who hasn't done well overseas. The art of playing spin is as artsy as playing the swinging and seaming balls.

Misbah, however, had a faltering start, failing (batting impact of less than 1) in his first five Test appearances for Pakistan. He made his debut in 2001 but was dropped in 2003, and not selected to represent Pakistan for the next four years.

Between October 2007, when he made his comeback, and the end of 2010, Misbah played sixteen Tests for Pakistan. Although he gave just a few high impact performances in this period, one particular facet of his batting stood out – a quality he would come to be identified with in the years to come.

An ability to absorb pressure

Pakistan was amongst the lowest-ranked Test teams in world cricket during this period (2007–10): they played twenty-four Tests, lost twelve, drew nine and won just three Tests. In fact, only West Indies and Bangladesh had a worse win: loss ratio.

Batting was their weakness and they had the lowest average score per batsman amongst all major Test-playing nations. Even at the start of his career, Misbah's ability to absorb pressure (of falling wickets) stood out. He was amongst the best in the world in this regard.

AC: Misbah-ul-Haq is not a Pakistani cricketer in more ways than one. He is a bit of an outlier. Most Pakistani batsmen of the past, whether you talk about Javed Miandad or Inzamam-ul-Haq or Saeed Anwar, have had a certain flair and elegance in their batting. And most of them have had a certain personality and charisma. Misbah is different. He is like a stone with no emotions, unfazed by whatever happens around him. Even when there are explosions around him, which is often the case with a volatile Pakistan team, Misbah is calm and stays focused without losing concentration. Thus, it is not surprising that he has absorbed a lot of pressure (of falling wickets) even when he was not producing the big performances consistently for Pakistan.

Post-2010, he added another quality to his batting – the ability to perform in big matches.

Excellent big-match temperament

Misbah has three series-defining performances in sixty-eight Tests. He has the fifth best matches to SD ratio for a Pakistani batsman after Inzamam (eight in 120 matches), Azhar Ali (three in 52 matches), Younis Khan (six in 110 matches) and Ijaz Ahmed (three in sixty matches).

It wasn't just about producing SD performances but also being enormously consistent in those series. This is why the value of his SD performances is among the highest in Test history.

His appetite for the big occasion can also be seen from his series-holding value (a high impact performance in a win or a draw which ensures that the favourable series scoreline remains intact), the highest for any player in the history of Test cricket, and big-match value (a high impact performance in a lost match which if won would have ensured that the player's team won the series or drew level from behind), the highest for any batsman in Test cricket.

In fact, if we take only the big-match attributes (which is the cumulative value of the SD value, the big-match value and the series-holding value), Misbah is second only to Bradman (amongst all batsmen) in the history of Test cricket – a fact that is nothing short of sensational.

This is the main reason why he has a higher impact than Miandad (five SDs in 124 Tests), Mohammad Yousuf (one in ninety), Saeed Anwar (two in fifty-five) and Hanif Mohammad (none in fifty-five), despite not being a prolific run-scorer. All of these other cricketers have a higher Runs-Tally Impact than Misbah but are lower in impact.

Vs New Zealand, Hamilton, 2011. *New Zealand post 275 in the first innings. Pakistan are in a spot of bother when Misbah comes out to bat at 104 for 3 which soon worsens to 107 for 4. He puts together 149 for the 5th wicket with Asad Shafiq; Pakistan reply with 367. The home team collapse for 110 in the second innings. Pakistan win by 10 wickets.*

Vs New Zealand, Wellington, 2011. *Misbah scores 99 and a match-saving unbeaten 70 (from 42 for 3, facing 226 deliveries and occupying the crease for 312 minutes) in the last innings of the second Test in Wellington. Pakistan, chasing 274, bat out 92 overs and end with 226 for 5.*

They win the series 1–0. This is Misbah's first SD performance.

Interestingly, he was made the captain of Pakistan in only the previous series against South Africa. And that almost immediately elevated his batting and brought out the big-match player in him. Misbah's career turned a corner from here.

The transformation

Misbah has been the second highest impact batsman in the world in Test cricket after only A.B. de Villiers since 1 January 2011. With age not exactly on his side (he is forty-two now), this is a particularly impressive achievement.

All his three SDs have come in this period (2011–16) in forty-seven Tests.

Vs Sri Lanka, Sharjah, 2014. *Sri Lanka led the series 1–0. Batting first, they posted 428. Pakistan replied with 341 with Misbah contributing 63. Sri Lanka were bowled out for 214 in the third innings. Pakistan needed 302 for victory. The match was in balance at 186 for 4 when Misbah joined Azhar Ali at the crease. The pair put together a match-winning 109-run stand for the 5th wicket. Misbah remained unbeaten on 68 as Pakistan registered their second highest chase (at the time; now third) by 5 wickets.*

The series was levelled at 1–1. Misbah recorded his second SD.

Vs England, Dubai, 2015. *Misbah scores 102 (from 85 for 3) and then 87 (from 83 for 3) in the second innings. Pakistan win by 178 runs.*

Vs England, Sharjah, 2015. *Misbah top-scores for Pakistan with 71 (from 88 for 3) in the first innings. Pakistan post 234. England reply with 306. He then scores 38 (from 152 for 4) in the second innings and puts together a significant 93-run partnership with Mohammad Hafeez. Pakistan go on to win by 127 runs.*

Misbah gets his third SD for two high impact performances in the series and his rise as a batsman coincides with his stint as Pakistan captain and his country's rise to the top.

AC: The cricketing world has not given Misbah his due for his achievements in the UAE. He has faced a lot of criticism regarding his age and brand of cricket but that hasn't bogged him down or forced him to change his style. To Misbah's credit, he has taken it in his stride and continued to perform consistently day in and day out for Pakistan. This shows his character and phenomenal mental strength.

Pakistan's surge in Test cricket

Since 2011, Pakistan has the second highest win: loss ratio in Test cricket after South Africa. Misbah has been one of the architects of this resurgence. Pakistan has played nineteen Test series since then, winning ten, losing three and drawing six (including their recent series-levelling effort in England).

Vs England, Lord's, 2016. *The crucial opening Test; Pakistan are 77 for 3 on the first day when Misbah walks in. Thanks to him and Asad Shafiq, Pakistan stabilize but for the next five hours, only one man holds an end down, till Misbah is finally dismissed for 114. Pakistan's 339 is destined to be the highest innings total in the match, as they win eventually by 75 runs. This is to be Misbah's highest point in the series, but it is a crucial contribution in a 2–2 series.*

Their continuous rise in the last six years meant that Pakistan reached the No. 1 position in the ICC Test rankings (in August 2016) for the first time ever – quite an achievement by a team not fancied by many and branded as unattractive.

Misbah has been Pakistan's highest impact batsman in this period (2011–16), marginally higher than the next highest, Younis Khan. In other words, the additional burden of captaincy has actually brought out the best in Misbah the batsman too. It says a thing or two about his mental strength and temperament.

AC: I have one criticism of Misbah. See, he has a bit of Miandad in his batting technique. He is an accumulator and not a free-flowing stroke maker like Inzamam or Mohammad Yousuf. He has a couple of releasing shots – the most prominent being the slog sweep, but he is not a big boundary hitter and plays a lot of dot balls. He also has a grip like Miandad's wherein there is a considerable gap between his two hands. This actually makes it difficult to play the big shots, especially down the ground, and is ideally suited to be a grafter. Not surprisingly then, he has a batting strike rate of only 44.88. Considering he plays most of his cricket on flat subcontinent tracks, that is poor.

Misbah bats at No. 5 in a team with not too many batting stars. While he absorbs a lot of pressure when wickets fall around him, it is a shortcoming that he fails to accelerate on many occasions when batting with the tail. He has the third lowest strike rate from the No. 5 batting position among all twenty-five batsmen who have scored a minimum of 1,000 runs since his debut.

He made 82 in 243 deliveries and 45 in 87 deliveries against India in Delhi. He could have accelerated, especially in the second innings which might have helped Pakistan set India a stiffer fourth-innings target. India went on to chase down their target of 203 with 6 wickets in hand.

Another classic case was his 33 in 120 balls and an unbeaten 79 in 181 balls (chasing 264) against Zimbabwe. Pakistan were bowled out for 239 in 81 overs in the fourth innings.

NN: In the Delhi Test, Misbah came out to bat at 59 for 3 in the first innings. Wickets continued to tumble and Pakistan were reeling at 142 for 8 before Misbah put together 87 for the 9th wicket with Sami (who contributed just 28). Yes, there was a case for him to have taken a risk in the second innings but that would have also meant a higher chance of getting out. Thus Misbah played to his strength and accumulated as many runs as he could for Pakistan, which was the need of the hour.

Similarly, in the Zimbabwe Test, Misbah came out to bat at 90 for 3 and had to play the role of the pivot, which he did successfully, but others around him failed, which resulted in a humiliating loss for Pakistan.

AC: Herein lies my bigger grouse. Why come at 59 for 3 and 90 for 3 when he could've walked in at 42 for 2 or 80 for 2 or such like?

NN: One must remember that Pakistan was not a world-beating side during this period. Their batting was amongst the weakest in the world. So, the need of the hour was to score runs. If Misbah were part of an all-conquering side, yes, maybe he could have been more daring and taken more risks as there would be others who could be trusted in the lower order. But Pakistan were just rebuilding after a period of great struggle. And Misbah was practically forced to play risk-free cricket. And there is no match in Misbah's entire career where one can clearly say that his sluggish batting adversely affected the team's result.

On the contrary, this proves that Misbah had the bigger picture in mind even at the cost of personal reputation. Against New Zealand in Wellington in 2011, he walked in to bat at 42 for

3 (chasing 274) and remained unbeaten on 70 in 226 deliveries. Pakistan played out 92 overs and ended with 226 for the loss of 5 wickets. The match was drawn but, more importantly, the series was won (Pakistan had won the first match in the two-Test series).

Since his debut, Misbah is the third highest run scorer from the No. 5 batting position, but, more significantly, the sixth highest impact batsman at that position in Test history (minimum forty matches) after A.B. de Villiers, Steve Waugh, Colin Cowdrey, Michael Clarke and Vivian Richards. His batting average of 52.96 is by no means inadequate. So, he more than made up for his 'slow' and 'boring' batting with the sheer amount of runs he scored and the impact they had in his team's cause.

Also, we must remember that conventional strike rate measures how fast a batsman scores his runs, irrespective of the rate of other batsmen in the match. This means that it gives you little indication of whether a high strike rate actually affected the result of the match.

This is where Strike Rate Impact comes in. It is attributed very rarely to batsmen in Test cricket. Not only does a batsman have to score at a strike rate higher than the match norm but also ensure that his performance helps his team to win or draw the match.

Now, the shocking part. Though Misbah has the lowest strike rate for a recognized batsman in Pakistan's Test cricket history, his Strike Rate Impact is the second highest only after Wasim Akram's. In Misbah's case, it means that he scored at high strike rate (much above the match norm) in a number of matches which Pakistan ultimately went on to win.

Here is a list of all substantial match performances (match aggregates) by Misbah in which he had a strike rate of 60 or above.

Vs Bangladesh, Mirpur, 2015: 91 in 94 balls; Pakistan won by 328 runs

Vs Australia, Abu Dhabi, 2014: 202 in 225 balls; Pakistan won by 356 runs

Vs Sri Lanka, Sharjah, 2014: 131 in 185 balls; Pakistan won by 5 wickets

Vs New Zealand, Abu Dhabi, 2014: 102 in 162 balls; Pakistan won by 248 runs

Vs West Indies, St. Kitts, 2011: 127 in 209 balls; Pakistan won by 196 runs

Vs South Africa, Abu Dhabi, 2013: 128 in 213 balls; Pakistan won by 7 wickets

Pakistan went on to win all these matches. This included the joint fastest century in Test cricket (in 56 balls against Australia) – a record only recently broken by Brendon McCullum. This basically tells us that Misbah has another gear. He has the ability to take any bowling attack to the cleaners if the situation so demands.

The fact that he has chosen to bat in a different manner for most part of his career is not so much a question of his ability but of the needs and demands of a volatile Pakistani batting line-up. Misbah knows that he would maximize his and his team's chances by being a grafter rather than an aggressor. So, whereas he could have accelerated batting with the tail and perhaps scored more hundreds, in the larger interest of his team, that would have been futile and, in some cases, counterproductive.

AC: Let's not view individual hundreds as a selfish effort, for if he adds 20 more to his total, the partnership would be worth 35 more. Not scoring more hundreds while batting at No. 5 (and not No. 7) is an indicator of the fact that he batted too slow for someone at that number.

There's always a counter-narrative to everything. If the numbers suggest that whenever he accelerated, Pakistan won, there is also a strong case for him to bat faster in most matches and not in select few. While he's been a part of a volatile line-up, it is equally true that he batted alongside Younis quite a bit too. Also, batting with the tail is an art and one rule of thumb is to bat faster if you are to maximize the chances of winning the game.

38

THE MOST CONSISTENT BATSMAN IN PAKISTAN'S TEST HISTORY: AZHAR ALI

A batting average of 46 in fifty-two Tests doesn't signify greatness. At best, it shows a batsman who is adept at the rigours of Test cricket rather than being special in it. These averages, it will no longer surprise the reader, completely belie Azhar Ali's contribution to Pakistan's cricket history and his place in it.

Ali made his Test debut in 2010. But the dicussions around the last few years about the most promising new batsman in the Test arena have invariably revolved around Kane Williamson, Steve Smith, Virat Kohli and Joe Root. Along with their impressive records, the flamboyance and stroke play of these four have played a part in this. Ali, in contrast, comes from the dour school of batting, not exhilarating to watch but mightily effective.

Standing in Pakistan's Test history

In Pakistan's Test history, for a minimum of fifty Tests, Azhar Ali emerges as the fourth highest impact batsman after Younis Khan, Inzamam-ul-Haq and Misbah-ul-Haq and the reason is not only the number of series-defining performances he has produced in a short career. The major reasons behind Azhar Ali's high standing are consistency and his ability to absorb pressure.

Vs Australia, Leeds, 2010. *Pakistan were 0–1 down going into the last Test of the series after being thrashed in the first one. Australia, batting first, were blown away for 88. Pakistan responded with 258, with Azhar Ali, playing in only his second Test match, contributing 30. Australia fared better in their second innings and set Pakistan a tricky target of 180 runs. Pakistan lost an early wicket, that of Salman Butt, with the score at 27 when Azhar Ali walked in. With Imran Farhat for company, the pair steadied the ship with a 110-run partnership in the face of some hostile bowling. Farhat scored 67 while Azhar Ali scored 51, and the match seemed destined to end in Pakistan's favour. A typical Pakistani collapse, however, saw them then scrape through by only 3 wickets. The manner in which the Pakistani batsmen struggled to score runs after his dismissal showed how significant Azhar Ali's contribution was. It was a promising start to a burgeoning Test career.*

Amongst the ten most consistent batsmen from the No. 3 spot in Test history

It is not a mystery why the No. 3 spot is the most challenging and responsible spot in any batting line-up in Tests. This is doubly so in Pakistan's case, and especially during Azhar Ali's career, when there have hardly been any stable openers in their side. Therefore, more often than not, Azhar Ali has had to come after the loss of an early wicket. The way he has absorbed the pressure and yet maintained his consistency is his true legacy as a batsman. For a minimum of fifty Tests, Ali emerges as the second highest Pressure Impact batsman in Pakistan's Test history after Younis Khan. Astonishingly, with a failure rate of only 33 per cent, he is amongst the ten most consistent batsmen from the No. 3 spot in the history of the game. It also means that he is the most consistent batsman in Pakistani Test history (irrespective of batting position).

Another consequence of coming in early to bat is facing the new ball, and when it comes to New Ball Impact (which is the ability of a batsman to either occupy the crease or score runs against the new ball), Azhar Ali's standing is the second best in Test history for any non-opener after Kane Williamson.

Vs Sri Lanka, Sharjah, 2014. *Trailing 0–1 and going into the final Test, Pakistan were almost shut out of the series by the Sri Lankan batsmen in their first-innings score of 428. Pakistan responded by scoring 341. Sri Lanka scored 214 in their second innings to set a target of 302 in a minimum of 59 overs. Both Pakistani openers were dismissed with the score at 48. Azhar Ali, then, contrary to his characteristic slow and steady approach, started a measured run chase in the final session of the game with Misbah-ul-Haq. Under fading light, Pakistan pulled off their second most successful run chase then in Test cricket. Though Ali got out just minutes before the end, his 103 off 137 balls won him the Man of the Match award.*

Pakistan's rise not a coincidence

Between 2006 and 2011, Pakistan struggled miserably in the Test arena, having the least but one win: loss ratio amongst the major Test playing nations (after West Indies). Since 2011, though, Pakistan's win: loss ratio has been the second best for any team after South Africa and they haven't lost a single series at 'home'. Needless to say, Azhar Ali's contribution has been massive.

It can be said that a lot of Azhar Ali's runs came in the UAE where pitches are considered to be flat, but his performances helped Pakistan win Test matches and series after a long hiatus. Even overseas, Ali was part of a historic Pakistan team which achieved the No. 1 ranking in Tests after drawing 2–2 against England away from home. Ali didn't produce big scores in the series but still had the highest New Ball Impact amongst all Pakistani batsmen. It shows the quiet effect he has had on the team.

In the new era of Pakistani dominance (2011–16), Azhar Ali has produced three SDs, the joint most by any Pakistani batsman, bowler or player (along with Misbah-ul-Haq and Younis Khan). In fact, his rate of producing an SD performance every seventeen Tests is the second best for any Pakistani batsman and the fifth best after Don Bradman, Inzamam-ul-Haq, Hansie Cronje and Graeme Smith in the history of Test cricket (minimum fifty Tests).

It is ironic that Azhar Ali's name is in discussion nowadays after his triple hundred against West Indies – appropriately not even amongst his ten highest impact Test knocks.

AC: This comes as a surprise because Pakistan cricket, for whatever reason, is not talked about and written about so much. Maybe it has something to do with the fact that they hardly travel overseas, so it is really a subcontinental story and not really a world story and the same is true for Azhar Ali. A good way to judge a player over a period of time is to see if a batsman is scoring around 1,000 runs in every eleven or twelve Tests, and Ali is doing well on that count. In fifty two matches, he has scored around 4,200 runs.

He has 11 centuries and 22 half-centuries which basically means that in thirty-three out of his ninety-eight innings, he has a 50-plus score which in turn means that he is taking approximately three innings for one 50-plus score, which is phenomenal. His is still a young career and it will grow further, but these numbers are definitely promising. It remains to be seen how Ali fares when he travels. He has played twenty Tests outside Asia, where he averages 33 in ten Tests in England, 34 in two Tests in New Zealand and only 22 in three Tests in South Africa. His numbers must get better overseas if he is to be remembered as a great batsman. For an Asian batsman, overseas conditions will always remain a yardstick and will be held against him till he starts scoring away from home.

SS

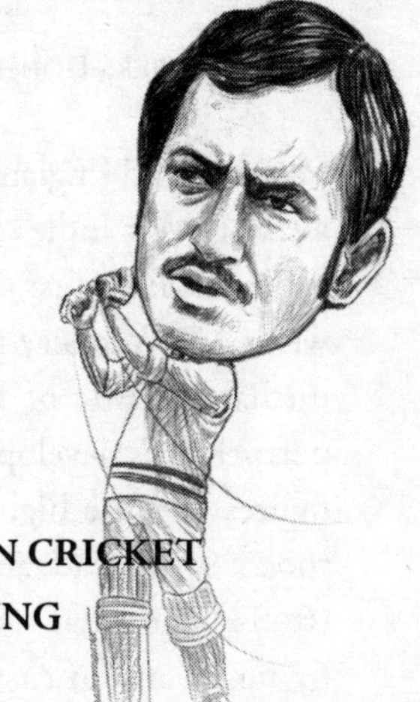

39

AJIT WADEKAR CHANGED INDIAN CRICKET HISTORY WITH HIS BATTING

He is famous as a very successful Test captain, but cricket pundits would be loathe to ascribe batting greatness to Ajit Wadekar. After all, he averaged just 31 in thirty-seven Tests and scored just 1 Test hundred – the time-honoured, and greatly flawed, measures for evaluating a batsman.

As it happens, if we take thirty Tests as a minimum (which we normally would not when we prepare all-time lists), Ajit Wadekar comes up as the fourth highest impact Test batsman for India ever, after Cheteshwar Pujara (more on him later), Rahul Dravid and Sachin Tendulkar.

The impeccable timing of some of his finest performances and the role that he played in changing Indian cricket history are stories that have been ignored for too long.

A landmark beginning in New Zealand

It was February 1968. The Indian cricket team reached New Zealand for a four-Test series. India had never won a Test series abroad in their thirty-six-year-old cricketing history. New Zealand had never won a Test series, home or away. But the Kiwis were getting hard to beat at home lately; they'd drawn their last home series with South Africa,

Pakistan and England (and they would go on to draw their next series against West Indies too).

In the first Test, New Zealand made 350, and India were 39 for 1 when Ajit Wadekar, playing in his fourth Test series, walked in. Highly uncharacteristic of Indian batting overseas at the time, continuous partnerships developed – every single Indian batsman reached double figures and the highest scorer was Wadekar with 80. India actually took a 9-run lead. And then, with some magic from E.A.S. Prasanna (6–94), the Kiwis were dismissed for 208, leaving India 200 to win, by no means an easy target in New Zealand. It was 30 for 1 when Wadekar walked in and once again took charge. First with Engineer, then Surti, Wadekar top-scored with 71 in two-and-a-half hours and took India within 37 runs of victory. Uncharacteristically, India did not make heavy weather of that and won by 5 wickets. It remains among India's best fourth-innings wins, given what had gone on before it.

But New Zealand came right back and won the next Test by 6 wickets. In the third Test, Prasanna and Surti helped reduce the Kiwis to 186, and India were 18 for 1 when Wadekar walked in. It became 78 for 2, then 98 for 3. Then, Pataudi, Borde, Jaisimha all departed with small contributions but Wadekar kept it together. When he was finally dismissed at 295, he had batted more than six hours for 143. India added a few more runs and, by then, the fight was comprehensively knocked out of the Kiwis. They were dismissed for not much (thanks to Nadkarni and Prasanna), India won comfortably and then dominated the next Test (thanks mostly to Prasanna and Borde) to win their first overseas series 3–1. Ajit Wadekar was the highest impact player for India (by a distance) in the first two crucial wins.

This ability to play at his best at the most crucial times would be showcased again and again in his career – a history-changing quality for a team that did not win much those days.

Mini-triumph against Australia

In December 1969, India would draw level with Australia at Delhi in the third of the five-Test series. After Bedi and Prasanna ripped through the Australians to finish them off for 107, India were set a not-so-easy 191 to win with more than two days to go. At 16 for 2, it seemed as if the Australians had it in the bag, but first with nightwatchman Bedi and then with a delightful Viswanath, playing only his second Test match, Wadekar stood firm and kept an attack of McKenzie, Connolly, Gleeson and Mallett at bay. His unbeaten 91 would give India a famous win (by 7 wickets), but India would lose the next two Tests to lose the series 1–3 (despite Wadekar scoring the most Indian runs in those two games).

In the very next series (almost fourteen months later), Wadekar would lead India to their first series win in West Indies. Though he didn't contribute much with the bat, the whole team was buoyed by the presence of the most sensational debut player in Indian cricket history: Sunil Gavaskar.

Epoch-making victory in England

That team would go on and make history in the next series as well, in England that same year.

The opening Test in an English tour has always been a crucial one (in fact, till 2014, every time India won the series in England, they had managed to not lose the first Test). On 23 July 1971, Wadekar came out to bat at 1 for 1 as India squared up to England's first innings of 304. John Snow was on fire and, with Gavaskar gone soon too, it was 29 for 2. Snow attacked with bouncers, which Wadekar hooked with conviction and changed the temperature with his calm at the crease. In about three hours of batting, he took the score to 125, out of which he made 85 before being dismissed. Thereafter, youngsters Viswanath and Solkar took their captain's lead and patiently applied themselves to their fullest to actually give India a slight first-innings lead. India drew that Test and the next one.

The final Test at The Oval, which India won to secure the series, is remembered as B.S. Chandrasekhar's Test for his landmark 6 for 38, which dismissed the English for 101 in the third innings. However, the highest impact player of that match was actually Wadekar for his doughty and critical batting at No. 3 in both innings, stabilizing the side from 21 for 2 in the first innings and 2 for 1 in the second, to score 48 and 45 (in a fourth-innings chase again) of the most valuable runs he would ever make, in what rapidly became a low-scoring game (Dilip Sardesai kept him company for most of those two innings with an invaluable hand too).

Wadekar played valuable support roles with the bat in his hat-trick of series wins as Indian captain when India beat England at home next. In a short span of time, and for the first time in its history, India was amongst the best two or three teams in the world. It was a landmark moment that defined much of modern Indian cricket.

The next series was in England again, seventeen months later, and an off-colour India was comprehensively beaten 0–3 (being dismissed for 42 would be one of the low points); Wadekar did not have a great series. He lost his place both as captain and player. At the age of thirty-three, his career was over after just one bad series.

In the end, Ajit Wadekar retired having played just thirty-seven Tests, with barely 2,000 runs at an average of 31, with just 1 Test century and 14 fifties. Not quite the numbers of a world beater. And this is where conventional figures get it so wrong.

Wadekar played in ten Test series, out of which India won four and drew one, only losing 50 per cent – an astonishing return given the past he emerged from.

The man produced the highest impact Indian performances in the matches that swung two of the three landmark away Test series India's way, which went on to change the history of Indian cricket.

Please digest this: India have just won two Test series in England forty-three years after that 1971 triumph. Even more surprisingly, they have won just one Test series in New Zealand (in 2009) after the one in 1968. This is how landmark that was.

Historical significance, anyone?

The timing of Wadekar's best performances was his most remarkable quality, one that cricket romantics have failed to give pride of place to.

In fact, at the end of his eight-year Test career, if we take just that duration into account, Ajit Wadekar was the sixth highest impact batsman in the world after Sunil Gavaskar, Geoff Boycott, Ian Chappell, Bill Lawry and Basil D'Oliveira (minimum ten Tests). This is a moment worth pausing in.

As mentioned before, if we take thirty Tests as a minimum, Wadekar comes up as the fourth highest impact Indian batsman of all time, after Cheteshwar Pujara, Rahul Dravid and Sachin Tendulkar. Of course, the high value of his two series-defining performances in tandem with his low sample size of thirty-seven Tests causes a skew, but at the same time, his SD to matches ratio of 18.5 is among the highest in history for any Test-playing nation.

So, really, could a batsman who averaged 31 be a great batsman (or even a very good one)? Consider this: Until as late as 1981 (after almost fifty years of Indian Test cricket had gone down), Wadekar was the only Indian Test batsman to have two SDs.

And for those who feel that Impact Index provides too high a value to SDs, let's just consider the proportion of runs made by Indian batsmen relative to their teammates and the opposition in all the matches they played: the runs tally impact (the only element of subjectivity here is a slightly higher value if the contribution came in a back-to-the-wall win, like with a third-innings recovery or a fourth-innings chase, a rare occurrence in Wadekar's time anyway). For Indian batsmen till 1990, Ajit Wadekar comes third on that list – after Sunil Gavaskar and Vijay Hazare, ahead of batsmen like G.R. Viswanath, Vijay Manjrekar, Dilip Sardesai, Dilip Vengsarkar, M.A.K. Pataudi, Polly Umrigar, Mohinder Amarnath and Chandu Borde. And if we take all of Indian Test cricket (1932 to present day), he is ahead of even Virender Sehwag, V.V.S. Laxman, Sourav Ganguly, Gautam Gambhir and Mohammad Azharuddin.

Every one of these batsmen has a higher batting average, often considerably more, than Wadekar. It just suggests how well timed Wadekar's better performances were and how, despite not piling up the big individual scores when set in easier conditions (which is what boosts averages), he was such an important contributor to his side.

Wadekar's batting failure rate of 43 per cent provides a significant cue to how regularly he did it. It is lower than the batting failure rates of Polly Umrigar, Vijay Manjrekar, Virender Sehwag, Sourav Ganguly, V.V.S. Laxman, Dilip Vengsarkar and many others, including contemporary stars like Virat Kohli and Cheteshwar Pujara.

In the end, the point is not about all-time rankings at all (where we usually begin with a minimum of fifty Tests anyway, when the skews reduce considerably) but about giving credit to players who contributed the most towards changing their country's history. It is obvious that many of them have not got due credit, and there really is no alternative to reading contributions in context.

Clearly, greatness needs a different measure.

AC: I actually claim to be someone who follows Indian cricket closely, who takes a little bit of pride in knowing what people have done, including the older names. But you have not seen them play, so you rely on what people tell you about them, or whatever documentation or literature there is on those players. Ajit Wadekar – of course that's a name I know in the context of someone who has had an influence on Indian cricket and is a big name as a captain – but with the conventional batting average of 31 in thirty-seven Tests, you kind of tend to not think of him as a top-quality batsman.

Winning overseas in the 1960s and '70s was much tougher than winning in 2000s, simply because there was very little history and no footage. For an Indian team to go there and do so well is huge, as is Wadekar's contribution as a player in them.

So, this story is a fascinating one for an Indian fan's perspective. In 2009, the only other time India won in New Zealand, those were uncharacteristically flat pitches for Kiwi conditions. But to do that such a long time ago, when conditions did not favour India, and to pull off such a victory, with the spinners also contributing – this has been a big finding for me. We hardly ever go through these scorecards, and this is a huge story in that respect.

JV

40

G.R. VISWANATH IS ALMOST AS HIGH IMPACT AS S.M. GAVASKAR

However great many consider Gundappa Viswanath to be, to see him in the same league as Sunil Gavaskar sounds dangerously close to blasphemy. After all, Gavaskar scored 10,122 runs at an average of 51.12 in 125 Tests while Viswanath made 6,080 runs at an average of 41.93 in 91 Tests.

But consider this: India never lost a match in which Viswanath scored a century. But that's still only fourteen occasions. Whereas Gavaskar hit thirty-four Test hundreds – the world record at the time.

The reason is, simply, series-defining performances. Viswanath registered three SDs in his career, while Gavaskar, in a longer career, registered two (including one in his debut Test).

Viswanath's three SDs constituted these.

Vs West Indies, Chennai, 1979. *Though made against a Packer-hit West Indies side, this was the only result Test in a six-match series. On a difficult pitch, West Indies managed 228. Viswanath walked in at 11 for 2, and produced 124 of the most enterprising runs before being last out at 255. Then, West Indies were knocked over for 151 and in a chase of 124, India were 17 for 3, till Viswanath stabilized the innings for a while, making 31. In the end, a blitzkrieg from Kapil Dev helped India win by a narrow margin of 3 wickets. This match is a good example of* *how favourable pitch conditions can make even lower-rated international bowlers major threats.*

Vs Australia, Melbourne, 1981. *Down in the series 0–1 and in the last Test, things didn't look good for India at 22 for 2 when Viswanath walked in to bat. Lillee and Pascoe were sizzling and, at 91 for 4 and 115 for 6, the end seemed nigh. But Viswanath was still there and the Australians knew only too well that the innings was far from over. So it proved to be. Viswanath added 51 with Kirmani (who made 25 – the second highest score in the innings), then 26 with Ghavri (who made precisely 0), then 40 with Shivlal Yadav – before he was ninth out at 230 (for 114 off 222 balls with 11 fours). India managed just 7 more, but Viswanath's extraordinary one-man show had inspired the team once again. Its complete manifestation had to wait till the second innings though, when, after being 182 behind, Gavaskar and Chauhan put on 165 for the first wicket, the team managed 324 (Viswanath contributed 30), and then dismissed the Australians on a wearing pitch for 83 (Kapil Dev 5–23, though not fully fit) to win by 59 runs. For the first time in their cricket history, India had not lost a series in Australia.*

Vs England, Mumbai, 1981. *In a bizarrely low-scoring opening Test of a six-match series, both teams were more or less even after England made 166 in reply to India's 179. Then, Viswanath came out to bat at 24 for 2 on a pitch where nothing seemed certain, and batted like no one had before – he made 37 in 38 balls, unthinkable in those circumstances and it shifted the momentum India's way. Then, Kapil Dev, at the peak of his powers, made 46 in much the same mould and India reached 227 with help from the middle order and the tail. England were knocked over for 102, which further accentuated the impact of those early runs. The series scoreline eventually was 1–0 to India.*

These are Gavaskar's two SDs:

Vs West Indies, Port-of-Spain, 1971. *Gavaskar began his Test career with an SD. He made 65 in his first Test innings out of India's 352 (only Dilip Sardesai with 112 scored more than him), as India took a lead of 138. West Indies rallied but could set India only 125 to win, not an easy task in* *a fourth-innings chase, especially in those days. But Gavaskar controlled the chase with assurance; the impending danger at 84 for 3 when Sardesai was dismissed was transformed to a slight hiccup as India won by 7 wickets – their first Test win in West Indies. It turned out to be the only result Test in the series, one in which Gavaskar made 774 runs overall.*

Vs Australia, Melbourne 1981. *India faced a deficit of 182 runs in the first innings as Gavaskar and Chetan Chauhan came out to bat. Gavaskar had had a dreadful series with the bat, it was 0–1 in the series, and this was the last chance to make amends. A remarkable fightback ensued, as they put on 165 for the opening wicket, when Gavaskar was given out lbw to Lillee by umpire Rex Whitehead, who had stood in all three Tests and made several poor decisions, mostly against India. Gavaskar was distraught as he was convinced he had inside-edged it. As Lillee got more vocal, Gavaskar lost it and pulled Chauhan along with him, staging a potential walkout. But manager Durrani and assistant manager Nadkarni ordered Chauhan to go back, who lost concentration and was out soon too. Still, the middle order fought and India managed 324, setting Australia 143 to win. Thereafter, on an increasingly two-paced wicket, India dismissed Australia for 83 and drew their first ever series in Australia.*

So, both Viswanath and Gavaskar got SDs in this match, as did Chauhan.

As SDs go, it is so often about luck too, or right place, right time. In 1979 at the Oval, when India chased an impossible 434 to win, Chauhan and Gavaskar again gave India a big start (213); Gavaskar went on to make 221 but India eventually ran out of overs as they finished at 429 for 8. If, say, Kapil Dev, who made 0 here, had made just 9, Gavaskar would have got an SD for this match, as a win would have made the series scoreline 1–1.

Similarly, at Bengaluru in 1987, India chased 221 to win in the fourth innings, and Gavaskar came out to play his final Test innings. The series was still 0–0 after four Tests and this was the final Test. The pitch was turning viciously and though Wasim Akram knocked out two batsmen, Iqbal Qasim and Tauseef Ahmed bowled pretty much unchanged thereafter. Gavaskar batted for almost five-and-a-half hours, playing one of his finest Test innings but was eighth out for an agonizing 96. If, say, Kapil Dev had made 18 instead of 2, India would have won, and Gavaskar would have had an SD. Instead, India lost by 16 runs, and Pakistan won a series in India 1–0.

Gavaskar was unlucky, no doubt – arguably the unluckiest Indian Test batsman ever on this count. Both those innings, among the finest Indian Test innings ever, deserved SD status. He would have been neck and neck with Tendulkar on impact otherwise, which would have been remarkable as Gavaskar played for a considerably weaker Test team relative to world standards.

Still, Gavaskar's incredibly low 36 per cent failure rate keeps him at higher impact than Viswanath, even if not by a great deal.

AC: While conventional numbers have Gavaskar far ahead, almost everyone who has seen Viswanath play, including Gavaskar himself, feels that Viswanath was a more talented batsman. This respect of your peers and your opponents is really what you play for.

Both their performances against those famed fast bowlers are astonishing, really, because they never got that kind of practice; they were playing a quality of bowling alien to them. Now, for example, we have bowling machines, and we can crank them up as much as we like, so you get that practice even if your team does not have a fast bowler. In those days, you really had to focus on your skills and find a way out.

I had this chat with G.R. Viswanath once and asked if he was scared of getting hit by all those fearsome fast bowlers he had faced. I was pleasantly surprised because his answer was, yes, there was a genuine injury scare. I asked him how he dealt with it. He said he would model his technique in such a way that he wasn't getting behind the ball all the time, and stayed inside or outside the line. Secondly, on the eve of the game, he said he would visualize himself getting hit and how he would react. That was a huge eye-opener, because I had never actually thought about these things – that I would get hit and this was how I was to feel the pain. He said that since it was such a distinct possibility, facing it and being prepared for it was much better. This was something that stood out for me, how differently cricket was played in those days.

Of course, everyone was in the same boat. Sunil Gavaskar too, but I do know that he realized later that wearing a skull cup was a mistake, because if he had been hit there the chances of getting seriously injured were actually higher as the impact of the ball would have been more concentrated with no give. He was fortunate he was never hit on the head when he was wearing the skull cup under his cap. Indian cricket was fortunate as well.

JV: There's a small caveat here, though, about Gavaskar's success against fast bowling. The four greatest fast-bowling challenges faced by India in a series happened in India when West Indies visited in 1974-75 (with Andy Roberts at his absolute best), in Australia 1980-81 (Lillee and Pascoe), in Pakistan in 1982-83 (Imran at his fearsome peak then) and immediately after that in West Indies in 1983 (just before the World Cup). If you must look at averages, Gavaskar averaged 27 at home against West Indies (in two Tests; he was injured for most of the series), 20 in Australia, 48 in Pakistan and 30 in West Indies. In every one of these series, someone else in his team excelled or did better than him at least – G.R. Viswanath, Sandeep Patil and then Mohinder Amarnath twice, respectively.

You can add two more series against West Indies to this, if you must. First, West Indies in 1976, but all Gavaskar's big runs were made at Port-of-Spain on slow pitches where spinners Jumadeen and Padmore were the main opposition bowlers. Whenever the pace ante was upped, someone else was left standing: Viswanath in the first Test at Bridgetown and Mohinder Amarnath in the last Test at Kingston. This was that series at the end of which Lloyd decided it was going to be pace all the way for the West Indies – it went on to change cricket history, of course.

The other one was in 1983, when West Indies came to India, looking to emphatically avenge the wounds of their World Cup loss. Gavaskar played two outstanding innings in the series (which India lost 0–3) while it was still open – a famous almost run-a-ball 121 made to equal Bradman's world record of 29 centuries at Delhi. And another innings, at a breakneck pace (relatively) in the very next Test at Ahmedabad, of 90 on a bad pitch. The Delhi Test was a high-scoring draw, where Vengsarkar outscored Gavaskar with 159. The Ahmedabad Test was lost by 138 runs, as India collapsed for 103 in the second innings (Gavaskar made 1 there). He failed 8 out of 11 times in that series (innings), and it was only because of his knock of 236 not out in the last Test in a dead rubber (walking out to bat at 0 for 2 though), a high-scoring draw, that his average touched 50 in the series.

This is just curious, because Gavaskar's ability to play fast bowling (in those pre-helmet times) and his rock-like importance to Indian cricket is beyond doubt.

AC: While I understand what these stats are suggesting, a batsman's form is something that goes up and down from time to time, and it'll be unfair to be reading too much into numbers that are a few years apart. One series here and there will always be below par and that shouldn't take the sheen off a wonderful career.

JV: These are not exactly cherry-picked series, but objectively the specific ones which posed the maximum pace challenges during the period Gavaskar's career ran. Anyone would pick these series for those reasons and his performances are in black and white. Of course he was a great player and had an outstanding career; in fact, the following facts confirm that even more.

Altogether, there were seventeen overseas tours during Gavaskar's career and India won or drew seven of those. Of those seven, Gavaskar was the leading Indian batsman thrice, which is perhaps a slight departure from expectation. Ajit Wadekar, Sandeep Patil/G.R. Viswanath, Ravi Shastri and Dilip Vengsarkar were the ones who did this in the others.

And there were fourteen Test series at home (single Tests not included), out of which India won or drew nine. Gavaskar played the leading role with the bat four times in those series. Farokh Engineer played it once, and Gavaskar actually shared the leading role with Viswanath twice and Vengsarkar and Shastri once each.

So, that's seven out of sixteen times overall where he played the leading role for India, and another four occasions when he shared the leading role, which is absolutely remarkable. These are figures only for series where India did well. There were several where India didn't and Gavaskar shone in many of those too (and India's losing had quite a bit to do with his failures). Add to this his two narrowly missed SDs (where India lost 0–1 in both cases) and you see why his influence on Indian cricket is so significant, but averages barely tell the real story even there.

JV

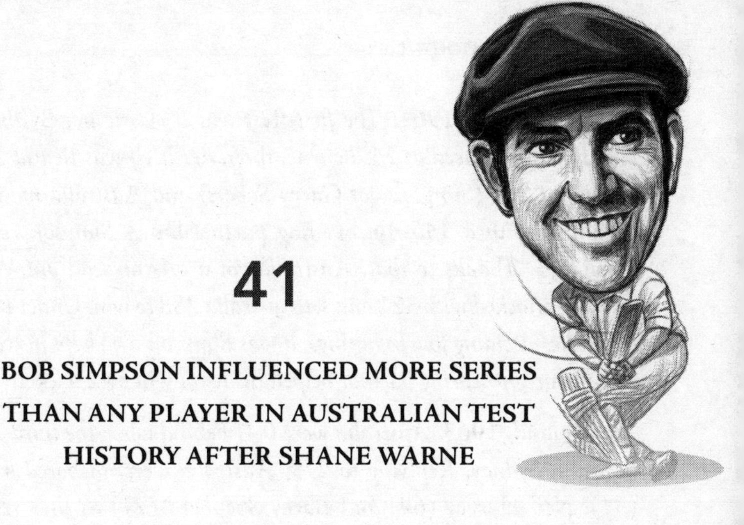

41

BOB SIMPSON INFLUENCED MORE SERIES THAN ANY PLAYER IN AUSTRALIAN TEST HISTORY AFTER SHANE WARNE

It's interesting what a batsman who averaged 47 with the bat in sixty-two Tests actually achieved. Bob Simpson was no all-rounder either – he took 71 wickets at about 42 apiece.

However, he has six series-defining performances in his career, the most by any Australian Test cricketer (Steve Waugh also has six SDs but in 168 Tests), save Warne, who has eight. In fact, in the history of Test cricket, for those who have played more than fifty Tests, he has the joint highest rate of producing an SD, with Don Bradman – one every ten Tests.

Here is what's going on.

Between 1957 and 1968, Simpson played fifty-two of those Tests, during which he was Australia's highest impact Test batsman (minimum thirty Tests), playing a big part in Australia's dominance in world cricket. Australia were the best Test team in the world for most of that period. They also did not lose a single home Test series in the 1960s and that had a fair amount to do with him too.

The main reason for his high impact was his propensity to play big innings when it really mattered. He has three SDs in those fifty-two Tests, a remarkably high SD to match ratio. All of them came in crunch situations.

Vs West Indies, 1961. *The first Test was a classic tie. By the time the last Test commenced at Melbourne, the series itself was tied at 1–1. West Indies got 292 (Simpson got Garry Sobers) and Australia made a strong beginning with a 146-run opening partnership – Simpson contributing a solid 75. Thanks to that, Australia got a 64-run lead but West Indies counter-attacked with 321 and set Australia 258 to win. Under the pressure of a series-deciding fourth innings, it was Simpson who kept his calm with a three-hour top-scoring 91 that helped his team win by 2 wickets.*

Vs England, 1963. *Australia were 0–1 behind when the third Ashes Test began at Sydney. Replying to 279, Australia were anchored by Simpson (91), Neil Harvey (64) and Barry Shepherd (71) as they replied with 319. Alan Davidson and Graham McKenzie then dismissed England for 104 – match pretty much done. Simpson later top-scored again with an unbeaten 34 as Australia won by 8 wickets. The series was 1–1, which stayed the final scoreline as the next two Tests were drawn.*

Vs England, 1966. *Series at 0–1 to England after the third Test. In the next match at Adelaide, England posted 241 and Simpson, batting for about nine hours, almost matched that on his own with a mammoth 225. Australia made 516 and won by an innings. Once again, the series scoreline was 1–1.*

Then there were two more SDs in that same period, where his bowling played a significant part too.

Vs England, 1961. *The series was level at 1–1 after three Tests. Australia batted first in Manchester and made 190 (Simpson failed). England dominated thereafter, and seemed to have the match at 358 for 6, when Simpson came on and took 4 wickets for 9 runs, including the two well-set batsmen (Barrington and Allen). Australia then came out and batted hard – Simpson put on 113 for the opening wicket with Bill Lawry before falling for 51, but it set the foundation for the eventual score of 432. England, set 256 to win, were 150 for 1 when a famous Richie Benaud show began. His 6 for 70 destroyed England; Simpson chipped in with a wicket too as Australia secured a famous win, which eventually decided the series scoreline too.*

Vs India, 1964. *In a three-Test series that ended 1–1, Simpson produced big performances in the two matches Australia won and drew. At Chennai, he produced 30 and then top-scored with 77 in a low-scoring Test. In the third and final Test at Calcutta, with the series at 1–1, he top-scored in both innings with 67 and 71 and also took 4–45 in India's only innings as the match ended in a draw.*

Simpson left the scene after a failure in the final Test against India at Sydney in January 1968. His run of scores before that Test was 55, 103 and 109. He was just thirty-one. It was a most peculiar departure.

He made a remarkable comeback after almost a decade to Test cricket in end-1977 as the forty-one-year-old captain of the Packer-hit Australian team. Coming out of retirement, he played ten Tests in two series against India and West Indies (the latter similarly Packer-affected) before retiring one last time as a player.

Even in that brief five-month period as player and captain, he produced another SD against India. Australia won that series 3–2, and Simpson produced big performances in all three Australian wins. In the first Test, he made 7 and 89 (after Australia were 7 for 3). In the second Test, he made 176 (out of Australia's 394) and 39, and even picked up two wickets. Then, in the fifth and deciding Test, he made 100 and 51 in a high-scoring Test where India made 445 in the fourth innings to lose by 47 runs. It was truly a captain's performance.

Simpson would come back as coach and ally to Allan Border in the mid-1980s, during a very significant phase for Australia.

As a pure batsman, he remains Australia's eighth highest impact Test batsman (minimum fifty Tests), higher impact than even Steve Waugh who averaged considerably more than him.

In the end, that ability to play at his best under crunch circumstances defines Bob Simpson's legacy as a batsman in Test history. Instead, cricket pundits talk about his triple century, his dedication, his limited stroke play, his ability to steal singles, his comeback at the age of forty-one, his second innings as coach – everything, except the most important thing he did for Australian cricket.

AC: It's almost preposterous that Bob Simpson would be a higher impact batsman than Steve Waugh. Not that the average of 46 with a 50-plus score in every third innings is mediocre, no matter how you look at it, but Waugh's achievements seem colossal in comparison. After all, we are talking about thousands of more Test runs. But when you look closely at the series-defining and match-winning performances, yes, Simpson's contribution inspires reverence. Not to forget a Test century at the age of forty-one, a decade after calling his time.

42

DURING AUSTRALIA'S MARCH TO WORLD DOMINANCE, MARK TAYLOR WAS HIS TEAM'S HIGHEST IMPACT BATSMAN

He is better known as Australia's epoch-changing captain in the mid- to late 1990s when Australia became the best team in the world and one of the greatest all-time sides. Such was Australia's dominance then, they won nine of their ten Tests series under Taylor, and lost just one (in India).

Impact Index identifies Mark Taylor as a high impact batsman, despite a batting average of 43.49 – not at all considered extraordinary in the modern age. Though his failure rate of 42 per cent was reasonably low, Taylor comes up as Australia's seventh highest impact batsman on this system primarily because of his four series-defining performances.

Interestingly, all four of them came before Australia became a world-beating side in that famous 1995 series in West Indies.

Australia in England, 1989. *Taylor produced 136 and 60 in the opening Test and 219 in the fifth Test as Australia won the series 4–0.*

Pakistan in Australia, 1990. *Taylor came up with 52 and 101 in a relatively low-scoring opening Test in a three-match series; this was the only result Test in the series.*

India in Australia, 1991–92. *Taylor made 94 and 35 not out as*

Australia won by 10 wickets in the opening Test. Then, 11 and 100 in the fourth Test, the second knock coming when Australia were behind in the match. Australia won that Test by 38 runs and eventually the series 4–0.

Australia in West Indies, 1995. *In the opening Test of the famous history-changing series, after Brendon Julian landed the first punches that had West Indies tottering at 195 all out, Taylor stabilized the situation for his team with a three-hour, measured 55, which gave Australia the start they needed to go and dominate the match. He made a relatively inconsequential 16 not out in the second innings, as Australia won by 10 wickets and set the cat among the pigeons, as it were. This is marked as a rare momentum-changing Test; what followed would change an era.*

'Right place, right time', some would argue, but isn't history mostly about that?

However, it is hard to argue with his influence as the second highest impact opening batsman in the world (after Gooch) in the period his career ran (1989–99) – even if it is not something that is still part of public memory.

AC: Mark Taylor wasn't your typical elegant southpaw; he was someone who took his time, built his innings brick by brick. It looked like he was taking the Allan Border legacy forward in more ways than one. He was an astute captain, like AB was, and even batted like him ... unattractive but effective. While the average of 43 isn't deemed extraordinary, it is impressive enough to be acknowledged. He scored over 7,000 Test runs and played in an era that was not so easy for batsmen around the world. Add to that his ability to take catches in slips, he was a proper match-changing player in the longer format.

Also, in Taylor's case, the lack of glamour is another thing that went against him, for he had far more eye-catching players around him – they are the ones who got all the media attention.

JV

43

THE SECOND HIGHEST IMPACT NEW ZEALAND BATSMAN IN TEST CRICKET: CRAIG MCMILLAN

He was always considered an outsider; a stoutly built, aggressive batsman capable of producing the odd brilliant innings. His Test batting average of just 38.46 is the eighth highest for New Zealand (minimum forty Tests), and he is only the thirteenth highest in terms of runs tally.

And yet, Craig McMillan is the second highest impact New Zealand batsman in their Test cricket history, after Kane Williamson.

McMillan played a pivotal role in changing New Zealand's Test cricket history

New Zealand had not won a Test series against a major Test side since beating Australia in a one-off Test at home in 1990. They had played twenty-seven Test series since then, lost eighteen, drew six and won only three (two against Zimbabwe and one against Sri Lanka). They had the worst win: loss ratio amongst all Test teams (0.34), barring Zimbabwe, during this period.

Vs India, Wellington, 1998–99. *The first Test is abandoned without a ball being bowled. In the second Test, New Zealand, set 213 for victory, are in trouble at 50 for 2 (effectively 50 for 3 as Nathan Astle is retired hurt) when Craig McMillan comes out to bat. It becomes worse for the* *home side as Horne, Adam Parore and Paul Wiseman depart in quick succession, leaving them reeling at 74 for 5. Chris Cairns joins McMillan at the crease. The pair add a match-winning 137 for the sixth wicket. McMillan remains unbeaten on 74 off just 122 deliveries as New Zealand win by 4 wickets. It was the highest ever chase at the Basin Reserve till then.*

Vs India, Hamilton, 1998–99. *In the third Test, McMillan plays two counter-attacking innings back-to-back. First, coming in at 95 for 3, he smashes 92 off just 102 deliveries in the first innings and then makes 84 off 102 in the second (from 76 for 3 which worsened to 85 for 4). New Zealand bat out enough time and overs to ensure that the match ends in a draw.*

New Zealand won their first Test series against a major side in nine years. The win gave them new energy and confidence and marked a radical transformation in New Zealand's Test cricket history.

Craig McMillan was the highest impact batsman and player of the series. He got a series-defining performance in the second Test – only the ninth Test of his career. There were other invaluable performances to follow:

Vs England, The Oval, 1999. *The series is tied at 1–1 when the fourth Test begins. New Zealand, inserted, post 236. England are bowled out for 153. McMillan walks out to bat at 22 for 4 (which soon becomes 37 for 5 and 39 for 6) in the second innings and scores a crucial 26 in 42 deliveries (the second highest score of the innings). He puts together an invaluable 40-run stand with Chris Cairns for the seventh wicket. Cairns blasts 80 in 93 balls. New Zealand score 162. England, set 246, are cleaned up for 162.*

New Zealand win their first Test series against the English in thirteen years (and till date, only the second series they ever won in England), and overall their third in twenty-eight Test series over sixty-nine years of Test cricket against them.

Vs Pakistan, Hamilton, 2001. *It is the third Test, 0–1 down in the series, the New Zealand pace attack destroys Pakistan in both innings. Three of their batsmen score big runs against them – openers Mark Richardson* *and Matthew Bell, and Craig McMillan. His 97-ball 98 is easily the most explosive innings of the match. New Zealand win the match by an innings and draw the series 1–1.*

This is McMillan's second SD.

Vs England, Auckland, 2002. *Again, 0–1 down in the series at the start of the third Test, New Zealand, batting first, post 202 in the first innings. McMillan scores a brisk 41 in just 59 deliveries (from 19 for 4). Tuffey and company rout England for 160. McMillan again scores a crucial 50 in just 51 balls in the second innings as New Zealand declare at 269 for 9, setting England 312. Tuffey, Drums and Adams ensure the visitors fall well short. New Zealand win by 78 runs and draw level the three-match series 1–1.*

McMillan gets his third and final SD.

This was New Zealand's first Test win against England at home in eighteen years and only their seventh win in eighty-five Tests against the same opposition.

McMillan was a big-match player. He had three SDs in just fifty-five completed Tests. Only three other New Zealand batsmen – Brendon McCullum (100 completed Tests), Stephen Fleming (109) and Kane Williamson (fifty-three) have three SDs in their Test careers.

This makes McMillan's matches to SD ratio the second best for any New Zealand batsman (after Williamson) and amongst the best in Test cricket history.

He was also the third highest impact batsman in the world (minimum twenty Tests) for a period of approximately three-and-a-half years (between December 1998 and April 2002) after Graham Thorpe and Mahela Jayawardene.

McMillan produced more series-defining performances and absorbed more pressure than Martin Crowe

Crowe is considered New Zealand's greatest Test batsman. His talent was in absolutely no doubt, but it is interesting that he did not produce as many big-match performances as a batsman of his calibre is presumed to have done (more on this in the introduction to this book). His two SDs (fine performances but not overly central ones) came in matches dominated by Richard Hadlee, and his failure rate of 50 per cent was higher than a few other New Zealanders.

Craig McMillan's failure rate wasn't much better (49 per cent) but he absorbed slightly more pressure of falling wickets than Crowe did, and he had a decidedly higher Strike Rate Impact than Crowe. Both these qualities were an inherent part of his batting in Test cricket.

McMillan's forte was his ability to score under pressure at a high strike rate

McMillan's ability to score tough runs under pressure (of falling wickets) at a strike rate much higher than the match norm made him a dangerous middle-order batsman.

His Pressure Impact in Tests is the fourth best for New Zealand after Kane Williamson, Stephen Fleming and Chris Cairns.

As we've said before, Strike Rate Impact is rarely attributed to batsmen in Test cricket. A batsman has to consistently bat at a considerably higher strike rate than the match norm throughout his career to earn a positive Strike Rate Impact in matches that his team wins. McMillan did that often enough and, in fact, is the eighth highest Strike Rate Impact batsman in the history of Test cricket after Adam Gilchrist, Ian Botham, Chris Cairns, Vivian Richards, Virender Sehwag, David Warner and Sanath Jayasuriya.

Vs India, Ahmedabad, 2003. *New Zealand had won just two out of thirty-one Test matches (one each in 1969 and 1988) in India. McMillan was making a comeback into the New Zealand Test side after a poor 2002 (after the home series against England).*

He scores 54 (from 108 for 4), helping New Zealand post 340 in reply to India's 500. India score 209 in the second innings, setting the visitors 370. McMillan again comes out to bat under pressure (86 for 4), curbs his natural instincts and makes an unbeaten match-saving 83 off 190 balls. He bats out time and overs (67.2 overs were bowled during his stay in the middle) to salvage a brilliant draw.

India save the second Test after being made to follow on. The visitors secure a second drawn series in eight visits to India.

New Zealand won nine series, drew six and lost ten during McMillan's career (November 1997 to March 2005) – a monumental improvement over their record just before that period.

McMillan's ability to score tough runs under pressure, at a strike rate higher than the match norm in crucial matches, changing not only the course of the match but the entire series, and in turn changing the history of cricket in New Zealand – that's his legacy.

Unsung legend? Like hell.

AC: Once again, we see the importance of context: for someone who batted with the tail more often than not, the numbers must be read differently. McMillan was the bridge between the top and the lower order, and hence his ability to bat faster was his strongest suit. Also, when you bat at that number, you're likely to face the second new ball, which often results in wickets falling around you and, therefore, you are forced to absorb more pressure. Also, we have this tendency to judge batsmen by the number of centuries they scored, and so anyone who bats with the tail is easily written off. Like Laxman for India, McMillan would've, perhaps, ended up with more centuries had he batted higher in the order. His consistency otherwise isn't too bad, for he did manage a 50-plus score once in four innings that he played, which is a really good return at the highest level.

NN: His failure rate was 49 per cent, and the Laxman example is well taken. Martin Crowe's was 50 per cent and Ross Taylor's is 52 per cent too.

NN

44

S. RAMESH WAS A VERY HIGH IMPACT TEST BATSMAN

Indian opener Sadagoppan Ramesh played international cricket for barely two-and-a-half years (1999–2001). In nineteen Tests, he averaged about 38 with just 2 centuries. Not the numbers of a world beater.

Yet, on an impact scale, he registers very high. If we take ten Tests as a minimum (we normally take fifty), he comes up as India's third highest impact batsman (after Pujara and Dravid), a very surprising finding.

It is a bit like Andy Ganteaume topping Bradman on averages. Although, to be fair, Ramesh did play more than one Test. The thing is, in his nineteen Tests, he registered two series-defining performances.

Neither of his SDs are remembered now.

60 and 96 Vs Pakistan, Delhi, 1999. *No one recollects Ramesh in this Test because of Kumble's historic 10–74 in the second innings (as Pakistan chased a well-nigh impossible target of 420). In the second Test match of his career, in the first innings, Ramesh made 60 out of India's 252 with only captain Azharuddin (67) playing a significant hand with him. Pakistan were dismissed for 172, and India batted well in the second innings, making 339 – Ramesh top-scoring with 96. Then came that legendary statistical achievement by Kumble. India drew level with Pakistan in the series, and 1–1 was the final scoreline, making this a series-defining Test.*

AC: One of S. Ramesh's biggest qualities was his touch; he was a touch player. Someone who wouldn't move his feet too much. But he had great hands, he could time the ball really well. He was not perturbed by pace. And he was happy playing against the likes of Wasim, Waqar, etc. In fact, he used the pace to his own advantage. In the match against Pakistan at Delhi, it wasn't an easy pitch to bat on and the SG ball in the hands of the Pakistani bowlers was a deadly combination because it was reverse-swinging. Even though both Wasim Akram and Waqar Younis were not at their pomp, they were still lethal. But Ramesh was unruffled. That was a very special innings.

Vs New Zealand, Kanpur, 1999. *In his sixth Test match, Ramesh and fellow opener Devang Gandhi had a 162-run opening partnership in response to New Zealand's 256 (a significant improvement from India being dismissed for 83 in the previous Test, which was eventually drawn). It set the foundation for a comfortable victory in a series where this was the only result Test.*

This was a strong New Zealand side (which had won a Test series in England very recently) and was a relatively hard-fought series too.

There was a poor series in Australia thereafter, where every Indian batsman except Tendulkar failed. And in 2001, when Australia visited, in the deciding match of a famous series at Chennai, Ramesh made 61 in the first innings and then 25 in a nail-biting fourth-innings chase of 155.

Thereafter, on tour in Sri Lanka, his sequence of scores was 42, 2, 47, 31, 46 and 55.

And then, he was dropped, at the age of twenty-six.

It remains one of the most unexplainable decisions in Indian cricket history. Initially, there were injury issues but more loud was the talk about how his footwork was poor. People focused on what he didn't have rather than what he had and, more importantly, overlooked what he had been able to accomplish.

It was a huge waste.

During Ramesh's time, India were struggling to find Test openers. The batsmen India tinkered with during this period were: Shiv Sunder

Das, Devang Gandhi, Deep Dasgupta, Sadagoppan Ramesh, Wasim Jaffer, V.V.S. Laxman, M.S.K. Prasad, Sameer Dighe, Hemang Badani and even Rahul Dravid. That's ten Test openers in a space of thirty-one months. Curiously, the most successful one amongst them was Ramesh. Indisputably. He had the lowest failure rate amongst the ten batsmen who opened then – and by a distance.

In fact, Ramesh's failure rate of 37 per cent remains one of the lowest in Indian Test history. During his career, Ramesh had the joint lowest failure rate amongst all openers in the world (minimum fifteen Tests), along with Michael Atherton. He was better in this respect than the likes of Justin Langer, Sanath Jayasuriya, Herschelle Gibbs and Gary Kirsten.

S. Ramesh belonged to international cricket. It was snatched away from him.

AC: Ramesh's Test career was cut short for the same reason that mine was as well. He got consistent 30s and 40s but not 100s. So, whenever you have a look at somebody's career and see a lot of 40s, you feel that he is consistent. Impact Index will obviously tell you that his failure rate is quite low, which is great, but only to a certain extent. What you do with the low failure rate is equally important. So, when he was getting those 30s and 40s consistently, nobody was stopping him to convert them into big ones. He did not make those starts count and, once you do that, eventually the selectors will start looking elsewhere – especially because he had an apparent weakness against swing bowling due to his lack of feet movement. The thing that went against him eventually were also his ODI numbers. He played some amount of cricket outside India, including the 1999 World Cup in England, and when you see a batsman getting out to slips due to an obvious shortcoming against swing bowling, you pretty much make up your mind. To add to that, he had a poor tour of Australia in 1999, where almost every Indian batsman failed. Eventually, that is what went against him. So, even though he was consistent in Tests and had a low failure rate, the question of why he was dropped was complex.

SS: Was it unfair?

AC: I don't think it was terribly unfair. Let me explain this through the example of my own career. I may hold a grudge about the fact that I wasn't given enough chances, but I also have to admit that I didn't convert my starts. You can't score 40s and stay alive because there will be a bad patch. What you do on a good day is what keeps you alive on a bad day. So, if your good day is only 45-odd runs and your bad day is as bad as anyone else's, it is hard to stay in the team that way. But it is a curious case, of course, and one worthy of discussion. That is what Impact Index brings to the fore.

JV/SS

45

CHETESHWAR PUJARA HAS SCORED A HIGHER PROPORTION OF HIS TEAM'S RUNS THAN MOST IN TEST HISTORY

Before making his debut, Cheteshwar Pujara was touted as the next 'Wall' for India after Rahul Dravid, given his penchant for scoring big and stonewalling his way through bowling attacks. It was silly, because he was yet to make his Test debut and also because the yardstick he was to be measured against was of India's highest impact Test batsman ever.

But thirty-eight Tests down the line, he has done the comparison no harm. In fact, for a minimum of thirty Tests, Pujara emerges as the highest impact Indian Test batsman of all-time ahead of even Dravid.

Just to clear the air, this in no way means that Pujara is a better batsman than Dravid, Tendulkar, Gavaskar, Sehwag or Laxman.

It just means that for a minimum of thirty Tests, if we combine all his performances, Pujara emerges as a higher impact Test batsman than all Indians.

AC: Cheteshwar Pujara's is a phenomenal case in Indian cricket and it has come at a wonderful time. In a day and age where T20 cricket is more glamorous and rewarding, Pujara is a throwback to the times when Test cricket was the be-all and end-all. In some way, Pujara is a misfit in this day and age, but he is also making Test cricket glamorous.

Pujara's high impact is not just because of his series-defining performances

In many Impact Index stories, a batsman registers a high impact because of his series-defining performances. Not in Pujara's case, though.

The real differentiator between Pujara and the rest of the Indian batsmen is his Runs Tally Impact (proportion of runs scored in a match context) – not only the highest for any Indian batsman but also the third highest in Test history after Don Bradman and Jack Hobbs (minimum: 30 Tests). It is almost 10 per cent higher than the next best Indian: Virat Kohli. To further compare, Pujara's Runs Tally Impact is 25 per cent higher than Dravid's and 27 per cent higher than Tendulkar's. This is a pretty sensational finding as it underlines not just his prodigious run-scoring capacity but also the high value of those runs to his team.

The average runs per batsman in Tests in India since Pujara's debut is 31, which is the fourth lowest amongst the major Test-playing nations – after only West Indies, Sri Lanka and South Africa. Pujara's average in those Tests has been 66 (the next best Indian is Kohli with an average of 47). This explains Pujara's high runs tally impact.

A very high Runs Tally Impact also indicates consistent contributions in team wins and this holds true for Pujara. This fact reflects in conventional statistics as well. For a minimum of fifteen won Tests, Pujara's batting average of almost 66 (compared to his career average of 49) is the highest for any Indian batsman in Test history (followed closely by Dravid). In fact, Pujara's average in a winning cause is higher than even the likes of A.B. de Villiers, Jacques Kallis, Brian Lara, Hashim Amla, Kevin Pietersen and Ricky Ponting.

Amongst Indian batsmen, Pujara ranks high in most of the other batting parameters as well. When it comes to New Ball Impact, Pujara is second to none amongst non-openers in Indian Test history, not even Dravid. And when it comes to Partnership Building Impact, Pujara's is the second highest for any Indian batsman, after Dravid's.

AC: An interesting facet about Pujara is that when he gets 100s, he gets big 100s. Not many in this day and age have the patience and hunger to do that. Pujara's is also an interesting case because it showcases the importance of first-class cricket. It was critical for the Indian first-class system that he does well. If a successful cricketer in the domestic set-up fails to show up on the big stage, what's the point of that whole exercise? This also reflects how good India's first-class circuit is. In my opinion the Indian first-class system is quite robust – better than that of many other Test-playing nations. Even though there are some question marks, it has still produced a guy capable of scoring runs at the highest level.

Vs Sri Lanka, Colombo (SSC), 2015. *Making his comeback into the Indian Test team as an opener in the series decider, Pujara came under early pressure as India were reduced to 14 for 2. Wickets kept falling at the other end, and India's situation worsened to 119 for 5 and then to 180 for 7. Helped along by a partnership with Amit Mishra (59), Pujara produced a masterclass in batting with the tail-enders, to guide India to 312. Pujara remained unbeaten on 145 as he became only the fourth Indian opener to carry his bat through. Sri Lanka responded with 201, a crucial 111-run lead was compounded further by India's second innings score of 274. Sri Lanka, chasing 386, fell 117 runs short. This ended up being a series-defining performance by Pujara as India beat Sri Lanka away in a Test series for the first time in twenty-two years.*

AC: Pujara's innings against Sri Lanka was the most significant innings of his Test career, and it came at a time when his name was not even being considered amongst the top five Indian batsmen in the set-up. There seemed to be a clear shift in tactics, with a preference for stroke makers. It was hard for Pujara after a middling tour of England, a poor tour of Australia, a no show in Bangladesh, a middling county season and being dropped for the first two Tests in Sri Lanka. It is always harder to make a comeback than to make a debut. A player knows that there's a reason why he was dropped previously. I was covering this particular game and Pujara was made to open on a green track. The ball was darting around and, as a batsman, you were never set on that kind of a track, a wicket-taking ball was never too far away. For Pujara to not just bat his own demons but to then bat through the tough conditions, it was remarkable. After a long time I saw a batting innings that defined a Test match. If he hadn't played that innings, India could easily have lost that series 1–2.

Standing tall amongst his contemporaries

Amongst all the contemporary batsmen in the world, only four batsmen are higher impact than Pujara: Younis Khan, A.B. de Villiers, Kane Williamson and Misbah-ul-Haq. Pujara's Runs Tally Impact is the best amongst all his contemporaries.

Pujara's only major failing is his relative inconsistency (due to a poor run of games away from home), which his failure rate of 44 per cent shows. Most of his contemporaries are far superior to him on that count. Steve Smith leads the way with a failure rate of only 29 per cent, followed by Warner (35 per cent), Joe Root (35 per cent) Azhar Ali (35 per cent), Kane Williamson (36 per cent) and Hashim Amla (38 per cent).

In no way, though, should his relative inconsistency mask the impact he has had on Indian cricket since his debut. Nor should there be, in an ideal world, question marks on his spot in the Indian Test team.

With the new Indian Test captain showing a marked preference for stroke-makers in the set-up, Rohit Sharma was preferred over Pujara for a few Tests. Then Pujara made a roaring comeback by producing an SD against Sri Lanka away from home in his comeback Test match. The debate over Pujara's spot refused to die down though. He played a crucial role in the home series win against South Africa where he was India's third highest impact batsman after Murali Vijay and Kohli. Pujara then faced 226 balls in his first two innings during India's tour of West Indies in 2016 but was dropped in favour of Rohit for the third Test – the importance of a No. 3 batsman worryingly lost on the team management.

The volatility of Pujara's position in the team not only puts him under continuous pressure but perhaps also sends out a wrong signal to the rest of the players trying to play for the team's cause. The debate over Pujara's spot is unlikely to die down in the future as well, the moment his form drops even a bit, but the team management would do well to remember that he is the real game changer in this current Indian Test team, especially in subcontinental conditions.

AC: Pujara is only a Test cricketer – something that is not discussed. It is tough playing only one format of cricket. There's a good chance that he might play only two Test series in eight months without any domestic matches in between and then be expected to stand fully prepared and Test-ready. It is hard to retain Test form over a long period without practice. His numbers are outstanding at the moment and it has to be judged keeping in mind that he plays only one format. For Pujara, it will always be a lot tougher than people who play ODIs as well.

Pujara's strength is that he is technically competent and has the ability to concentrate for long periods of time. He knows the art of batting time and tough sessions which is getting lost in this age and day. He is happy to score ugly runs and is not someone who will choose flamboyance over effectiveness. It separates him from his peers and is a great quality. He still has a few chinks in the armour which were exposed in England and then in Australia. He leaves a gap between bat and pad and tends to play beside the ball. That said, I have seen him evolve from a domestic batsman to an international batsman and I am sure he will improve on that and, hopefully, by the time he tours again, he would have addressed all his issues.

SS

46

INDIA'S MOST UNDERRATED BATSMAN IN BOTH TESTS AND ODI CRICKET: NAVJOT SIDHU

Navjot Sidhu as a higher impact Test batsman than Sehwag and Azharuddin, despite averaging just 42.13 with the bat and registering only 9 tons, will raise eyebrows. But when one analyses the significance and timing of his contributions, Sidhu emerges as the fifth highest impact batsman in India's Test cricket history, after Dravid, Tendulkar, Gavaskar and Viswanath (minimum 50 Tests).

Despite a relatively high failure rate, Sidhu's high New Ball Impact and Partnership Building Impact suggest his effectiveness as an opener. But the big reason for his high impact are those two series-defining performances he registered in just fifty-one Tests.

In India's only Test match win (also series win) outside its own shores in the 1990s against Sri Lanka (1993), Sidhu was India's highest impact batsman (with 82 and 104).

Then against Australia in the famous momentum-changing Chennai Test of 1998, Sidhu was India's second highest impact batsman (with 62 and 64) and in the second innings, with India still in the arrears, he began a famous assault of Shane Warne (which Tendulkar continued spectacularly with his classic unbeaten 155). India came back from behind to win this match and later, the series.

The frequency at which he produced a series-defining performance is the main reason why he is higher impact than Virender Sehwag –

the latter had three SDs in 104 Tests compared to Sidhu's two in fifty-one.

Also, Sidhu scored a higher proportion of runs in the matches he batted (Runs Tally Impact) than Azharuddin, and thus is of marginally higher impact than him with the bat.

Interestingly, Sidhu's longevity is not as low as his tally of fifty-one Tests suggests, because his Test career actually lasted sixteen years.

AC: This is a somewhat shocking revelation. There are any number of legends in Indian batting history that I would have thought are higher impact than Sidhu's. Of course, you cannot deny the series-defining performances. But there are two things to it. One, as a batsman, you can't really know if a performance will be a series-defining performance, unless it is in the last Test match, which neither of these performances was. Sometimes, it is luck; when you score runs, you might just happen to be on the right side of a result, and that also happens to be the right match.

JV: That's absolutely right, if you're only looking at a player's propensity to register SDs. But the fact is also that many series are decided on the only result-oriented pitch of the series; at least, that was the case in the 1980s and some part of the 1990s too. Most significantly, this is about history, and what a team's fortunes were, and how they got decided and who contributed the most when it got decided. Whether it is luck or not, the contribution is measured in black and white.

AC: I'm not denying the contribution; that's there for everyone to see. But there's something that goes against him here – his overseas record. His numbers overseas are completely different. So, there are two Navjot Sidhus who played for India. Despite a double century in the West Indies, his Test average drops to almost half outside Asia, to 27. He crossed 50 only four times in thirty-two innings outside Asia. With Indian batsmen, that will always be a yardstick – how good your performances are outside Asia. And that is why Sidhu's performances are taken with a pinch of salt. Also, remember, opening in the subcontinent is one of the most productive batting positions in cricket.

JV: But doing well in India, or Asia, cannot just be dismissed, can it? India won a single Test series abroad in the 1990s, but they were unbeaten at home (in a series context). That single win abroad had Sidhu as the highest impact player, and the most important series win that decade, against Australia in 1998, had Sidhu as the second highest impact batsman. Are these not significant contributions, regardless of how he played abroad? It's a bit like the Kumble argument, isn't it?

AC: No, I disagree. Kumble went on to take 600 wickets, which means he learnt to adapt overseas too. Also, batsmen score runs in all kinds of conditions – for example, in the same Test match, a lot of batsmen score runs irrespective of the pitch conditions, but that's not the case with bowlers. On a dustbowl, all fast bowlers in the game are rendered useless; similarly, on green pitches, spinners from both sides are equally ineffective. There's no such thing for a batsman. If you don't score consistently outside Asia, it'll be, quite rightly, held against you.

Sidhu is India's sixth highest impact ODI batsman of all time

After Sachin Tendulkar, Virat Kohli, M.S. Dhoni, Rohit Sharma and Shikhar Dhawan, Navjot Sidhu is India's highest impact one-day batsman ever (minimum sixty matches).

Who would think that, with his batting average of 37 in 136 matches (131 completed games) at a strike rate of about 70, or his 6 centuries?

Impact portrait

Sidhu's high ODI batting impact comes from unexpected quarters. Strike rate has very little to do with it (despite his famous propensity to hit spinners over the top).

With the exceptions of M.S. Dhoni, Virat Kohli and Shikhar Dhawan, no Indian batsman has been more consistent in ODIs than Sidhu. His 43 per cent failure rate is exceptional, especially for a top-order batsman.

When it comes to Runs-Tally Impact, only Kohli, Tendulkar, Dhawan and Sourav Ganguly are ahead of Sidhu in Indian ODI history.

And most significantly, Sidhu had three series- and tournament-defining performances from his 131 (completed) matches. It suggests that he was amongst the most decisive players for India when it came to series results.

Sidhu's one-day career began in the best way possible. Selected directly for the 1987 World Cup, this was Sidhu's sequence of scores: 73, 75, 51, 55 and 22. It made him the second most consistent batsman of the tournament (after Mike Gatting), even though India did not go beyond the semi-final.

But his most influential period came a few years later.

Sidhu was the second highest impact ODI batsman in the world between 1993 and 1995

During this period, if we take forty matches as the minimum, Sidhu was the second highest impact batsman in the world in ODI cricket, after Azharuddin.

With a failure rate of just 36 per cent in forty-two matches, he was also the second most consistent ODI batsman in the world at the time, only after Carl Hooper.

All his three SD performances also came in this period.

Vs England, 1993. *First, with India 0–2 down in the series, Sidhu produces 76 in a chase of 199 at Chandigarh. And later, from 2–3 in the series, a magnificent unbeaten 134 in a chase of a formidable 257 at Gwalior. Sidhu is Man of the Series and the highest impact Indian batsman in the seven-match series (reduced to six, which ultimately ends 3–3).*

Vs West Indies, 1994. *Sidhu played just the first three matches in the five-match home series, and produced two big performances at Faridabad and Mumbai, helping India win. The series eventually finished 4–1 to India. In the second ODI (after India had lost the first), India were 2 for 2 when Sidhu, first with Azharuddin, then with Kambli, took India to a victory in a rain-shortened match with an unbeaten 65. In the next game, he produced an unbeaten 114 off 103 balls to steer India to 260 for 4 in 44 overs; India won by 4 runs.*

Vs Sri Lanka, 1995. *The final at Sharjah. Sri Lanka get 230. Sidhu comes in at 48 for 1, which soon becomes 58 for 2. With Azharuddin (90), Sidhu (84) takes India to a thumping win.*

AC: Again, his ODI batting average is over 43 at home and 33 elsewhere. In ODI cricket, opening the batting is even easier than opening in Tests, with 15 overs of the power play. He has played 113 ODIs out of 136 in his career in Asia. That does take the sheen off.

JV: He did average 49 in six matches in New Zealand though.

AC: Well played for those games. But you do get the drift about in and outside-Asia argument, which has its merits. And yes, he has produced some outstanding performances in World Cups, both in 1987 and 1996, against good sides. You can't take that away from him, of course.

Taken together, the picture that emerges is of an extraordinarily high impact batsman who was clearly underrated during his playing days.

Sidhu's legacy should be his big-match temperament across formats. That can't be mere coincidence.

47

M.S. DHONI IS THE MOST CONSISTENT PLAYER IN THE HISTORY OF CRICKET

About an hour after playing the World Cup-winning knock in 2011, there's a story that has Dhoni sitting quietly in the dressing room when someone asked him what that precise moment was when he knew India would win the World Cup. Dhoni shook his head and said that he never expected India to win it. When asked why, he went back to an interview of Tendulkar's about two weeks before the World Cup began. Tendulkar had claimed that not winning the World Cup was the only regret he had in his career. Dhoni's reasoning was that since no human being gets everything, Tendulkar's wish would not be fulfilled this time either.

Apocryphal or not, this anecdote has Mahendra Singh Dhoni written all over it. That propensity to not get stuck in the details of the moment but go way beyond to the big picture is a very rare quality, especially in sportspeople.

AC: My earliest memory of him was that he was carefree but not careless. He was never overawed by the situation but was also aware of what he wanted in life. He didn't seem particularly ambitious but he was not lackadaisical either.

I remember travelling to Zimbabwe with him in 2004. He was not the primary keeper then (Dinesh Karthik was), and therefore not a key player. Dhoni would bowl in the nets, and as someone who shared a room with him then, I used to tell

> him not to bowl and, rather, focus on batting because surely he wanted to play at some point. And he said, 'Look, I like bowling and I'll bowl to you too if you like. But don't tell me not to bowl. I don't care too much about batting; I'll bat when my turn comes up in the session.' He was that kind of guy. I used to tell him, cut your hair, it doesn't look nice, Indian cricket will not accept you like this; there's never been an Indian cricketer with this look. He responded by saying, if they have to accept me, they'll accept me the way I am. And eventually, of course, the entire country adopted his hairstyle for a little while.
>
> That was typical of him – a very shy guy who knew where he belonged and what his limitations and his strengths were.

No doubt Dhoni himself does not believe that he has achieved everything there is in the game, but the evidence, examined from a helicopter view, suggests he has. He has done a lot he is not appreciated for.

His tangible captaincy accomplishments are commonly known – two world titles in 50-over cricket, one world title in the Twenty20 format, besides IPL and Champions League titles too (two apiece). And, more than a few forget that when India held the No. 1 position in the Test ICC rankings for a short while, Dhoni was the captain.

All the while, keeping wickets (a specialized and demanding physical role), captaining the side (which must be mentally draining in a country where the sport means so much) and being a key batsman who was often expected to deliver the most under pressure, consistently. Which he did, for the most part.

Besides all that, from his repertoire of predominant bottom-hand batting, Dhoni even introduced the cricket world to a new kind of shot, christened the 'helicopter shot', which accomplishes something considered impossible till barely a decade ago, hitting a proper yorker for six.

If this is not everything, what is?

Why does he then get such a big black mark for being a strangely passive and unimaginative Test captain, 2011 onwards? Why is he expected to be superhuman? Why is he considered a mediocre Test player without accounting for his wicketkeeping role?

Dhoni is a giant in Indian cricket in all three formats. Internationally, he is a giant in the ODI format – that's the bird's-eye view.

So let's dwell more on the ODI format first and determine his true place in that.

India's highest impact ODI player

M.S. Dhoni is the highest impact Indian ODI player (minimum sixty matches). Kapil Dev has the same impact as him but in fewer matches. Sachin Tendulkar follows them from a distance, where Ravindra Jadeja and Irfan Pathan also roughly dwell.

It should not be surprising that the best all-rounders are the highest impact players in ODI cricket. Their dual skills help them contribute more consistently in matches. Dhoni contributed in three ways – as wicketkeeper, captain and significant middle-order batsman.

Purely as a batsman, Dhoni is India's third highest impact player ever, after Sachin Tendulkar and Virat Kohli. Both of them batted in the top four positions most of the time in ODI cricket; Dhoni batted mostly at No. 6 or 7, from where he had far less opportunity to have a say consistently. The next highest impact batsman in this position is the eighteenth highest impact Indian batsman – Ajay Jadeja.

Dhoni is higher impact as an ODI batsman than the likes of Azharuddin, Ganguly, Gambhir, Yuvraj, Dravid, Sehwag, Vengsarkar and Gavaskar, a few of whom also bowled a bit, but were mostly specialist batsmen.

Interestingly, five batsmen absorbed more pressure (of falling wickets) than Dhoni across eras: Kohli, Dravid, Azharuddin, Amarnath and Yuvraj. And only three batsmen have been higher impact chasers than him: Kohli, Gambhir and Azharuddin.

AC: All these batsmen have been top-order batsmen. When you're chasing, you'll really only need Dhoni if things go wrong, even horribly wrong. Like if he comes in at 25 for 4 or whatever, which obviously does not happen too often. Even if he comes in at 150 for 4 or 5, he is getting that much less opportunity to score runs, which in turn reduces his batting impact. Nine out

> of ten times, none of these seven batsmen are at the crease in the last 10 overs, which is the toughest time to bat, especially in a chasing situation. There's no time to get set. There is an older ball, which is tougher to get away. Field restrictions are not there then, so it is tougher to get boundaries. The asking rate is climbing. The overs from the less effective fifth bowler are almost always consumed by then. Wickets have been lost; you're probably the last recognized batsman. So, you have to really tread carefully. Conventional averages can never do justice to a player overcoming these circumstances at that batting position.

Dhoni's batting failure rate of 40 per cent makes him India's most consistent ODI batsman.

All of this is just remarkable for someone who came in to bat at the position he did mostly – Nos. 6 and 7, even though some of his most famous innings came when he played higher up the order.

Vs Pakistan, Visakhapatnam, 2005. *In just the fifth ODI of his career (after four failures), Dhoni came out to bat at No. 3 with the score at 26 for 1, Tendulkar gone. First with Sehwag (74 off 40), then with Dravid (52 off 59), he took the Pakistan bowling apart with primarily shots in the V. He was in the sort of zone where he did not even feel the need to lie down as every other player did when a swarm of bees invaded the ground. It was tiredness that ended his innings at 148 (with India at 281 for 4), fifteen fours and four sixes adorning it. India won that match, one of the only two it would win in a series where Pakistan triumphed 4–2.*

Dhoni also got nine series/tournament-defining performances in his career, in 283 ODIs (till November 2016). Only Tendulkar (twelve) got more than him in 463 ODIs whereas Yuvraj also has nine in 293 ODIs.

He is also India's highest impact wicketkeeper with Mongia and More after him. And finally, Dhoni is the highest impact Indian captain by a distance, followed by Azharuddin, Ganguly and Kapil Dev.

Let us look at his overall consistency in an even broader context.

A giant on the world stage

Dhoni is the eleventh highest impact player in ODI history (minimum sixty matches), after Viv Richards, Dennis Lillee, Adam Gilchrist, Andrew Flintoff, Imran Khan, Shane Watson, Shane Warne, Greg Chappell, Kapil Dev and Brett Lee (Kapil goes above Dhoni here because of the latter's relatively lower impact in his three matches for Asia XI).

He got nine SDs/TDs in his career. In terms of SD tallies, five players got more than him – Gilchrist (thirteen), Tendulkar (twelve), Jayasuriya (twelve), Afridi (eleven) and Akram (eleven). Six other players in ODI history also registered nine SDs – Brett Lee, Glenn McGrath, Shaun Pollock, A.B. de Villiers, Muttiah Muralitharan and Yuvraj Singh.

Vs Sri Lanka, Mumbai, 2011. *World Cup Final. India chasing 274 was 31 for 2 at one stage with Tendulkar gone. Gambhir and Kohli had stabilized the innings somewhat but when the latter departed at 114 for 3, instead of Yuvraj, many were surprised to see captain Dhoni walking in, perhaps to keep the right–left combination going with Gambhir, probably to neutralize Muralitharan. The rest is emphatic history – 91 not out off 79 balls, with a six over long on to accomplish the biggest run chase in World Cup final history. And becoming the second India captain to win the World Cup (and an SD to go with it).*

Dhoni has also had the highest impact as a wicketkeeper in ODI history. Most curiously, he has conceded the least byes in ODI history in proportion to matches played.

AC: Dhoni actually started out as someone who could bat brilliantly but was a very average keeper and never looked likely to be a wicketkeeper for the long term. He was slightly better than a stopper but never likely to be a wicketkeeper for the long term. In his own inimitable style, he has actually gone on to redefine the way you generally keep wickets. The time-honoured way of receiving the ball and then the hand going forward is what coaching manuals tell you to follow. But Dhoni's own way has no give. (It is relevant to say here: don't try this at home because this stunt is performed by a professional.) Of course, he has great hands to pull this off, but he has also worked very hard at it. The results are there for everyone to see. He is one of the most effective keepers in world cricket and definitely the best one-day keeper at the moment. For someone who did not even start as a wicketkeeper, that demonstrates enormous evolution as a player.

As a batsman, Dhoni is the twenty-fourth highest impact ODI batsman ever. Specialist batsmen like Kane Williamson, Brian Lara, Azharuddin and Gary Kirsten are below him on the impact list. More significantly, only two batsmen ahead of him have also been full-time wicketkeepers (so that excludes A.B. de Villiers) – Adam Gilchrist and Kumar Sangakkara.

Vs Sri Lanka, Jaipur, 2005. *Chasing Sri Lanka's 298, a formidable score for its era, Dhoni was sent up at No. 3 by captain Dravid. He walked in at 7 for 1, Tendulkar gone for 2. Sehwag made 39 off 37, Dravid 28 off 34, Yuvraj 18 off 24 and Venugopal Rao 19 off 39. And yet, India won by 6 wickets with almost 4 overs to spare, only because of Dhoni's 183 off 145 balls – hitting on the up and through the line for the most part, with fifteen fours and ten sixes to show for it. It was the twenty-second ODI of Dhoni's career, a colossus unequivocally announced.*

Amongst middle-order batsmen, especially those who batted at No. 6 or 7 for the most part of their careers, only Michael Bevan was higher impact than Dhoni.

AC: I consider Dhoni to be the best finisher the world has ever seen. I rate him higher than Michael Bevan because of two qualities he had. His acute awareness of the game situation – no one reads a game better than him. And that dual ability he has of hitting the long ball at will, but also knowing the importance of taking singles and doubles, and just generally pushing the field and knowing exactly when to go for the big one. He does not give in to the temptation of hitting a big shot just because he can. Which bowler to go after, which bowler was to be respected, which situation has to be respected a lot, how to take the game forward – all of this. And, of course, he could hit sixes and fours much better than Michael Bevan could.

Finally, and crucially, his consistency. Thanks to contributing on three levels (batting, wicketkeeping, captaincy), Dhoni's failure rate is a ridiculously low 9 per cent, the only one to not touch double digits. Gilchrist is at 11 per cent, Quinton de Kock, in an ongoing career like Dhoni's, is at 11 per cent and the great all-rounders follow thereafter (with Sarfraz Ahmed slotting in between) – Shaun Pollock, Kapil Dev, Richard Hadlee and Greg Chappell. (Imran Khan was a little less consistent in this format.)

Vs Pakistan, Lahore, 2006. *After losing the Test series in Pakistan, this five-match ODI series had great significance for India, which was at 1–1 when they landed at Lahore. Chasing Pakistan's formidable 288, India were 12 for 2 at one stage, but recovered thanks to Tendulkar and Yuvraj. But two quick wickets around the 35th over had India at 190 for 5 when Dhoni walked in. With 99 required in 92 balls, the stage was set for a one-of-a-kind genius. Dhoni hammered 72 off 46 balls, with thirteen fours and no six, some one-handed off-side shots still memorable, as India won by 5 wickets and went 2–1 up. The series was won in the next match, where R.P. Singh and Irfan Pathan led the way with the ball, leaving very little for the batsmen to do. In the last match at Karachi, with Pakistan desperate to bring some parity back, India chased a formidable 286. Gambhir and Dravid set a solid foundation, as Dhoni joined Yuvraj at 141 for 2 in the 31st over. Halfway stage on paper and spirit, but made a mockery of by Yuvraj in the form of his life, and Dhoni, more mentally balanced than any new player in world cricket. After stealing a few singles and playing out a few tight overs, they gradually speeded up. As the Pakistani bowlers (including Mohammad Sami and Mohammad Asif) began to visibly crack, Dhoni simply exploded – he made his last 50 runs in 27 balls, and India finished off the match in the 47th over, winning the series 4–1.*

AC: I don't remember a single instance of Dhoni throwing his wicket away when he should not have. He may get out, all of us have done that, but he wouldn't throw away his wicket because he has just hit a six, and therefore wants to hit another one to feel

> good. It is actually very interesting. He never did things in the middle just to feel good – that is just against his basic nature. Yet, all his life he pursued things that felt very good to him, like his dogs, his bikes, just things he enjoyed doing, but he would never play a rash shot following a big shot, just because it felt good.
>
> He has amazing control over his mind and has a remarkable ability to process the information in front of him in a way that it is advantageous to him and his team. He has been just remarkable.

Dhoni's consistency curiously gets even more magnified in the longer format.

Dhoni in Tests

Despite a relatively considerably lower impact overall here (compared to ODIs), Dhoni still comes up with the lowest failure rate in Test history – a jaw-dropping 6 per cent. He is followed by Adam Gilchrist, Joel Garner, Kamran Akmal, Shaun Pollock and Fred Trueman.

In the history of Test cricket, amongst full-time wicketkeepers or those who kept for the majority of their careers (thus excluding the likes of Kumar Sangakkara, A.B. de Villiers, Alec Stewart and Brendon McCullum), M.S. Dhoni is the sixth highest impact batsman in the history of Test cricket. After Adam Gilchrist, Andy Flower, Alan Knott, Kamran Akmal and Matt Prior (minimum fifty Tests).

This means that, in 139 years of Test cricket, only five wicketkeepers batted more decisively than him in Tests.

As a Test batsman, Dhoni is India's eighteenth highest impact batsman (minimum forty Tests). Specialist batsmen (or nearly), like Mohinder Amarnath, Chandu Borde, Vijay Manjrekar, Pankaj Roy, Yuvraj Singh and Anshuman Gaekwad, were of lower impact than Dhoni overall with the bat. His batting failure rate of 59 per cent sits incongruously with these numbers, but not when you look at them in the context of all-rounders (or as a wicketkeeper). Kapil Dev has a 65 per cent batting failure rate, Ravi Shastri 59 per cent and Vinoo Mankad a massive 77 per cent. Amongst wicketkeepers, Syed Kirmani had a 71 per cent failure rate, Nayan Mongia 74 per cent and Kiran More 73 per cent; only Farokh Engineer with a magnificent 39 per cent was better, but he used to open the innings, which is, of course, very significant.

AC: There are again two Dhonis – one a Test batsman in Asia, and one, outside Asia. The reason is that he is an outstanding player of spin, so along with his situational awareness, it made him a force to reckon with in these conditions. Outside Asia, he had a slight technical incompetence to deal with what was on offer in Australia, South Africa and England, particularly. There, you need to be more technically equipped and tighter to score runs. He did find his way; for example, in the last tour to England, he came up with a technique that only worked for him – he just started walking across the stumps or stepping out, forcing people to bowl straighter or shorter. He thus managed to avoid what troubled him the most – the cover drive against the moving ball outside the off stump.

So, when you look at it from the prism of his technical competence, you would have to say that he overachieved as a Test batsman. In limited overs cricket, there is no doubt that he has been an absolute match winner, but Test cricket is built around the knowledge of where your off stump is, how good your defence is, how long can you bat without making a mistake, how good your cover drive is and things like that. These were never Dhoni's strongest suit, so for him to achieve what he did with the bat in Test cricket is remarkable.

He made up for a lot of his deficiencies with his courage. For example, in England in 2014, he took a lot of body blows but stood his ground.

JV: He showed that mettle in 2007 too, in the very first Test he played in England, at Lord's. India were 145 for 5, chasing 380 in the last innings, when he walked in. He batted for almost three-and-a-half hours and pretty much saved India the match, with a little help from the rain gods. India finished at 282 for 9, Dhoni 76 not out. India went on to win the next Test, which eventually won them the series. It was a huge contribution.

So, Dhoni is no mediocre Test player either, even if he was a far superior ODI player.

Vs Sri Lanka, Port-of-Spain, 2013. *Fresh from the Champions Trophy* *win in England, Dhoni's team had reached the tri-series final in West Indies. On a bowling pitch with uneven bounce, Sri Lanka made 201 anchored by Sangakkara's well-confirmed greatness that produced 71. In reply, India were 152 for 7, Dhoni watching from the other end, not quite helplessly though. He was not fully fit and refused quick singles, watchfully waiting. After 16 balls, his score was 4. Soon it was 167 for 8 and Dhoni began to refuse even easy singles and take charge himself. At 182 for 9, a jittery Ishant Sharma joined him, and was chided by Dhoni more than once for nervously taking off for a run. Soon it was 17 required off 9 balls. Dhoni calmed Ishant down, asked him to just survive. Two runs came off the next two balls and Ishant let the last ball of the 49th over go through. Dhoni signalled to the dressing room for a heavier bat as Eranga got ready to bowl the last over, with figures of 2 for 34 from his 9 overs so far. Dhoni missed the first ball. The next one went for a massive six. Sri Lankan body language on the field changed. Still 9 required off 4 balls. The next ball was sliced over point for a four. Still, 5 runs off 3 balls would normally be worth fighting for but Eranga's ostensible nervousness suggested no such thing. It was amply confirmed by the next delivery, a somewhat resigned-length ball, which Dhoni hit over extra cover for a six. His 52-ball 45 comfortably won him the Man of the Match award.*

Dhoni's thought-out method to take the match to the last over, relying on the bowler's nervousness as much as his own ability, paid dividends throughout his career, considerably more than logic would ordinarily suggest. This quality manifested the most in T20s.

Dhoni in T20s

Dhoni's sample size in T20 Internationals is not much, but given his three roles, he comes up as the third most consistent player in the world with a failure rate of just 14 per cent after Graeme Swann and Kumar Sangakkara.

However, contrary to popular assumption, he is not as much of a giant in T20s as he is in ODIs. He is India's third highest impact T20I player (minimum twenty matches), after Virat Kohli and Irfan

Pathan. As a batsman, he is India's fifth highest impact batsman, after Kohli, Gambhir, Yuvraj and Dhawan. This is not surprising, given the limited opportunity he gets in his batting position in a 20-over match, but it is curious that his Strike Rate Impact and Chasing Impact are also relatively low. His eye-catching performances (especially when he finishes a match) here and there give a wrong impression overall; he does not quite do it as often, or perhaps he does not need to.

As captain of Chennai Super Kings, who won two IPL titles and two Champions League titles, he has led inarguably the most successful franchise in T20 history.

In IPL history, he is the eleventh highest impact player (minimum thirty matches), after Andrew Symonds, Shane Watson, Adam Gilchrist, Moises Henriques, Suresh Raina, David Warner, Shane Warne, Michael Hussey, Robin Uthappa and Harbhajan Singh.

A superhuman workload

No proper analysis of Dhoni can ignore his workload. He is the most active cricketer in the history of the sport, the most overworked. Crouching down 540 times on a full Test match day, 300 times in an ODI and 120 times in a T20 match and concentrating on every ball – this is the most underrated aspect in any assessment of him. (Impact Index accounts for a wicketkeeper's job by giving a flat value to the role he does, adjusting it for increased probability of taking catches.) It is wrong to judge him without accounting for this.

In end-2014, it was calculated that since the beginning of IPL in 2007 till then, Dhoni spent 668 days on the field for India or CSK. If you include travel days around these matches, and the attendant energy that is spent, that kind of workload boggles the mind.

The above only accounts for physical energy. Then there is the mental energy that comes with being captain in all three formats of the most hysterical cricket nation on earth. Consider this – in the history of Test cricket, only five players captained their sides in more Tests (Smith, Border, Fleming, Ponting and Lloyd), and they were all batsmen. In fact, the next eleven captains after Dhoni on that list were all primarily batsmen too. In ODI cricket, only two players captained their side in more matches (Ponting and Fleming), both batsmen and the next four on that list after Dhoni were batsmen too. You rarely spot an all-rounder or a wicketkeeper on those lists.

Couple this with being an important batsman expected, literally expected, to rescue the team from tough situations, especially in the limited overs formats. All this has led to a situation where Dhoni did not even last a decade in Test cricket (he retired from the format in December 2014, when he was just thirty-three). Or, to look at it another way, he lasted nine whole years playing all these key roles, with considerable success overall.

All this with the kind of consistency that has never been seen before or since. No cricketer in any format has ever justified his place in the team as often as Dhoni has.

There is no other way to say it, really: M.S. Dhoni is cricket's most consistent player ever.

AC: It is good that we're talking about this. No wicketkeeper in the history of cricket has actually done as much as Dhoni has. Adam Gilchrist comes close, of course, but you have to keep in mind that keeping in Australia is a lot easier than keeping in India – you are crouching fully here. And of course, the pressure of captaincy in all three formats. No one and nothing can really quantify the level of workload this one cricketer has had over the years. No one will come close to doing what he has done. If he were to take off his shirt, Dhoni would probably have a Superman cape under it.

JV/SS

48

ZIMBABWE'S HIGHEST IMPACT PLAYER – IN BOTH TESTS AND ODIS: HEATH STREAK

When it comes to Zimbabwe, Andy Flower's name tends to dominate discussions – yet another instance of how much more glamorous batting is as compared to bowling.

Of course, Andy Flower is easily Zimbabwe's highest impact batsman in both formats. Given that he was also wicketkeeper during a lot of this, one would expect him to easily be right on top of any impact chart. Interestingly, he is second to Heath Streak in both Test and ODI charts.

If we keep single Tests aside, and make Bangladesh the exception, Zimbabwe has won just one Test series in its history – against Pakistan in 1998. And that too in Pakistan. In Peshawar, Streak took 4–93 and 2–19 and contributed a useful 24 in a low-scoring Test. Zimbabwe won by 7 wickets and the next two Tests were rain-hit, thus giving the match a series-defining status.

Their only other notable Test result in fifteen years came in 2001, when they drew 1–1 with India in 2001. After being 0–1 down, Zimbabwe dismissed India for 237, with Streak taking 3–69. Then, in the third innings, as India dealt with a deficit of 78 runs (thanks partly to Streak's innings of 40 as well), Streak and Andy Blignaut destroyed the Indian batting, dismissing them for 234 and giving themselves a target of 157, which they made with 4 wickets to spare. Blignaut got the Man of the Match award, but Streak was over 60 per cent higher impact than him in the game as a whole.

Overall, Streak's 31 per cent bowling failure rate and 22 per cent failure rate as an all-rounder in his sixty-five-Test career are only indications of what he could have accomplished if not part of a largely pushover side for most of his career.

In ODI cricket too, he emerges as Zimbabwe's highest impact player, with three SDs, more than any other Zimbabwean. The most famous of these performances came in a pulsating finale at Auckland in 2001, after the series was at 1–1. In the decider, Streak took 2–34 as New Zealand finished with a seemingly secure 273. But an unbeaten 79 from Streak, including a last-wicket partnership of 19 in which he contributed all the runs, took Zimbabwe home with 1 wicket to spare.

Streak was much more effective as an ODI batsman than in Tests, even though he was almost a genuine all-rounder in the latter as well. And he was their highest impact bowler in both formats.

The political turmoil in Zimbabwe no doubt affected him too. While sport continues to be about right place, right time, it is important to not forget the deeds of those who transcend them somewhat, if only for a short while.

AC: Heath Streak was one of the true all-rounders, i.e., he could make it into the team on either of his two skills. Of course, when you open the bowling and carry not just the burden of the unit, but also the hopes of your nation, your batting is likely to suffer a little bit, and that's reflected in his career stats too. His averages of 22 and 28 – in Tests and ODI, respectively – don't really do justice to his batting abilities. He could take the ball away from right-handed batsmen, and the feature that stood out in his bowling was his intent to pitch fuller and making batsmen play. He wasn't afraid to get driven but he was shrewd enough to invite the drive through covers and not mid off – the moment the batsman goes through covers, he shows the face of the bat partially and hence brings the slip cordon in play. It would also be fair to say that he was the only Zimbabwean bowler who could've walked into any international side purely as a bowler.

As for his Impact vis-à-vis Andy Flower, it's a slightly

skewed comparison for the simple reason that they didn't win enough. When that's the case, even though the purpose of this exercise is not to cherry-pick, you end up doing that by default. Andy has scored runs around the world against all types of bowlers and on all surfaces, and if those runs didn't amount to results, it's just unfortunate. In any case, batsmen can't really win matches; they can only set up matches for the bowlers to convert into results. Andy did that and more.

JV: But Streak and Andy Flower played for the same team. In their entire Test careers, they got very limited opportunities for SDs for obvious reasons. When they came, Streak registered it twice, Flower not even once. They were in the same team, so that's in black and white. Agreed that in the first Test against Pakistan they wouldn't have known that the match would eventually become a series-defining one, but against India in 2001, it was the last match of the series so there was everything to play for.

In ODIs too, Streak has one SD more, which is also interesting, given that batsmen dominate bowlers in ODIs. Both were all-rounders, as Flower kept wickets.

JV

49

SHAKIB AL HASAN IS AMONG THE FIVE MOST CONSISTENT ALL-ROUNDERS IN ODI HISTORY

Great players in weak teams are at a disadvantage. Despite standing out within their teams, the collective mediocrity of the side drags their impact down too, on a career level.

Shakib Al Hasan is the highest impact ODI bowler and the third highest impact ODI batsman (after Tamim Iqbal and Mushfiqur Rahim; minimum fifty matches) for Bangladesh. This makes him the highest impact Bangladeshi ODI player ever, by a distance. In fact, the next highest impact player, Mashrafe Mortaza, has a 44 per cent lower impact than Shakib, which is massive. In fact, the players coming after Mortaza are clustered together on impact, further accentuating the gap between Shakib and everyone else.

All-rounders of this stature are rare. In any other international team, Shakib would have been one of its key players. That even having Shakib amidst them could not lift Bangladesh to greater heights suggests how much they struggled as a team collectively.

AC: Shakib's contribution to his team goes beyond the runs he scores and the wickets he takes. He plays in a team which was used to losing, but through his performances, Shakib lifts the morale of entire team and gives them the belief they need to compete at the highest level. Bangladesh cricket owes a lot of their recent successes in ODI cricket to Shakib – the hero who makes the current lot of players believers and dreamers. He raised the bar for others, and because of his sustained excellence, his team itself is changing now. Therein lies his greatness.

Shakib's impact for Bangladesh

For a side not used to winning, it automatically takes away the possibility of registering series- and tournament-defining performances. In Bangladesh's history, these are players who have single SDs: Mohammed Rafique, Abdur Razzak, Mohammad Mahmudullah, Tamim Iqbal and Mushfiqur Rahim. Shakib is the only one who has three – in West Indies in 2009 (against a weakened side, but still in West Indies), against New Zealand in 2010 and against South Africa in 2015.

Otherwise, Bangladesh has only won sporadic matches against the stronger teams. Their series wins against West Indies, New Zealand, Pakistan, India and South Africa remain their only true sustained achievements so far. Of these five series, Shakib provided SD performances in three.

Even in the World Cups, Shakib was Bangladesh's highest impact player in the 2011 edition, and their second highest impact player in the 2007 (after Mortaza) and 2015 editions (after Mushfiqur).

Vs West Indies, Barbados, April 2007. *Twenty-year-old Shakib Al Hasan comes out to bat at 26 for 3 against England during the Super Eight stage in the 2007 World Cup. Wickets keep falling around him, 40 for 4, 47 for 5, 65 for 6. Bangladesh is dismissed for 143 in 38 overs. Shakib is unbeaten with 57 off 95 balls. He comes out and bowls 6 overs for 19 runs, and though England eventually win by 4 wickets, Shakib is noticed by the cricket world.*

Shakib's standing on the international stage

On a world stage too, Shakib is an all-time great. He is actually the twenty-sixth highest impact ODI player in history (minimun sixty matches). This is sensational because the SD component – which is the highest impact entity in this system – is fairly nullified in Shakib's case.

However, if you take away the value of SDs from everybody's impact, Shakib is the highest impact player in ODI history (minimum sixty matches). Even Viv Richards, Dennis Lillee and Adam Gilchrist, otherwise the highest impact ODI players of all time, come later on that list. Is there anything left to be said?

A good part of this has to do with his consistency – his failure rate is just 15 per cent, Shakib is the fifth most consistent all-rounder ever, after Shaun Pollock, Kapil Dev, Richard Hadlee and Greg Chappell.

AC: Shakib Al Hasan is the only world-class player in Bangladesh. He could walk into any limited-overs side in the world as he brings two skills to the table – two skills he is almost equally adept in.

NN: Could he walk into Australia and South Africa?

AC: He could. Certainly. He will guarantee ten overs with the ball (in ODI cricket) and then could bat anywhere from Nos. 4 to 6. He is equally useful in T20 cricket.

NN: Yes, not surprisingly then, he is the only Bangladeshi player who plays in the IPL.

Even after considering SD performances, Shakib is the twenty-fourth highest impact ODI player, which means he is higher impact than the likes of Richard Hadlee, Shahid Afridi, Muttiah Muralitharan, Ricky Ponting and Sourav Ganguly. If this sounds outlandish, keep in mind that this is the impact a consistent all-rounder has on the game, and why he is the most sought-after entity in one-day cricket. Also, in a weak team, the great all-rounder does not end up sharing as much impact with other teammates.

Amongst Asians, Shakib is the fifth highest impact all-rounder ever after Imran Khan, Kapil Dev, Wasim Akram and Sanath Jayasuriya. All four of them have won world titles for their teams.

AC: I don't think there is a better all-rounder in ODI cricket today. I will go on and say that Shakib is amongst the top ten all-rounders in ODI cricket history.

NN: He is certainly the highest impact all-rounder in contemporary ODI cricket. If we consider the entire history of ODI cricket, he comes up as the fourteenth highest impact all-rounder of all time – a phenomenal achievement, given that he is in the Bangladesh team.

Just for perspective, he is a higher impact all-rounder than Shahid Afridi, Ravindra Jadeja, Andrew Symonds, Richard Hadlee, Mohammad Hafeez, Lance Klusener and Chris Cairns amongst others.

Vs Zimbabwe, Chittagong, November 2014. *Zimbabwe has Bangladesh at 31 for 3 when Shakib Al Hasan walks in. It is 70 for 4 not a lot later. But his 101 off 99 balls helps take Bangladesh to a formidable 281. And Shakib's 4–41 plays the biggest part in dismissing Zimbabwe for 194. Standard operating procedure when it comes to Shakib.*

Shakib as a batsman

He is Bangladesh's third highest impact ODI batsman (minimum fifty matches) after Tamim Iqbal and Mushfiqur Rahim.

When it comes to proportion of runs scored (Runs Tally Impact), only Tamim Iqbal, who is a specialist batsman, is ahead of Shakib.

Only two batsmen scored runs at a faster pace than Shakib – Mashrafe Mortaza (who does not cross an impact of 1 as a batsman, therefore cannot be considered a proper batsman) and Aftab Ahmed.

Only Khaled Mashud amongst Bangladeshi batsmen has absorbed more pressure (Pressure Impact) than Shakib in their ODI history. When it comes to chasing down targets also, only Tamim has a higher Chasing Impact than Shakib.

AC: Shakib as a batsman has been phenomenal for Bangladesh. He has the ability to bat like the playmaker and also hit big and be the finisher – a quality which one does not usually associate with him. He has produced a number of cameos, especially in T20 cricket.

Vs Sri Lanka, Dhaka, January 2009. *A strong Sri Lankan outfit is dismissed for a mere 147 in 30-odd overs. In reply, Bangladesh are 11 for*

3 in 4 overs. Twenty-one-year-old Shakib Al Hasan (then Saqibul Hasan) slams an unbeaten 92 off 69 balls with ten fours and two sixes, with Muralitharan and Ajantha Mendis mere onlookers, as Bangladesh win by 5 wickets in the 24th over. Bangladesh captain Mohammad Ashraful calls it their greatest ODI victory ever, especially because Bangladesh had to win this last league match to progress.

Shakib as a bowler

He is Bangladesh's highest impact ODI bowler, a consequence also of being the most consistent Bangladeshi bowler ever.

His hallmark as a bowler was his high Economy Impact – no one even comes close in Bangladesh ODI history. He is of more than 50 per cent higher impact than the next one on that count, Abdur Razzak.

Only Rubel Hossain has been more of a wicket taker than Shakib; he is, of course, a specialist bowler.

No Bangladeshi bowler has broken more partnerships than Shakib.

> **AC:** Shakib is a very clever limited-overs bowler. He sometimes bowls slower, inducing a mistake from the batsman, but is mostly very restrictive and can be banked upon to bowl a tight spell of 10 overs in almost every match. He is very reliable as a bowler.

Vs West Indies, Chittagong, October 2011. *A West Indian batting line-up including Marlon Samuels, Darren Bravo, Kieron Pollard and Darren Sammy is dismissed for 61 off 22 overs. The best bowling figures are Shakib's as he takes 4 for 16 in 5 overs.*

Shakib in his own era

During the period Shakib has played (August 2006 till present day), he has been the sixth highest impact ODI player in the world (minimum sixty matches), after Shane Watson, A.B. de Villiers, Kumar Sangakkara, M.S. Dhoni and Quinton de Kock.

And if we do not consider SD performances, he has been the second highest impact ODI player after Sangakkara.

All this makes him the most consistent all-rounder in the whole world right now.

In other formats too, Shakib has been peerless. In Tests, he has been Bangladesh's highest impact bowler and player ever. In T20Is, he has been Bangladesh's second highest impact batsman (after Sabbir Rahman) and their highest impact player ever.

But it is in ODI cricket that Shakib's current colleagues have started delivering incrementally, leading to some good results gradually. Bangladesh reaching the World Cup quarter-finals and winning bilateral series against Pakistan, India and South Africa – a telling manifestation of the promises ahead for this team.

All of this could lift Shakib Al Hasan's impact and make him an even more noticeable player in world cricket. More importantly, it could help Bangladesh finally fulfil their true potential as an ODI team.

AC: Undoubtedly, Shakib is the greatest player in Bangladesh's cricket history. He could be the one reason because of which the country turns a corner for good.

50

R. ASHWIN IS WELL ON HIS WAY TO BEING THE HIGHEST IMPACT PLAYER IN TEST HISTORY

Those who have been following the career of Ravichandran Ashwin closely may not be entirely surprised by this. The man has seven Man of the Series awards in thirty-nine Tests, which means, in more than half the Test series he has played in, he has been Man of the Series. This is as close to fantasy fiction as it gets in cricket.

It is important to remember that we're talking about a genuine all-rounder here, who averages 34 with the bat and 24 with the ball – impressive conventional numbers, those.

Now, for a view through the Impact Index lens.

Ashwin is the highest impact Test player in 139 years of Test cricket and the highest impact all-rounder ever. Yes, this is for a minimum of thirty Tests, which is not substantial by any means, but it is not that inconsequential either. So, as a player, Ashwin is higher impact than Bradman and Sobers even, which is, obviously, blasphemy.

However, consider this. He is the highest impact Test bowler of all time, ahead of Muttiah Muralitharan and Clarrie Grimmett. Yes, minimum thirty Tests again, but still. If we consider just this point of their respective careers (thirty-nine Tests), Ashwin has 26 per cent higher impact as a bowler than Shane Warne, 39 per cent higher impact than Kumble and 67 per cent higher impact than Muralitharan.

Consider his Man of the Series tallies again. Ashwin has seven of those in 14 series. Just for perspective, Wasim Akram has seven in 43 series, Shane Warne eight in 46 series, Imran Khan eight in 28 series, Jacques Kallis nine in 61 series, and Muttiah Muralitharan eleven in 61 series.

In impact terms, Ashwin has five series-defining performances (in just thirty-nine Tests – the second highest SD to matches ratio in Test history, after Alan Davidson (minimum thirty Tests). These SDs have come against West Indies, Australia, South Africa and New Zealand at home, and against West Indies away.

Even more remarkably, he emerges as the highest impact player of all time even if SDs are left out of the calculations. He has 12 per cent higher impact then than the next highest impact player, Muralitharan. And 14 per cent higher impact than the one after, which is Hadlee.

The sole reason for this is Ashwin's awe-inspiring consistency. His 5 per cent failure rate makes him the second most consistent Test player of all time in history (after, curiously, Bruce Yardley). Roughly every two Tests or so, Ashwin has produced a high impact performance that has knocked the stuffing out of the opposition. This ratio too is amongst the highest in Test history, and the sole reason why Ashwin has been the highest impact player in the world since his debut in 2011.

If we take a minimum of fifteen home Tests, Ashwin is the highest impact bowler in Test history in home conditions. Davidson and Muralitharan follow him on that count. His three lowest impact bowling performances in home conditions came against England in 2012 in the sole home series defeat for a side that was on the cusp of generational change – the only blot so far.

In away conditions, against the stronger sides, he has a lot of work to do still. He averages 55 with the ball in Australia in six Tests, and 34 in England in two Tests and he didn't take a wicket in 42 overs in the only Test he played in South Africa – a noticeable failure, given how close India came to famously winning that Test. Unless he improves his record in these countries, he will perhaps never be universally considered an all-time great player, which would be a great pity.

Given that 2016–17 is filled with home series for India, that impact will almost certainly go higher. But, since he is likely to have a long career, it will be interesting to see if he can carry the confidence of his home performances overseas. Ashwin will probably have a side that will complement him well on that count.

As of now, Ashwin is also the sixth highest impact bowler for India in ODIs too. He has not done enough with the bat in this format yet to be called an all-rounder here, but he still remains the most consistent Indian bowler in ODI history. Clearly, this is the defining feature of his game.

Consistency and fundamental reliability makes Ashwin a potential legend – given his low sample size of Tests so far (just thirteen Tests outside the subcontinent so far), it's hard to be more concrete. We suspect that a large part of his story is yet to unfold – but what a foundation he has already laid.

AC: If you give a flat pitch to a batsman, he's likely to score a century. If you give a green pitch to a fast bowler, he's likely to pick 5 wickets. But if you give a spin-friendly pitch to Ashwin, he's almost guaranteed to win you the game, and I'm talking about a Test match and perhaps, the Test series. I remember saying the same about Kumble, and it's meant as a huge compliment.

They say that off-spinners are a bigger threat on turning pitches because they expose both edges of the bat, and Ashwin's presence is allowing India to indulge in preparing some turning pitches. What I like about him is the fact that he does it the orthodox way – the flight, the dip, the turn and the bounce. The other factor that must stand out is that other spinners playing in the same match on the same pitch don't get the same rewards as Ashwin, and that says a lot. If conditions are so tailor-made for spin, every spinner must do well, but obviously, that's not the case here.

Since we're at it, I must mention that there's a serious decline in the defensive skills of batsmen around the world and therefore we don't see many hard-fought sessions in Test cricket any more. If it swings and seams, the Asian batsmen falter, and if it grips and turns, the rest of the world bows down. While this can't be held against Ashwin, he must improve his overseas returns against stronger teams to take the focus away from the disparity in his home and away numbers.

JV

51

THE THIRD HIGHEST IMPACT BOWLER IN ENGLAND'S TEST CRICKET HISTORY: GRAEME SWANN

Graeme Swann was drafted into the England squad for the final Test in the home series against New Zealand in 1999 but did not play.

He made his ODI debut in 2000 but was written off for seven years after a solitary match. He made his Test debut a year later at the age of twenty-nine.

He finished with a bowling average of 30 and a strike rate of 60, which places him thirteenth and tenth respectively in England's Test cricket history (minimum fifty Tests).

For all English bowlers who have played at least fifty Tests and taken a minimum of 100 wickets, he played for the shortest length of time (five years). But he is amongst the highest when it comes to impact.

It is remarkable that Graeme Swann emerges as the third highest impact bowler in England's Test cricket history – after Fred Trueman and Darren Gough – given that conditions in England have traditionally favoured swing and seam bowling.

AC: Off-spinners are generally considered the easiest bowlers to face. As a kid, when you hold a cricket bat for the first time, a slog-over midwicket is your go-to shot. Thus, off-spinners – whether it's the invention of the doosra or the carrom ball – they have been forced to innovate the most to avoid extinction.

In cricket's history, no one has evolved as much as off-spinners. Muralitharan redefined off spin with wrist spin, Saqlain Mushtaq invented the doosra. In these times, there was a Grame Swann who was still the classic old-fashioned off-spinner and who rose to significant heights with hardly any change or innovation. He did not need to reinvent himself to be successful.

Also, we must remember that most off-spinners have been under scrutiny and there is a stigma attached to their bowling actions – how much they bend their elbow. The doosra is almost banned now. Great spinners like Muralitharan, Harbhajan and now Sunil Narine have had their actions questioned. But here was Graeme Swann – a beautiful traditional off-spinner with a smooth unquestionable action. Absolutely flawless.

Biggest series winner of his era

Graeme Swann was an exceptionally good big-match player. He rose to the occasion and performed consistently in decisive matches – the bigger the stage, the better his performance.

He has three series-defining performances in a relatively short career of sixty Tests. This is the main reason for his high impact. Only Bobby Peel, Ian Botham and Derek Underwood have more SDs (four each). Darren Gough and Fred Trueman have three each.

If we restrict the time frame to Swann's career (December 2008–December 2013), he emerges as the biggest series winner with the ball (along with Dale Steyn, who produced his three SDs in forty Tests as compared to Swann's sixty) in the world during this period.

Swann played in nineteen Test series during his career. England won twelve of those, lost five and drew two. They were the best side in the world for a short while during this period.

Great Ashes record

England were thrashed 0–5 in Australia in 2006–07; it was a demoralizing and humiliating defeat to say the least. The previous occasion a team had been whitewashed in an Ashes contest was in 1920–21.

The Ashes, The Oval, 2009. *It was 1–1 going into the fifth and final decisive Test. England, opting to bat first, scored 332. Broad and Swann ripped through the Australian order and cleaned them up for 160; Swann took 4–38. England declared at 373 for 9 in the second innings, setting Australia a target of 546. Swann picked up his second 4-wicket haul of the match (4–120 in 40.2 overs), which included the wicket of Michael Hussey (the highest scorer of the match) and three other top- and middle-order batsmen, as the visitors were bowled out for 348.*

England won the Ashes 2–1. Swann gave an SD in the series decider. He was the second highest impact bowler (after Broad) in the series.

Swann played a supporting role in the 2010–11 Ashes, where England beat Australia 3–1 to win their first Ashes Down Under since 1986.

In the 2013 home Ashes, which the hosts won 3–0, he was the leading wicket taker (26 wickets in five Tests) and the highest impact bowler for England.

Swann had been the pivot around which England's three consecutive Ashes victories were built – a feat previously achieved way back between 1953 and 1956 (which is till date England's best period in Test cricket).

AC: What worked in Swann's favour is the fact that he was born and bred in England where the pitches hardly offer any assistance to spinners. Thus, unlike spinners from the subcontinent who get a lot of purchase from the wicket (and sometimes tend to get lazy), Swann had to work doubly hard on his bowling to make himself a world-class bowler. He had to beat the batsmen in the air, because after pitching, the ball did not do much in England. He did this by putting more revolutions on the ball. This was his biggest strength, and it explains his great Ashes record.

Conquering the subcontinent

Arguably, this was an even bigger achievement. The subcontinent poses the toughest challenges in recent times for overseas teams, from low and slow turners to the hot climate to the partisan crowds. It was no different for England.

Vs Sri Lanka, 2012. *England had lost to Sri Lanka in their two previous tours in 2003 and 2007. Much to pattern then, Sri Lanka won the first Test at Galle by 75 runs.*

In the second Test at Colombo, Sri Lanka had recovered from 30 for 3 to 216 for 4 before Swann triggered a collapse getting rid of the centurion Jayawardene. The off-spinner picked up 3 more wickets to return with figures of 4–75 as the hosts were bowled out for 275. England's top order fired and they posted 460. Sri Lanka again succumbed to the spin of Swann in the second innings (6–106 in 40 overs) and were cleaned up for 278. England chased down 94 with 8 wickets in hand.

Swann registered his second SD performance as England came from behind to draw level the two-match series 1–1.

He was also the highest impact bowler and player of the series.

Vs India, 2012. *England's last series win in India was in 1985. They had lost three and drawn one series since then. Moreover, England had major spin woes. Their primary spinners – Phil Tufnell and Ian Salisbury had failed in 1993. Liam Dawson and Ashley Giles were largely ineffective and low impact in 2001 while Monty Panesar failed in 2006.*

India, although amongst the worst touring teams, were giants at home. Between 1993 and 2012, India had played thirty-three Test series at home and won a whopping twenty-three. They had lost just two – against South Africa in 2000 and Australia in 2004.

Again, much to expectation, India won the first Test by 9 wickets. Swann had taken 6–190 in 58.3 overs. Clearly, he needed support from the other end.

In the second Test at Mumbai, India, electing to bat first, scored 327. Monty Panesar stepped up spectacularly this time. He took 5–129 and Swann 4–70. Alastair Cook and Kevin Pietersen hit contrasting hundreds as England amassed 413. Swann and Panesar again wreaked havoc and picked up 4 and 6 wickets respectively, dismantling India for a paltry 142 in the second innings. England chased down 57 with all ten wickets intact.

The match completely changed the momentum of the series. England found a new confidence and beat the hosts by 7 wickets in the third Test at the Eden Gardens while the fourth Test in Nagpur ended in a draw.

England won their first series in India in twenty-eight years (after 1984–85) and as such Swann earned a momentum-changing SD for his feat in the second Test.

He was, once again, the highest impact bowler and player of the series.

A rampant wicket taker

Besides his big-match temperament, Swann's wicket-taking prowess was dangerous too; he could claim crucial opposition wickets, one after another.

England had traditionally used spinners as support acts. Their role was to restrict the runs from one end while the faster men attacked from the other. Interestingly, amongst the ten English bowlers with the highest Economy Impact, six are spinners.

Curiously, Swann is not even in this list, suggesting that economy was not his forte. But, as far as wicket-taking ability is concerned, Swann is third, next only to Alec Bedser and Fred Trueman in England's Test cricket history. He was the leading wicket taker in the world during his career with 255 wickets in sixty tests.

Swann also has the best Pressure Building Impact, after only Trueman in England's Test cricket history.

His bowling failure rate of 32 per cent is the lowest for an English spinner (minimum fifty Tests). Derek Underwood (34 per cent), Fred Titmus (40 per cent), John Emburey (48 per cent) and Ashley Giles (57 per cent) were all more inconsistent with the ball.

AC: The other strength that Graeme Swann had – something that Mushtaq Ahmed told me – was that he had a fast bowler's attitude. He was a fast bowler in a spinner's skin. He wanted the batsmen to go after him in order to pick up wickets. He loved a challenge. He never bowled on a defensive line outside the leg stump. He pitched the ball outside the off stump tempting the batsmen to go for the drive inducing a false shot. Stuart MacGill had once told me that it is a failure

> for a spinner if a batsman continuously manages to defend him successfully. A truly great spinner will make the batsman take risks against him in the hope of getting him out. Swann did that, luring the batsman to play strokes, always taking the game forward.

A comparison with Underwood and Laker

Besides Swann, the two leading English spinners in Test history are these two. Underwood took 297 wickets at 26 apiece in eighty-six Tests and Jim Laker 193 wickets at 21 apiece in forty-six Tests. Swann, with 255 wickets at 30 apiece in sixty Tests actually has a slightly higher Bowling Impact than Underwood, simply because he was a wicket-taking bowler (Swann had a higher propensity to pick top/middle-order wickets; his bowling strike rate of 60 is also better than Underwood's 74). Underwood, however, was a far more restrictive bowler.

Laker (played forty-six Tests) also had a lower propensity to pick top/middle-order wickets than Swann. He also had an SD less (two as opposed to Swann's three) but still had a higher overall impact with the ball due to his phenomenal consistency (failure rate of just 17 per cent).

Swann's place in history

Swann is the sixth highest impact spinner (after Muralitharan, Warne, Kumble, Benaud and Herath) in the history of Test cricket.

He is the third highest impact player in English Test history (after Botham and Wally Hammond). Although just half a batsman (an impact of about 0.5 in Tests), he chipped in with some useful contributions, batting lower down the order, as his average of 22 also suggests.

Swann was the third highest impact bowler in the world during his career after Steyn and Herath (minimum thirty Tests). And he was England's highest impact and most consistent player (non-wicketkeeper) in this time frame.

Swann retired midway into the Ashes of 2013–14, with his team down 0–3, citing a personal drop in form and body fatigue; he was almost thirty-five. He also stated that his inability to help England to a fourth consecutive Ashes win had triggered the decision, remaining to the last a fierce competitor who played to win.

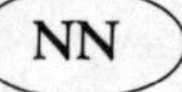

52

THE HIGHEST IMPACT PAKISTANI SPIN BOWLER IN TESTS: DANISH KANERIA

To have Danish Kaneria come up as Pakistan's highest impact spinner in Test cricket (minimum fifty Tests) was befuddling for us at Impact Index.

Conventionally, he is actually the fourth highest wicket taker in Pakistan Test history (after Wasim Akram, Waqar Younis and Imran Khan, and therefore the spinner with the most wickets), but his bowling average of nearly 35 per wicket takes away a lot of the sheen. Every major Pakistani spinner had a better bowling average than him: Abdul Qadir, 33; Saqlain Mushtaq, 30; Mushtaq Ahmed, 33; Iqbal Qasim, 28 and Saeed Ajmal, 28.

This has been attributed to several factors – the lack of a strong support spinner at the other end, a captain who could use him optimally, even a wicketkeeper who took all the chances he created. He also never quite had the kind of presence or personality that inspired the romantics to poetry, as Qadir or Mushtaq did, for example.

It is curious that Kaneria has very few high impact performances but several middle-range impact ones.

However, he had a low failure rate of 30 per cent, which made him more consistent than any Pakistani spinner who played more than fifty Tests. Qadir's failure rate was a considerable 45 per cent (something that should diminish some of his reputation), Mushtaq Ahmed's 37 per cent and Iqbal Qasim's 38 per cent. Only Saqlain's was better at 29 per cent but Kaneria did something Saqlain couldn't.

Kaneria registered three series-defining performances in his career, two more than both Saqlain Mushtaq and Mushtaq Ahmed, and as many as Qasim and Qadir. These three performances came against South Africa (2003) and Sri Lanka (2004) at home – oddly, the first time Pakistan did not lose against them at home in twelve years – and West Indies away (2005), all two-Test rubbers in which Kaneria performed big in Pakistan's only win in the series.

In fact, from the period of his first SD against South Africa in 2003 till end 2006, Pakistan played twelve Test series, losing only one home series (against India) and two away series (in Australia and England). During this period, Kaneria was the fourth highest impact bowler in the world, after Muttiah Muralitharan, Glenn McGrath and Shane Warne.

Kaneria's highest point was his second SD in 2004, against Sri Lanka. Trailing 0–1 in the series, in the second and final Test at Karachi, Kaneria took 3 of the first 7 wickets to fall in the first innings. Then, Younis Khan and Inzamam-ul-Haq scored centuries on a pitch that flattened considerably. Jayasuriya and Sangakkara then scored centuries as Sri Lanka made 406. During this innings, that lasted 142 overs, Kaneria bowled 60 overs, 20 maidens, gave away 117 runs and took 7 wickets. Despite a fourth-innings scare, Pakistan won by 6 wickets. By drawing the series, Pakistan managed to avert a home series loss against Sri Lanka for the first time in twelve years. They haven't lost since (there have been three series post-2004) – a good example of how a single moment can shift history for a considerable period.

His marathon performance in the above match received praise from his coach at Essex, Graham Gooch, and resulted in a further extension for him at the English County circuit.

In 2012, Kaneria was found guilty of match fixing in a 2009 Pro40 match while playing for Essex, which effectively ended his career at the age of thirty-one. It is tragic that he is remembered today for that, and for the smaller matter of being only the second Hindu to play Test cricket for Pakistan. What he did while playing those sixty-one Tests, and taking 261 wickets, is barely a footnote now.

AC: This comes as a surprise. When I think about Pakistani spinners, Saqlain Mushtaq comes to my mind as the one having the most impact. But then, if you think about it, Saqlain would have shared a lot of his impact with Mushtaq Ahmed, and not to forget Wasim Akram and Waqar Younis at their best. In such a case, wickets and impact get distributed amongst many good bowlers. It also becomes hard to have those series-defining individual performances when there are four to five good bowlers in a team. It is not Danish Kaneria's fault though that others were on the decline and that he didn't have an equally competent spinner at the end. So, you have got to give credit where it's due and Kaneria has obviously done well.

With Kaneria there was no beauty to his action, and I think that's how we end up judging a lot of leg-spinners. In a leg-spinner's craft, we concentrate a lot on the drift, dip and then the prodigious turn of the ball. To be honest, Kaneria didn't have all of that, nor did he have a dramatic action like Mushtaq Ahmed or Abdul Qadir did. He was consistent and didn't bowl as many loose balls as most leg-spinners but he wasn't photogenic. There is a lot of romanticism in cricket and we tend to revere those bowlers and players more who are visually appealing.

As for match fixing and how that took the sheen off Kaneria's achievements and contributions, well, I think that is only fair. If a player brings disrepute to the game, everything else becomes irrelevant. Mohammad Azharuddin was such a brilliant batsman; he was a great match winner. But you don't really see him in that light any more. That's the nature of the beast – if you are found cheating, you will carry that stigma for the rest of your life.

JV

53

A HIGH IMPACT TEST BATSMAN WITH AN AVERAGE OF JUST 36: ARJUNA RANATUNGA

Arjuna Ranatunga led Sri Lanka to the 1996 World Cup win. He was praised for his innovative ideas and daring in that tournament, as well as his calm, useful batting (much in evidence in the World Cup final at Lahore).

His role in building Sri Lanka into a formidable team in One-Day International cricket is well recognized; yes, but not what he did for their Test side. Nor is he given due credit for his own Test batting. His batting average of 36 is eleventh on a list of Sri Lankan batsmen who have played more than forty Tests. He is eighth on a runs-aggregate list.

However, through the Impact Index sieve, he comes out as the third highest impact Test batsman for Sri Lanka. The names ahead of him are Kumar Sangakkara and Mahela Jayawardene. The names below him include the great Aravinda de Silva, batting average 43; Thilan Samaraweera, 49; Hashan Tillakaratne, 43; Tillakaratne Dilshan, 41; Sanath Jayasuriya, 40; Asanka Gurusinha, 39 and Marvan Atapattu, 39.

Sangakkara and Jayawardene played at a time when the Sri Lankan team won quite a bit, especially at home, served as their team was for a long time by the highest impact bowler in Test history, Muttiah Muralitharan, who was nurtured in his formative years by Ranatunga, his captain. Aravinda de Silva, considered by many to be the most talented batsman Sri Lanka has produced, like Ranatunga, did not have the advantage of playing for an assured and accomplished team for as long as Sangakkara and Jayawardene did.

Ranatunga's impact breakdown

The 1996 World Cup is a good place to have as a signpost. Winning that was clearly a landmark moment in Sri Lankan cricket and even though it is a drastically different format, their Test fortunes changed too – a combination of new-found assurance and some great players developing at the same time.

Before the 1996 World Cup, Sri Lanka played sixty-six Tests and won barely 10 per cent of those. After the 1996 triumph, until Ranatunga retired in 2000, Sri Lanka played thirty-nine Tests and won 31 per cent of them.

In fact, if we go back a year, to the beginning of 1995, from when the turnaround ostensibly began, it is apparent that the team was on an upward surge. Between January 1995 and December 1998, four straight years, Sri Lanka were the fourth best team in the world in terms of win: loss ratio (after Australia, South Africa and Pakistan). They won their first away series in Pakistan in 1995 and their first Test in England in 1998 (a one-off Test) and they continued being hard to beat at home.

In that period, Ranatunga was Sri Lanka's highest impact batsman. He had two series-defining performances in this period – in Pakistan and against a fine New Zealand side at home. In fact, in those four years, Ranatunga was the seventh highest impact batsman in the world, after Steve Waugh, Ijaz Ahmed, Gary Kirsten, Nasser Hussain, Mark Waugh and Brian Lara (minimum twenty Tests).

If we look at Ranatunga's entire career – February 1982 to August 2000 – he was the highest impact Test batsman for Sri Lanka.

He absorbed the most pressure in Sri Lankan Test history then, only after Aravinda de Silva. (Today, it is Angelo Matthews.)

Only Muralitharan (four) got more SDs for Sri Lanka during Ranatunga's (three) playing days. He was the twenty-ninth highest impact batsman in world cricket in that nineteen-year period (minimum fifty Tests) – ahead of Saleem Malik, Allan Border, Mike Gatting, Sunil Gavaskar, Dilip Vengsarkar, Graham Thorpe and Graham Hick, amongst others. Absolutely remarkable for a batsman in a team that had just begun playing Test cricket.

Writing Sri Lankan Test history

Ranatunga was there at almost every milestone in his country's cricket history, often as a significant contributor. Here's a quick recall of those moments.

During Sri Lanka's **first-ever Test series win**, against India in 1985, Ranatunga top-scored with 111 in the first Test after coming in at 118 for 4. It gave Sri Lanka a first-innings lead from which they dominated the match, which though drawn, set the pace for the series. Sri Lanka won the next Test and drew the third.

Sri Lanka won a match and **drew a series against Pakistan** (perhaps the second best side in the world then, after West Indies) for the first time in 1986. After being 1–0 up, in the second Test, on a pacer-friendly pitch, Pakistan were dismissed for 132. The Sri Lankan innings was anchored by Ranatunga who made 77 in five hours of batting. It gave Sri Lanka a substantial lead and the pacers did their job again, for a famous win. This was Ranatunga's first series-defining performance. A half-century and a century from Ranatunga in the last Test went some way towards drawing the game and the series.

Sri Lanka's **first win against New Zealand** and their second series win ever in 1992 had Ranatunga anchoring the middle order with a 76 that eventually led to a comfortable 9-wicket win.

Sri Lanka's **first win against England** in a one-off Test in 1993 had Sri Lanka generating a spirited response to England's 380. Ranatunga's 64 played its part in the first innings and in the second, set 140 to win, Sri Lanka were at 61 for 4 with Ranatunga and Hashan Tillakaratne at the crease, both yet to open their accounts. They both took Sri Lanka through, with Ranatunga unbeaten on 35.

Sri Lanka's **first overseas Test win** was in New Zealand in 1995, when Ranatunga top-scored with 55 in the first innings of 183, then pitched in with 28 in the second when the Sri Lankan batsmen – primarily Tillakaratne and debutant wicketkeeper Chamara Dunusinghe – took the game away. Chaminda Vaas blew New Zealand away and Ranatunga scored 90 in the next Test to help Sri Lanka draw that match and win the series.

In the deciding Test of an exciting series in 1995, when Sri Lanka **won in Pakistan for the first time**, Ranatunga came out to bat at 87 for 3 in the third innings, with the match, and the series, entirely at stake. His calmly compiled 87, made over almost five hours, changed the direction of the match, as Sri Lanka managed to set a target of 357, which proved too much for Pakistan. This was Ranatunga's second SD.

Sri Lanka's **first Test win in England**, in 1998, is famous for Jayasuriya's 213, de Silva's 153 and particularly Muralitharan's 16 wickets, but Ranatunga too chipped in with a nifty 51.

To **beat a strong New Zealand side** in 1998, Sri Lanka had to come back from 0–1 down to win two consecutive Tests. First, Ranatunga contributed 36 – the second highest score in an innings dominated by sensational newcomer Mahela Jayawardene (in his fourth Test) who made 167, in a match the hosts won by an innings. This was followed by a tight deciding Test where Sri Lanka were 36 for 4 in the second innings, before Ranatunga's 64 helped take them to a score from where Muralitharan could destroy the Kiwis. This gave Ranatunga his third SD.

In Sri Lanka's **first Test win against Australia** in 1999, Ranatunga contributed right at the end. Chasing 95, Sri Lanka were at 60 for 4; with an unbeaten imperious 19, he finished the match off.

Beating Pakistan in their backyard in 2000 needed Ranatunga's calm at the fag end of the first Test as Sri Lanka were 177 for 8, chasing 220 for victory. An injured Ranatunga (no longer captain) took Sri Lanka home with a calm, unbeaten 29 while wicketkeeper Kaluwitharana gave him productive company with 36. Sri Lanka won by 2 wickets and took the lead in the series. Ranatunga was injured in the next Test, which Sri Lanka won to pocket the series.

Sri Lanka **drew against a formidable South African side** in 2000, though the second Test almost won them the series. Chasing 177 to win, Sri Lanka were 21 for 4 when Ranatunga walked in to bat. With just Russell Arnold and later Upul Chandana for support, he steered his team within 16 runs of victory before he was caught at short leg for a memorable 88. A jittery Sri Lanka collapsed to give South Africa a 7-run win.

This was Ranatunga's penultimate Test match. He had scored 49 and 88. In his final Test innings, Ranatunga walked in at 119 for 4. Sri Lanka were set a target of 263 to win the series. But they had run out of overs and Ranatunga stayed not out with 28 as he helped a youngster he had mentored, Mahela Jayawardene, score a century. It was a fitting handing over of the baton.

Influential captain

Ranatunga became captain in December 1989 and was at the helm for almost ten years, until February 1999. In that period, the strides Sri Lankan cricket made in all formats are second to none for a new cricket nation, which they were in the 1980s.

Sri Lanka had played fourteen Test series before Ranatunga became captain and won only once (against India).

With him as captain, Sri Lanka played twenty-six Test series, won eight, lost twelve and drew six. In terms of Test matches, the record reads – played fifty-six, won twelve, lost nineteen, drew twenty-five. Again, truly remarkable for an emerging cricket nation.

Ranatunga mentored many young talents who went on to become forces for their country. None more than Muralitharan, who would go on to be the highest impact Test bowler of all time, whose success is even more remarkable when it is examined closely.

It is hard to forget sometimes that Sri Lanka as a Test cricket-playing nation is just thirty-four years old. But it should not be difficult at all to trace Arjuna Ranatunga's influence in that, both as an inspiring leader and as a canny soldier.

AC: This is an incredible story. While nobody underestimates Ranatunga's contribution in shaping Sri Lankan cricket, not many give due credit to his contribution with the bat. Perhaps, it's only fair that he hit the winning runs in the final of Sri lanka's biggest ever win – the 1996 World Cup final. I think it's his charisma and contribution as a captain that hides his batting contributions, for the moment you think of Ranatunga, you think of him taking his team off the field against Australia because the umpire called Murali for chucking. You remember him for making Jayasuriya and Kalu open in the World Cup, you remember him for instilling self-belief in a team that wasn't expected to win but this chapter opens our eyes to his contribution with the bat too, and that too, in Test cricket.

JV/NN

54

MATTHEW HAYDEN WAS THE HIGHEST IMPACT AUSTRALIAN BATSMAN IN AN ILLUSTRIOUS GENERATION

Matthew Hayden played 103 Tests for Australia between 1994 and 2009. During almost all of that time, it was the best team in the world.

On the team were also Steve Waugh, Ricky Ponting, Adam Gilchrist, Justin Langer, Damien Martyn, Michael Hussey and Michael Clarke. As in all great sides, Hayden had to share impact with many of them at different times, which makes it exceptional that he comes up as the fourth highest impact Test batsman in his country's Test history.

AC: Matthew Hayden's biggest strength has been intimidation. That is usually a quality associated with bowlers, but strangely Hayden, through his towering presence and aggressive style of batting, intimidated bowlers across the world. I think only Vivian Richards in the past has had that effect on the psyche of bowlers and opposition captains.

I remember playing against him. He used to step out against fast bowlers. But there was a calculated game plan behind this. Not only did he want to look the bowler in the eye to rattle him but also force him to bowl short, which would enable Hayden to play the hook and the pull – shots he had mastered with the advantage he got from his height. The bowler's confidence would be completely shattered; there is nothing more disheartening than a batsman coming down the track to a bouncer and smacking it away for a boundary or six.

As of February 2001, however, Hayden had played just thirteen Tests and – thanks largely to his unacceptable 54 per cent failure rate – he was Australia's lowest impact specialist batsman since 1994.

AC: It is truly praiseworthy how Hayden turned his Test career around after a poor start. He had played only a solitary Test each in 1994 and 1996 before his comeback in 1997. After five more Tests, and a string of failures, he was again dropped for a period of three years. After a lot of toil and hard work and performances in Australia's domestic cricket, he was finally recalled in 2000.

He went to the MRF Academy in Chennai where, initially, he looked at sea against the spinners, but he did not give up. Hours and hours of practice on dusty pitches meant that he was ready for the tour to India in 2001. He mastered the sweep shot and used his feet against the spinners hitting them down the ground – this made him special. Most batsmen who can sweep well are not good on their feet and vice versa. Also, for an Australian batsman to come to the subcontinent and conquer it and make it his own was almost unprecedented. There was no looking back for Hayden after the India series. He had finally arrived in world cricket.

But from February 2001 until the end of his career (January 2009), he was the highest impact Australian Test batsman in the best side in the world, and the fifth highest impact batsman (after Inzamam-ul-Haq, Kumar Sangakkara, Graeme Smith and Rahul Dravid) with a failure rate of just 39 per cent in ninety Tests. Therefore, he was also the second highest impact opening batsman in world cricket at the time.

AC: Hayden loved a contest. He was always in the bowler's face while batting, and never shy of a verbal spat. Even while fielding, he would walk up to batsmen and exchange a few words and sledge – it egged him on and inspired him to give his best. Even when the day's play was over, while walking back to the pavilion, he would not hesitate and say a few words.

> Most of the time, it was just nonsense, but he liked to get under the opposition skin.
>
> I remember I was fielding as a substitute at short leg in the Chennai Test in 2004. The ball was turning and gripping. India had to bat last. Hayden started chatting with me. He told me that the pitch will turn square and it will be impossible to bat on Day 5. I asked him why he was telling me this as I was not even playing the match. What I found remarkable was that he was sledging while batting – that is something one usually does not witness in cricket. He was just unique in more ways than one.
>
> There was another incident about which Justin Langer has written extensively in his book. It was the first day of the Boxing Day Ashes Test in 2002. While walking out to resume their batting post-lunch, Hayden expressed his desire (to Langer) to go down the track and hit Harmison for a six but was wary of the occasion – the opening day of an Ashes Test. Langer told Hayden to go for it if he is confident. Hayden did exactly that a few overs after lunch. This epitomized his mindset, his confidence and ability. It started a trend where Hayden would dance down the track and smash quality fast bowlers to all parts of the ground, intimidating them in the process.

His hallmark was the ability to build partnerships – no one built more partnerships in world cricket than he did in that 2001–09 period. In fact, when it comes to Australian Test history, he is second in that aspect only to Bradman.

> **AC:** Hayden had a weakness too. He could not cut the ball. As Indians, we left the point empty, bowled slightly short outside the off stump, tempting him to play the cut shot, hoping to induce a mistake. But he seldom fell for it. He was a smart and an astute batsman who made the bowler bowl to his strengths. He played the pull and the sweep and used his feet to hit the spinners over the top but rarely attempted the cut shot – for all his bullying and intimidation, he did not let his ego come in the way. In fact, I remember him sweeping some of our fast bowlers on the tour Down Under in 2003–04.

As an opening batsman, he got to set the tone for his team and did it so successfully, it transpires that he scored the third highest proportion of runs for his team (on a match-by-match basis) in Australian Test history, after Bradman and Neil Harvey.

Given the batting talent that followed him, there is little wonder that Australia were the most dominant team in Test history for as long a period as they were, after West Indies (between 1976 and 1995).

> **AC:** Hayden was a seriously hard-working cricketer. He spent hours and hours in the nets and went through one practice session after another. He would not remove his pads from 9 a.m. to 5 p.m. He would just bat and bat – first against the bowling machine, then in the nets. So, whatever he was doing on the cricket field with the bat, all that domination and aggressiveness, was a result of some serious hard work over a period of time.

He was a world beater in a world-beating team. Given all that he did, it is curious that he is somewhat underrated. Perhaps it has something to do with the fact that he is only sixth when it comes to batting averages among Australians who played more than fifty Tests.

Batting averages should really have no place in the twenty-first century.

55

GRAEME SMITH IS AMONGST THE FIVE BIGGEST SERIES WINNERS WITH THE BAT IN TEST CRICKET HISTORY

Sachin Tendulkar averaged 54 in Test cricket. Ricky Ponting 52. Mohammad Yousuf 52. Rahul Dravid 52. Shivnarine Chanderpaul 51. Steve Waugh 51. Matthew Hayden 51. Hashim Amla 50 (ongoing).

Graeme Smith averaged 48 but is higher impact than every single one of them.

> 'Watching Graeme Smith bat is like watching someone hacking an ox to death' – Andy Zaltzman

Graeme Smith is South Africa's second highest impact Test batsman ever (minimum fifty Tests) after A.B. de Villiers.

And the sixteenth highest impact batsman in the 139 years of Test cricket.

> 'I have come to see Amla and De Villiers, not Smith.' – Average Spectator

Smith has affected the series scoreline more regularly than most batsmen in the modern game, again far more than many names taken before his in the pantheon of batting greatness.

Only two batsmen in Test history have more series-defining performances than him – Rahul Dravid and Inzamam-ul-Haq.

'There is no uglier batsman in world cricket. He squats at the crease like an overgrown crab, legs splayed, bat wielded at an oblique angle in a chunky claw.' – Simon Hughes

When cricket romantics start treating what goes on in the middle less as a ballet performance and more as competitive sport, stories like these won't need to be told. All analysts can retire and clarity can prevail.

We're not even sure why you need any kind of analytics to know that Smith is one of the truly great fourth-innings batsmen. You don't need to be a great scholar of the sport to know that those usually are the toughest runs scored in this sport.

So let's get these simple signposts out of the way.

Amongst the best in the world

If we take fifty Tests as the minimum, Graeme Smith is the second highest impact South African batsman of all time, ahead of the likes of Jacques Kallis, Gary Kirsten, Hansie Cronje, Daryll Cullinan and Hashim Amla.

On a world stage, if we look at all of Test history (minimum fifty Tests), Smith is the sixteenth highest impact batsmen of all time with the likes of Sutcliffe, Hayden, Miandad, Dravid, Viv Richards, Boycott, Jayawardene and Tendulkar below him on an impact list. Perhaps a few jaws would have met floors by now.

Even during his career (2002 to 2014), Smith was the fifth highest impact batsman in the world after A.B. de Villiers, Jacques Kallis, Kumar Sangakkara and Ricky Ponting, ahead of many other luminaries. It means that he was the highest impact opener in the world during his Test career. It is then perhaps not surprising that Smith also has the second highest New Ball Impact after Gary Kirsten in South African Test history.

Joint most SDs by any South African

The SD is a player's true legacy. Smith's count of seven SDs in his career is jointly the most for any South African, along with Jacques

Kallis (although the latter achieved it in almost fifty more Tests). Smith's feat is even more astonishing considering that Kallis was a genuine all-rounder, and had more chances to register an SD, whereas Smith was a specialist batsman.

In fact, amongst batsmen in Test history, only Rahul Dravid and Inzamam-ul-Haq have more SDs than Smith (eight each). When it comes to matches to SD ratio, amongst modern-day batsmen, only Inzamam with one SD in every fifteen Tests is ahead of Graeme Smith, who achieved one SD every seventeen Tests. A.B. de Villiers matches Smith's ratio. Younis Khan (in eighteen), Sangakkara (in nineteen), Dravid (in twenty-one), Misbah-ul-Haq (in twenty-two), Kallis (in twenty-four), Lara (in twenty-six), Cook (in twenty-seven), Tendulkar (in thirty-three), Ponting (in fourty-two) are behind him. Historically, Greg Chappell (in seventeen), Hutton (in twenty), Miandad (in twenty-five), Hobbs (in thirty) draw the picture with broad strokes. Bradman (one in ten) couldn't have been entirely human, of course.

Conventional statistics show that no one scored more runs in the fourth innings in Test history, especially in a winning cause, than Smith. Among the more knowledgeable commentators and students of the game, this is seen as his greatest legacy. But nobody has really measured the timing of many of these performances – that they came when the series was on edge, when everything was still at stake.

Smith's high impact Test performances

Some of Smith's highest impact Test performances are listed below (both in a series context and a match context). They represent South Africa's modern Test history at its brightest.

47 and 125 not out vs New Zealand, Wellington, 2004. *Trailing 0–1, going into the final match of the three-match Test series, Smith produced the first SD performance of his career in a quintessential fourth-innings chase – a trait that was to become his forte for the rest of his career. Chasing 234, South Africa had collapsed to 36 for 3 with Gibbs, Rudolph and Kallis nursing their wounds when Smith, along with Kirsten, shepherded South Africa's reply under immense pressure. Not only did he score the* *bulk of the runs (53 per cent of the runs) but he also made sure that he stayed on till the end to see South Africa through.*

48 and 108 (Perth); 62 and 75 vs Australia, Perth/Melbourne, 2008. *The Test series in which South Africa dethroned Australia from their No. 1 spot in the ICC Test rankings ended Smith's most memorable year. South Africa won the first two Tests and the series, with Smith contributing every time. His fourth-innings century set the pace as his team chased 414, through the jitters of 19 for 1. Hashim Amla, Jacques Kallis, de Villiers and debutant Jean-Paul Duminy all carried on the good work started by their leader as they won by six wickets. Chasing a potentially tricky 183 in the second Test, Smith hammered 75 off 94 and once again took the lead in removing the bite from the situation as his team won by 9 wickets (and won the series). South Africa lost the third Test – interestingly, in a fourth-innings chase again (of 376) – but this time they were left hanging on for a draw at the end. An injured Smith walked in at 257 for 9 and played out 17 balls in 26 minutes before he was bowled by Johnson with just five minutes left. Smith's immediate despondency would have suggested they had lost the series 0–3. This is an SD for Smith's two big performances in the series.*

37 and 101* vs Australia, Cape Town, 2011. *In one of the most bizarre matches in the history of Test cricket, Graeme Smith was forced to come out to bat for the second time on the same day after two inexplicable collapses left South Africa chasing 236 runs to win the match. Given the flow of the match (with the second and third innings yielding 96 and 47 respectively), 236 seemed a huge target before Smith and Amla got their act together and breezed past the target in around 50 overs to give South Africa a 1–0 lead. This innings is very high on the impact charts because it came in a fourth-innings chase and also because of how low-scoring the game was.*

259 vs England, Lord's, 2003. *After cracking 277 in the first Test match in a drawn cause, Smith followed up with another double century in this game, this time in a winning cause. This innings registers a very high impact primarily because South Africa needed only one innings to win the match.*

234 vs Pakistan, Dubai, 2013. *After losing their first Test match in a span of twenty-two months and fifteen Tests, South Africa had it all to do against a potent bowling line-up in this two-match Test series against Pakistan. With talks about South Africa lacking a proper spinner, Imran Tahir picked up 5 for 32 in the first innings to skittle Pakistan out for 99 runs. The Pakistani spin duo of Saeed Ajmal and Zulfiqar Babar started off strongly against the South African batsmen but Smith and de Villiers (164) made sure they batted Pakistan out of the game with a mammoth 338-run partnership for the 5th wicket after they were 134 for 4 at one point of time. Pakistan managed to fare better in their second innings and scored 326 runs but it was not enough to make the South Africans bat again.*

7 and 154 not out vs England, Edgbaston, 2008. *South Africa were one up with two to go. In a frenetic four-day Test match that had seemed an even battle between bat and ball, South Africa were left to chase down 283. At 93 for 4, the series had seemed to come alive again – 22, 6, 5, 2, 27 were the contributions from the other end, and at 171 for 5, the proverbial chokers looked set to show those colours again. Instead, they eased to victory in style, with an astonishing unbeaten 154 from the skipper, as they closed down the series in a memorable triumph.*

> My mindset was not about technique but about the way I thought about the game. I always saw cricket as a transfer of pressure between batting and bowling. It was always more mental for me. – Graeme Smith

AC: Smith had strength of character. Anyone else would have imploded after the way he was ridiculed by critics for the ugliness of his batting style. There's a funny thing about the lack of aesthetics – while you're getting the runs, people talk about how effective the player is, but the moment he fails (which everyone must sooner than later), the same people shred your technique and the style (or the lack of it) to pieces. He had the most unorthodox way of playing (even more unorthodox than Chanderpaul, in my opinion), for he turned some of the fundamentals of the game on its head. Everybody is told about the importance of presenting the full face of the bat but he rarely did that (as if he never got a good deal from a bat sponsor). In Tests, bowlers reside on the line that's outside the off stump and the length that's drivable, for that brings the slip cordon in play, but Smith never played a proper drive. At most, he would push the ball through covers as if it was an obligation because the ball was just too full. For the rest, he kept rolling his bottom hand to drag the ball towards the on side.

His unique style of batting initially lured and eventually fooled even the best bowlers in the world to bowl straight to him, which was his strength. They saw his bat coming down at an angle with the face slightly closed as an opportunity to dismiss him, but it never worked out that way, for that was his strength. Captains tried innovative fields to guard the on side with as many as three catching midwicket fielders, but he kept eluding them. For him, it seemed that it was always about the runs and not about how good he looked while accumulating them.

Last-innings batting is all about the character, and it doesn't come as a surprise that he's produced the goods more often than not in the tricky fourth innings.

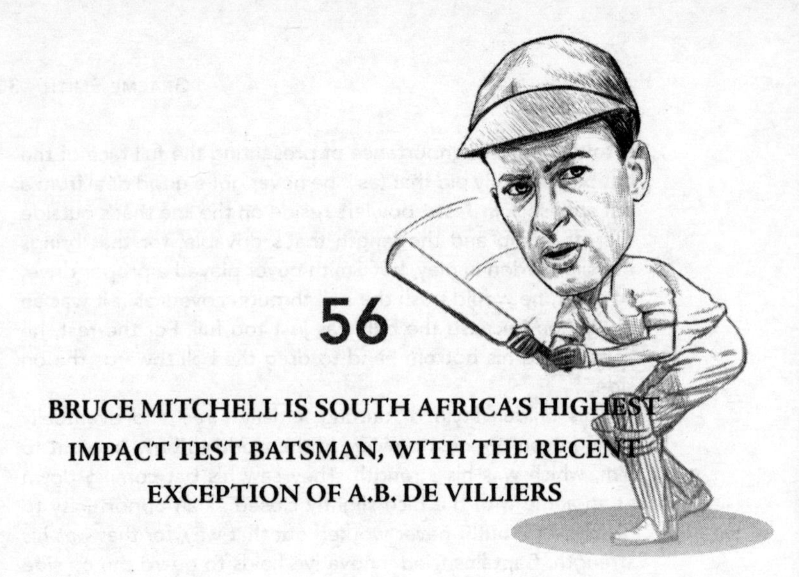

56

BRUCE MITCHELL IS SOUTH AFRICA'S HIGHEST IMPACT TEST BATSMAN, WITH THE RECENT EXCEPTION OF A.B. DE VILLIERS

That is, if we take a minimum of forty Tests (since there were far fewer Tests in that era). For sixty-five years (1949 onwards), until A.B. de Villiers's dream run, Bruce Mitchell was South Africa's highest impact Test batsman.

Bruce Mitchell played every one of the forty-two Tests South Africa played between 1929 and 1949. Of the nine Test series those matches constituted, South Africa won only three, losing the other six.

In those three series, Mitchell played the leading role, producing the most important contribution at just the right moments.

Vs England, Johannesburg, 1930. *In the opening Test of the series, Mitchell failed as South Africa were destroyed for 126. England took a lead of 67, significant in that era of uncovered pitches. Mitchell came out to bat again with the score at 34 for 1, which soon became 50 for 2. He batted for two-and-a-half hours, top-scoring with 72, as his team, inspired by his fight perhaps, set England a substantial 240 to win. South Africa won by 28 runs, and this turned out to be the only result match in the series (Mitchell produced very substantial contributions in the remaining Tests as well).*

Vs New Zealand, Christchurch, 1932. *In the opening Test of a two-match series, replying to New Zealand's 293, Mitchell anchored the South*

African innings with 113 (with opening partner Jim Christy also scoring 103) – setting the foundation for an innings victory. In the next Test, he scored 0 and 53 as South Africa won convincingly again, and, with it, the series 2–0.

Vs England, Lord's, 1935. *In the second Test of the series (with the series still 0–0), the match was on an even keel after the first innings, with South Africa having got a 30-run lead. Then came a five-and-a-half-hour effort from Mitchell, during which he scored a famous unbeaten 164 out of South Africa's 278 for 7, setting a demoralized England 309 for victory, which they couldn't even make half of. This was the only result Test in the series. Mitchell produced substantial performances in the rest of the series too that maintained the series scoreline.*

He authored other classics too, even if none of them were in a winning cause. The most memorable of them came at the Oval in 1947, after the series had been lost. As South Africa chased an unthinkable 451 for victory (Mitchell had made 120 out of his team's total of 302 in the first innings), he batted for seven hours and anchored a performance that is still remembered with awe – 189 not out as his team finished at 423 for 7, with an eighth-wicket partnership of 109, out of which he scored almost 70 per cent of the runs.

In his last Test match, the fifth in the series against England at Port Elizabeth, with South Africa trailing 0–1, and his team at 13 for 2, Mitchell scored 99 as his team reached a respectable 379. England responded with 395, with time running out of the match. Mitchell top-scored with 56 as South Africa declared at 187 for 3, with a last gasp bid to force a result. But England just about made the 172 required after losing 7 wickets, and won the series 2–0.

If Mitchell had played for a stronger team, and if the war hadn't robbed him of his finest years, perhaps he would have had the reputation of a George Headley or a Bradman. As it is, he was the fourth highest impact batsman of the period his career ran – after Bradman, Headley and Stan McCabe. His 38 per cent failure rate is second only to Bradman and Headley; in fact, in South Africa's Test history, only Jacques Kallis and Hashim Amla bettered him in this aspect (the same failure rate but over a higher number of Tests).

Mitchell's batting average of almost 49 in that era does reveal a story greater than conventional cricket stats can usually accomplish.

AC: Once again, a story that was never told. Yes, like you rightly mentioned in the end, the average of 49 on uncovered pitches must be worth a lot more. And Bruce Mitchell's heroics (can't think of a better word after reading the piece) deserve a lot more mind space and attention among cricket lovers. The best thing about such stories is that, even though their conventional numbers are good enough to be acknowledged, they seldom get documented in this fashion because of the lack of a compelling narrative. The moment you delve a little deeper, look at contributions in wins and the circumstances, the story becomes too strong to be ignored.

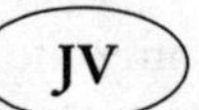

57

BRIAN LARA'S 375 AND 400 ARE NOT HIS HIGHEST IMPACT TEST PERFORMANCES

On 18 April 1994, at St. John's, Antigua, Brian Lara broke Garry Sobers's then Test record of 365 for the most number of runs in an innings with a pull off Chris Lewis's bowling. It was a monumental effort, given the physical and emotional strain of the innings. There was some early pressure, West Indies had been reduced to 12 for 2, but Lara fought back by stringing three consecutive 150-plus partnerships.

The innings had high romantic value, given the audacity of the shots played and the symbolic change of the flag-bearer of West Indian cricket for the next decade. Yet, looking from the context of the series and the match, Lara's 375 is not even amongst the twenty highest impact batting performances of his career.

The result of the last Test of the series was inconsequential as West Indies had already won it 3–1. Driven by Lara's 375, West Indies finished with 593 runs in their first innings, losing only 5 wickets. England, in reply, matched their total thanks to Robin Smith's 175 and Mike Atherton's 135. West Indies, in their insignificant second innings, finished with 43 runs for the loss of no wicket.

Overall, every wicket in the match was worth almost 82 runs.

Given the basic premise of Impact Index, which looks at the significance of an innings within the match context, it is not hard to figure out why Lara's innings doesn't stand out as a very high impact one. Yes, he absorbed pressure at 12 for 2, but after those two wickets, almost each and every batsman made merry on a perfect batting pitch. Given that the match resulted in a tame draw, Lara's innings stood out only for the longevity of it, not for his contribution towards a favourable match or series result.

> **AC:** That's generally the case with really big individual innings – the flat nature of the pitch is a given for this to happen. It's also quite likely that the rest around you were doing handsomely too, or you'd run out of partners. And on most occasions the opposition also responds with a high score (unless it is a brittle team). In short, these innings are great for record books (and they do mean a lot), but they rarely help the team to win the game/series.

Same story, ten years later

Ten years later, at the very same venue and against the same opponents, Lara smashed the world record again, this time scoring 400 (breaking Matthew Hayden's 380, set barely six months previously). West Indies finished with 751 runs for the loss of only 5 wickets. England finished with 285 in their first innings. On being asked to follow on, they finished with 422 for the loss of only 5 wickets. The match par for every wicket was almost 73 runs. Again, in the context of the match and the series, the innings was deemed inconsequential as England held on to draw the match and were already leading 3–0 in the series going into the last Test. Very much like his 375, even this innings doesn't register amongst his twenty highest impact Test innings.

Which, if not these?

Brian Lara's two highest impact Test innings actually came against Australia in 1999. Remarkably, both in the same Test series, in consecutive matches.

After going down 0–1, Australia were rolled out for 256 in the first innings at Kingston. West Indies, in reply, were 5 for 2 when Lara came in to bat. It soon worsened to 34 for 4. Lara's only point of support was

Jimmy Adams (93) with whom he shared a 322-run partnership. Lara himself scored 213 runs as West Indies finished with 431. Australia could manage only 177 runs in their second innings, with West Indies requiring only three runs to knock off in their fourth innings. There were only four batsmen (Lara being one of them) who crossed 50 runs in the entire match. The match par for every wicket was a meagre 29 runs. Lara's runs therefore came at a premium and, more importantly, sealed the match for West Indies. It remains the second highest impact batting performance by any West Indian in the history of Test cricket.

Remarkably, the second highest impact innings of his career came in the very next match. Australia, batting first, reached 490 after being 36 for 3 thanks to Steve Waugh's 199 and Ricky Ponting's 104. West Indies, in their reply, scored 329 with Lara managing only eight runs. Driven by Courtney Walsh's 5–39, an Australian collapse for 146 saw West Indies chasing 308 runs in their last innings. When Lara came out to bat in the second innings, West Indies were 78 for 3. It soon worsened to 105 for 5. Again, with Adams as a companion, Lara stitched a recovery, stringing a 133-run partnership. Another mini-collapse saw West Indies requiring 60 runs to win with only 2 wickets in hand. Ambrose and Walsh combined scored only 12 runs as Lara took West Indies home with only a wicket to spare. Lara finished with 153 not out, and helped West Indies gain a 2–1 lead in the series. The match par for every wicket was only 33 runs.

AC: This is one of my fondest memories of Brian Lara. I distinctly remember how tense I was just watching the match. It was a high-octane, high-skilled clash between two quality opponents. The Australian bowlers were at the peak of their powers, and so was Brian Lara. The thing that stood out was Lara's attacking instinct in the face of adversity. He didn't compromise his basic instinct while ensuring that he didn't commit a mistake. If I would pay to watch someone bat, it is Lara in full flow.

In both these cases, Lara played the defining innings under pressure, which won West Indies the match. Lara's back-to-back masterclasses against Australia also earned him a series-defining performance as he produced high impact performances to shape the series (even though Australia would go on to level the series in the very next and last Test). It was a far cry from his record-breaking efforts of 375 and 400, which didn't come in a match-defining cause and where most other batsmen too made merry on an easy batting wicket.

If cricket is to be seen and understood on the basis of the value of an innings within the match context and to a team's cause, Lara's 213 and 153 should always be placed on a higher pedestal than his 375 and 400. (It is ironic that those two innings do not even total up to 375.)

There is no separate chapter in this book on Brian Lara because the universal acknowledgement of his genius does not make for a hidden story. However, it is worth mentioning here that he is the fifth highest impact Test batsman of all time (minimum fifty Tests), after Don Bradman, Peter May, Younis Khan and Greg Chappell. The batsmen who immediately follow Lara on this list are Jack Hobbs, Inzamam-ul-Haq and A.B. de Villiers. At a glance, the most remarkable thing about this is that Lara is the only one who was not from a side that dominated world cricket for the more substantial part of his career (West Indies had lost its pre-eminent crown four-and-a-half years after his career commenced).

Furthermore, Lara has absorbed the most pressure (of falling wickets) in Test history, after Peter May, Andy Flower, Angelo Mathews and Kane Williamson (minimum fifty Tests, otherwise M.A.K. Pataudi would make this list too). He remains the sixth most consistent batsman in Test history, after Bradman, Len Hutton, Peter May, Jack Hobbs and Azhar Ali (an ongoing career of course, so that could change).

All these qualities were on display when he played his two highest impact innings in Test cricket.

AC: There were many comparisons between Lara and Tendulkar about who's the greatest. Well, my take on this is that, if I wanted to see technical competence, I'd see Tendulkar, but if I wanted to see sheer brilliance in batting, I'd go to watch Lara. His high backlift, the hop and the flair made for exciting cricket, and not even once did I see him alter his game because of the circumstances. That doesn't mean he didn't score runs when things got tougher but just that he could score runs in all situations without calling upon a different skill set. He was a genius.

SS

58

CHRIS GAYLE IS NOT THE HIGHEST IMPACT T20 BATSMAN IN THE WORLD

Chris Gayle's name is synonymous with T20s, with good reason. The big left-hander from Jamaica made his ODI and Test debut in 1999 and 2000 respectively. He had a reasonably successful career in both formats but it was not until the advent of T20s that he got a format in which he could try and lay claim to being the world's best.

For the cricket media, especially in India, he is the best T20 batsman ever. But is he really?

Overall T20 record

As of November 2016, Chris Gayle has played 272 T20s, scored 9,668 runs at an average of 42 and hit them at a strike rate of 151. Even though conventional numbers are unable to portray a player's true T20 prowess, these numbers are still mind-boggling. There is absolutely no doubt about Gayle's capability as a match winner in the format, but has he done it consistently enough? Has he won tournaments for his team? Or has he mostly made hay while the sun shone?

A major reason why Gayle has monstrous conventional figures in T20s is because of the big knocks which bump up his overall numbers. In Impact Index, though, we restrict the impact of any performance in a match at a career level, so that it doesn't skew the overall figures which therefore also takes into account the consistency of a player. And it is on this count where Gayle falls behind somewhat against his peers.

AC: Let us first acknowledge that he literally owned this format for several years and is, undoubtedly, the first legend of the T20 format. While conventional numbers do conceal a lot and reveal little at times, his near-10,000 T20 runs must be applauded for the astronomical strike rate of 151. He changed the course of many T20 games in his career and is, therefore, quite rightly, judged very highly in the first two-thirds of his T20 career. One must realize that T20 cricket has changed the dynamics of batting and the game itself quite a lot, for no format allowed one batsman to dominate the game and influence the result so much, and Gayle did influence many matches.

I also feel that he deconstructed the T20 batting quite nicely in that he was happy to bide time initially and then launch into bowlers of lesser pedigree. The thing that works in the batsman's favour in T20 is the fact that opposition's best bowler (irrespective of his form that day) rarely bowls more than 12 to 18 balls at a time (12 balls on most days because it's imperative to keep a couple of overs for the death) and nobody exploited this aspect more than Gayle. His ability to hit sixes without coming down the track also made him a dangerous batsman to bowl to.

Gayle has a batting failure rate of 44 per cent in 267 innings – sixteen batsmen have had a lower failure rate than him in T20 cricket around the world (minimum fifty innings).

In fact, in all T20s (minimum fifty matches, domestic and international, with a higher value to internationals against Test sides), Chris Gayle is the fourth highest impact batsman in the world after Imran Nazir, Suresh Raina and Quinton de Kock. To see him below these batsmen may seem shocking.

The drawback

The biggest downside to Gayle's career has been his inability to kick on in big matches/knockouts. Gayle has only three tournament-defining performances in 272 T20 matches.

Amongst batsmen, Suresh Raina, Dwayne Smith, Kieron Pollard and Imran Nazir top the list with five such performances each. In fact, amongst the forty-one batsmen who have produced two or more tournament-defining (TD) performances in their T20 career, Gayle's matches to TD ratio is amongst the worst. Only Hodge, Sangakkara, Yusuf Pathan, Gambhir, Warner and Yuvraj Singh have a worse matches to TD ratio than Gayle amongst these batsmen. Not flattering for the 'World Boss'.

And it is not because his team fails to deliver in the big games (though that inevitably happens with all players at some point). Gayle's failure rate as a batsman in big matches (in all T20 cricket) increases to 49 per cent (in thirty-three knockout games) compared to 43 per cent in group stage games.

Specifically, in the IPL, he has played seven big matches, and has had comprehensive failures in three. There have been only two instances in which he has given a high impact performance.

In IPL 2011, Gayle scored 89 in just 47 balls against Mumbai Indians in the second qualifier but failed in the first qualifier (8 off 9 balls) and then in the final against Chennai Super Kings (0 off 3 balls).

In IPL 2016, chasing 209 in the final, Gayle scored 76 runs off 38 balls against Sunrisers Hyderabad, but his teammates failed to close out the match to clinch the trophy. He had earlier failed in the first qualifier against Gujarat Lions (9 runs off 12 balls). Even in the WT20s for West Indies, Chris Gayle has clicked with the bat in only two out of six knockout matches, producing comprehensive failures in the remaining four.

While it is possible to blame his teammates for one or two of his performances that did not register as TDs (like in IPL 2016), it is also hard to ignore the fact that Gayle has produced a defining performance (where his team has won) in only three out of thirty-seven T20 tournaments.

Most pertinently, his overall big-match conversion rate of just 30 per cent (eleven performances in thirty-three big matches) is poor for a player of his stature. In comparison, Imran Nazir has a 52 per cent conversion rate, Suresh Raina 42 per cent, Michael Hussey 36 per cent and his fellow countryman Lendl Simmons has a 38 per cent conversion rate.

> **AC:** His lack of performances in the knockout games will always be held against him and in turn will take a little bit of sheen off his glorious T20 career. Batsman like Gayle and a format like T20 dictate the boom-or-bust kind of performances; unfortunately, his knockout numbers are more bust than boom. Is it because the quality of the opposition is superior in these games, teams find out a workable strategy against him during the league phase and implement them in the knockouts better, or because he's not someone who does well under pressure? The jury is still out on this.

IPL career

In IPL history (minimum of fifty matches), Chris Gayle is only the fifth highest impact batsman after Michael Hussey, David Warner, Suresh Raina and Dwayne Smith. All of them have produced a TD for their respective franchise and as a result have an IPL title to their name. Gayle does not.

T20I success

With the West Indians playing a massive role in almost all domestic T20 leagues around the world, it seemed only a matter of time before they would collectively go on to win the World T20 title. They did just that in the 2012 World T20 in Sri Lanka, where Chris Gayle finally produced a TD in the semi-final against Australia.

West Indies became the only team to win the title for the second time in 2016, but this time Gayle drew blanks in the knockout phase of the tournament.

Still, when it comes to T20Is (minimum of twenty-five matches), Chris Gayle is the third highest impact batsman in the world after Virat Kohli and Kevin Pietersen.

Other T20 leagues

Chris Gayle has plied his trade in many domestic T20 leagues around the world but has managed to produce only two TDs – in the Bangladesh Premier League in February 2013 and the Caribbean Premier League in August 2016.

Here's a look at Gayle's performances in some of the T20 leagues around the world:

Bangladesh Premier League (minimum five matches): Third highest impact batsman overall after Imran Nazir, Ashar Zaidi.

Ram Slam T20 Challenge (minimum five matches): Eighteenth highest impact batsman overall and the second highest impact batsman for Lions after Quinton de Kock.

Caribbean Premier League (minimum five matches): Fifth highest impact batsman overall and the second highest impact batsman for Jamaica Tallawahs after Andre Russell.

Big Bash League (minimum fifteen matches): Sixteenth highest impact batsman overall.

It is evident from his T20 records that, even though he made his mark in many of the domestic T20 leagues, he failed to influence and propel his team to silverware on most occasions.

In many ways, Chris Gayle is the face of T20 cricket, but as things stand, he is one of the best, rather than the best, batsmen in T20 history.

AC: The decline of Gayle over the last few years has been palpable and those who intend to see it have seen it already. The latest version of Gayle is an average batsman against quality bowlers (both seam and spin) and still a lethal batsman against certain kind of bowlers (read medium pacers and spinners bringing the ball back in). Also, his cult has something to do with his playing for the Royal Challenger Bangalore (RCB) at one of the flattest pitches in the world. His numbers while playing for the Kolkata Knight Riders (KKR) on a slow-low Eden Garden pitch weren't flattering and that's why he went unsold in one of the auctions. His comeback in the IPL through the RCB not just gave him a fresh lease of life but also propelled his T20 reputation to the sky. His decline could also be a combination of two factors –

playing only one format throughout the year (inferior quality in T20 leagues around the world) and age catching up with him. He's never been the swiftest of movers between the stumps, which meant he never had a B game to fall back on in case the big shots deserted him, and that's proving too costly now. Perhaps that's one of the reasons for his high failure rate in T20s. Although T20 teams do budget for high failure rate anyway – why else would you need six batsmen to last 50 overs and the same number for 20-overs cricket.

A final thought – you are (or should be) remembered for how you lived and not how you died, and Gayle's unbelievable T20 record for two-thirds of his career will always force people to consider him a T20 giant.

SS

59

THE HIGHEST IMPACT T20 PLAYER EVER: SAMUEL BADREE

This is the sort of thing that brings Impact Index a bad name. How can a specialist spinner, who has no other skill to speak of, be the highest impact T20 player ever (if we take sixty matches as the minimum) in a game where batsmen supposedly dominate?

How is he even the highest impact bowler? Has Sunil Narine not taken 241 wickets in 192 innings at an average of 18? What about Lasith Malinga, who has taken 299 wickets in 216 innings at an average of 18? In comparison, Samuel Badree has 146 wickets from 145 innings at an average of 20. What makes him higher impact than those two?

Master of restriction

In a sport that is, at its core, really all about who scores more runs in just 20 overs, Badree has the lowest economy rate in the history of the format, even below Narine's (5.61 to 5.68). No one has choked runs better.

In fact, Badree's contribution has been even more significant than these numbers suggest as he opens the bowling with his fast leg spin (where the ball doesn't turn much) and delivers very accurately in the power play when the field is up and batsmen look to hit over the top (he often bowls out). As is common in these circumstances, these batsmen often overcompensate when he is off the attack and provide breakthroughs to other bowlers. In this way, Badree has often set the pace for his team.

Curiously, despite the lower economy rate, Narine's Economy Impact is marginally higher, which means that when we factor in the scoring standards of each match, Narine has restricted runs a little more.

This then begs the question – if Narine's Economy Impact is higher, and clearly he is a much more prolific wicket taker, how can Badree be higher impact than him?

Big-match player

This is what makes Badree the highest impact T20 player ever (followed by Adam Gilchrist).

Badree has seven tournament-defining performances to his credit, more than any player, let alone bowler, in T20 history. This essentially means he produced a high impact performance in a play-off match when his team went on to win the tournament. Among bowlers, Harbhajan Singh has four TDs; Narine and Malinga three each, all of them in considerably more matches.

This is a staggering accomplishment and certainly belies his 37 per cent failure rate as a bowler, which, while being very good, is not among the lowest in T20 history. Narine, with 27 per cent, trumps him here too. But Badree is by far the better big-match bowler.

Badree has played in twenty-one big matches (play-off games in tournaments) in his career and produced a high impact performance in six of them, failed in just four and done reasonably well in the others. Narine has played twenty-two such matches, with high impact performances four times, with eight failures. Malinga has played twenty-four, with four high impact performances and ten failures. So, this is where Badree sails over the others, even though he has not even been the leading act sometimes.

In matches where Badree has got a TD, he has been the highest impact bowler twice, the second highest impact bowler four times and once even the third highest impact bowler. But he always set the tone at the top of the innings. In the end, Badree's impact in big matches is 25 per cent higher than Narine's and 78 per cent higher than Malinga's.

Badree's TD performances helped his team (Trinidad and Tobago) prevail in the **Caribbean T20 League** four times (in 2011, 2012, 2013 and 2015) and, earlier, in the infamous **Stanford** 'million dollar' tournament in 2008.

Most significantly, he was a key bowler in both of the West Indies' successful campaigns of the **World T20** title – neck and neck with Narine as the highest impact bowlers of the tournament in 2012 and the highest impact bowler of the tournament in 2016.

Badree has six high impact performances with the ball in fifteen World T20 games, with failures in only two of those matches, which is pretty staggering too. And he is **the only T20I bowler to have two TD performances to his credit.** This comfortably makes him the highest impact T20I bowler till date.

Badree played just one season in the Big Bash league in Australia – just eight matches in 2016, and was among the ten highest impact bowlers in the tournament. But the main cause of his modest reputation, despite what he has accomplished, lies elsewhere.

Mediocre in the IPL

Despite West Indies winning both the 2012 and 2016 titles in the subcontinent (the latter in India, in fact), it is inexplicable that Badree has played just five IPL matches till date, for two franchises (four for Chennai Super Kings (CSK) and just one for Rajasthan Royals (RR)). He did fail in three of those five matches, but also, he never was given a chance to settle down, and was never fitted in as a key bowler.

Given his pedigree and, more importantly, his style of bowling in these conditions, it is baffling that an IPL team has not identified him as a key constituent of its bowling attack. RCB did perhaps plan to do that in 2016, where he was under the spotlight after the West Indies'

World T20 championship win, but he got injured and had to miss the tournament.

Just like an English or Australian Test player does not find his stock going up unless he delivers prominently in the Ashes, the IPL is where T20 reputations are made. At thirty-five, Badree doesn't have too much time left to make his mark here.

AC: This is an astonishing finding – even if no one would dispute Badree's utility in the shortest format. But since IPL performances are so central to T20 reputations, Badree's no-show there has dented his reputation. Before going ahead with what makes him exceptional in T20s, it's worth finding out what goes against him in the IPL. Most IPL teams manage to source Indian spinners, but very few teams can boast of two quality Indian pacers and, therefore, the team selection is skewed against picking Badree. While Badree is a great power play bowler, he's rarely bowled in the death overs, and that's something all IPL teams crave for – an overseas death specialist. It's almost criminal to have an overseas bowler out of the game in the first 10 overs itself, and that tends to happen very often with Badree.

Now, let's focus on what's going right – Badree isn't an orthodox leg-spinner who turns a mile, and that happens to be his strength in the shortest format. Unlike other leggies, he's able to bowl a lot straighter with two men manning the fence on the on side (you can have only two outside the circle in power play overs). You can try to play him like a slow inswing bowler but the odd ball grips and turns away to create doubt. And like most leggies, his low point of release produces less bounce and that makes it difficult to get under the ball. The idea of going across to balls that aren't bouncing much is laden with risk.

The biggest aspect in this story is his impact in the knockout games. It's not easy to bowl leg spin (irrespective of style) with a new ball, because gripping the ball and being accurate isn't easy while the ball has lacquer on it. Not many teams would prefer Badree over Narine in a knockout game, but if both were assigned the same role, this finding shows why conventional thinking can be flawed.

60

THE UNLUCKIEST T20 PLAYER IN INDIA: ROBIN UTHAPPA

This one is about a batsman who should have been a certainty for the national team to play the World T20 2016. Why he did not make it neatly exemplifies one of the biggest mistakes made in cricket selections around the world.

After being a part of India's winning campaign in the inaugural World T20 tournament in 2007, Uthappa had played just four T20Is for India in the next seven years.

We break down Uthappa's comeback story beat by beat from early 2014.

A glorious run

Uthappa was in splendid batting form for Karnataka in the 2013–14 domestic season where his team completed a rare treble, and he carried it forward to the IPL.

Playing as an opener for KKR, he had an outstanding season (660 runs; average of 47; strike rate 138) where he top-scored with 42 off 30 balls in the play-off against KXIP. He won the Orange Cup comfortably, even if Glenn Maxwell got the 'Player of the Series' award, which was bizarre because Maxwell failed in all the play-off games.

KKR won the title, and even though he failed in the final, Uthappa was the highest impact batsman in that tournament and the most consistent (minimum ten matches; failed in just 4 out of 16 innings). He also kept wickets for KKR, so he was easily the highest impact player for IPL 2014.

The comeback

After this eye-catching run in T20s, Uthappa was called back for national duty, twenty-seven months after his last appearance – for ODI cricket, though.

On a tour of Bangladesh, Uthappa managed 69 runs in his three ODI innings but, oddly enough, was still the top-scorer for India.

Yet, Uthappa was not selected for the only T20I (against England) India played that year after the IPL. He then got a chance to play in the Champions League. Yet again, Uthappa was the highest impact batsman for KKR in the T20 tournament, and his team even finished runners-up.

He came back again only in the ODI squad for the home series against Sri Lanka, though – replacing an absent M.S. Dhoni as wicketkeeper, batting down the order too, from where he scored 35 runs in two innings. He was dropped after the series.

A persistent run

In IPL 2015, Uthappa did well again, scoring the highest proportion of runs for KKR in the season, although they failed to make the play-offs. Uthappa's performances with the bat still kept him in the national fray.

He was once again called up to play three ODIs and two T20Is against Zimbabwe. In the three ODIs, he produced 0, 13 and 31. The media began to speculate if he had blown his chances for India yet again, never quite grasping that he hadn't played a single game in the format where he had actually earned his comeback.

In the T20I series that followed, Uthappa was in his element even though he wasn't given his natural opening position. He scored an unbeaten 39 off 35 balls in the first T20I and then 42 off 25 balls in the second T20I. Significantly, he top-scored in both innings (and was the highest impact Indian batsman in the series), making it abundantly clear to anyone paying attention that he squarely belonged to the T20 format, certainly much more than ODIs.

And yet, when India began their preparation for the 2016 World T20, starting with the T20I series against South Africa in October 2015, it became clear that Shikhar Dhawan was being preferred over him as an opener. In the lead-up to the event, India played fourteen T20Is, Uthappa was not picked in the squad for even one of them.

He had been dropped for his ODI performances!

Better than his competitors

In the time period between World T20 2014 and World T20 2016, Robin Uthappa was the highest impact T20 batsman in the world (minimum thirty innings across all T20 competitions in the world). His failure rate of only 31 per cent and the proportion of runs that he scored was the fourth best in the world after Virat Kohli, Kane Williamson and David Warner.

In the same time frame, amongst his competitors for the opening spot, Uthappa's impact with the bat was 20 per cent higher than Rohit Sharma's, 86 per cent higher than Shikhar Dhawan's and 96 per cent higher than Ajinkya Rahane's.

In the two seasons of the IPL between the two World T20s, Uthappa was the highest impact batsman followed by Lendl Simmons and Rohit Sharma. Uthappa's consistency in these two seasons of the IPL was also the second best after Faf du Plessis (minimum twenty innings).

Interestingly, the domestic T20 tournament, Syed Mushtaq Ali Trophy, was pushed up the calendar before the 2016 World T20 to aid the selectors in the overall selection process. For a minimum of five innings, Uthappa emerged as the highest impact batsman of the tournament.

Still, he was not picked.

India's big loss

India's campaigns in the 2014 World T20 and the 2016 World T20 followed a similar pattern. The batting rested solely on Virat Kohli's shoulders with at least one of the two openers failing constantly.

The importance of openers setting the pace in T20s cannot be overstated. They almost invariably end up as the highest impact batsmen for their teams. Why then did the Indian selectors never address the opening issue? Instead, they opted for Shikhar Dhawan as Rohit Sharma's opening partner in the 2016 World T20 based purely on his ODI exploits. Perhaps he was captain M.S. Dhoni's choice too.

The setback was apparent in the IPL season following the 2016 World T20. Uthappa didn't bat his usual self, and finished as only the third highest impact batsman for KKR after Yusuf Pathan and Gautam Gambhir. More importantly, he wasn't even amongst the ten highest impact Indian batsmen in IPL 2016. Predictably, he was not named in the Indian squad for the three-match T20I series against Zimbabwe (which India lost 1–2) following IPL 2016. The selection committee maintained the status quo regarding Uthappa while naming India's T20 squad against West Indies in the USA as well.

For all his exploits in the two years leading up to the 2016 World T20 – as the highest impact T20 batsman in the world – Uthappa's 'reward', a non-selection in the final Indian squad because of his poor ODI returns, reeked of injustice. Talk about comparing apples with oranges.

Sometimes an injustice to a player can mean an even greater injustice to his team.

> **AC:** Another interesting finding that highlights how human preferences work. Good IPL returns have seen players donning the India cap in ODIs, and good ODI numbers get them a Test cap and in this case, good ODI performances saw Dhawan retaining his T20 spot for the second World T20 in a row. Whatever happened in the immediate past influences our decision making, irrespective of how flawed that judgement might be. You justify it with current form, winning combination, etc., but it can't hide the inaccuracy of judgement.

Robin's case is a curious one for a variety of reasons ... since India played very few T20s between the two World T20s, the opportunities weren't available easily, and when they did appear (before the World T20 2016), the team management stuck with Dhawan, for he started showing glimpses of what he could be in T20s.

The change in Robin's fortunes has a lot to do with his change of technique and approach, which came about due to Pravin Amre. He started as someone who was comfortable against pace, and often opted for a flat bat instead of a straight one, which in turn inflated his failure rate. His second coming in the IPL (the last three seasons) is all about playing down the V and caressing the ball instead of bludgeoning it. He's also shown great temperament in stitching partnerships with Gambhir. His consistency in a format that dictates inconsistency has been exemplary. It'll be a travesty of justice if he doesn't get his due at the top of the order before it's too late.

61

T20 CRICKET IS NOT AS MUCH ABOUT BATTING AND CHANCE AS MOST PEOPLE SEEM TO THINK

Too many people seem to trash T20 cricket as a 'game of chance' where 'bowlers have no role'.

There is a lot of talk about how bats have become so much better – resulting in shots that would be unthinkable even two decades ago – but almost no discussion on the rising standards in fielding, where we see things unimaginable two decades ago. There is also today an enormous amount of homework possible, thanks to video analysis and data churning, most of which is spent examining batsmen's weaknesses than bowlers'. Whether or not these even out things, there are certain other aspects no one seems to talk about or perhaps even notice.

Underdogs thrive more in 50-over cricket

For all the talk about T20 cricket being about the teams on the day, there are fewer upsets in T20 cricket than there are in 50-over ODI cricket. Since bilateral T20 series have not really been established as premier events yet in the manner bilateral ODI series have been so far, let us just look at respective world event results.

In ODI World Cups so far (from 1975 to 2015), there have been seventeen upsets in eleven tournaments. Here, if we remove dead rubber matches, where the match is really just a formality and has no impact on the tournament, it comes to fifteen upsets in eleven World Cups.

In the World T20 tournaments so far (from 2007 to 2016), there have been eight upsets in six tournaments. More importantly, if we remove dead rubber matches (and matches between associate nations), it comes down to just four upsets in six tournaments. Proportionately, this is considerably less.

England have been the side most upset in both formats – four times (including one dead rubber game) in World Cups and twice in World T20 tournaments. Curiously, after England, it is India and South Africa who have been upset the most in World Cups while in World T20s, it is West Indies and Australia who follow England in that respect.

Some of the upsets in the ODI World Cups are very memorable – Zimbabwe beating Australia in 1983, Zimbabwe beating England in 1992, Kenya beating West Indies in 1996, Zimbabwe beating India and South Africa in 1999, Kenya beating Sri Lanka in 2003 and reaching the semi-finals (thanks also to walkovers), Bangladesh beating India and Ireland beating Pakistan in 2007, Ireland and Bangladesh beating England in 2011, Bangladesh beating England in 2015. But what equivalent moments do we have in World T20s? England being beaten by Netherlands twice. Do we remember that anywhere near as vividly?

It is a curious fact, this. Perhaps the reason for fewer upsets in T20 matches lies in the nature of the format itself – there is simply too little time for a team to drop its guard?

AC: When T20 cricket was introduced, most teams started out even, since most hadn't cracked the T20 code. We saw teams causing a few upsets. But the moment teams understood its nuts and bolts, it became almost impossible for weaker teams to compete, let alone beat, the stronger team. There's room for mediocrity in ODI (middle overs with the bat and ball) but there's no room to breathe in T20 cricket. With every over being 5 per cent of the entire innings and 25 per cent of a bowler's quota, it just takes one weakness to be exploited enough to change the outcome. Perhaps that's why the salary-cap structure is necessary in T20 leagues; in its absence, the rich will just run away with the silverware all the time.

The stronger T20 teams actually do win

Since 2011, Impact Index has projected the four likely semi-finalists in eleven T20 tournaments (based on the performances of its constituent squad members), which is on record on our website, and 71 per cent of the time, it has got them right. That just suggests that this is not a game of chance as some people seem to think it is.

The best bowling sides do better than the best batting sides

Even casual followers can make this out – Sun Risers Hyderabad (SRH) was the best bowling side in the 2016 IPL. It is not just about one bowler or two but the whole unit together.

We found the following in a study through Impact Index of eleven tournaments since 2011 (six IPLs, three World T20s and two CLT20s):

One of the two highest impact batting sides *before* the tournament has gone on to reach the final 55 per cent of the time (six out of eleven tournaments).

While one of the two highest impact batting teams *during* the tournament has gone on to reach the final 81 per cent of the time (nine out of eleven tournaments).

And one of the two highest impact bowling teams *before* the tournament has gone on to reach the final 64 per cent of the time (seven out of eleven tournaments).

While one of the two highest impact bowling teams *during* the tournament has gone on to reach the final each and every time in the eleven instances (100 per cent).

For a sport that appears to run purely on batsmen (who garner a disproportionate part of the glamour), this is an interesting finding. Bowlers have at least as significant a role in T20 cricket as batsmen do, if not slightly more.

Perhaps the big mistake a lot of people make is compare Test and

ODI economy rates with T20 economy and come to the conclusion that an average of 8 runs an over means that it is a batsman-dominated game. T20 requires a reset in the mind. If Test and ODI crickets did not require the building of an innings, natural batting talent would be expressed much the way it is in T20 cricket. Yes, batting pitches are prevelant in this format, but is it really much more here than in the other two? And even on batting pitches, bowlers have a big role to play.

> **AC:** On most days you need two to three batsmen to last 20 overs but in every single T20 innings, you need at least five (if not six) bowlers to save you the day. This explains who is more important in the T20 context. But while a bowler will seldom produce a match-winning performance (he has only 4 overs to bowl), batsmen tend to do it more often (with no restrictions, he can bat for the entire 20 overs of the innings and play a match-winning knock). Also, the advent of T20 forced people to accept that failure is a necessary evil for the batsman but it's taken a lot longer to see bowlers conceding 8-9 runs an over. It takes a paradigm shift in the thought process, which shall take its own sweet time. This explains why batsmen are the glamour boys of T20 cricket.

The hustle of T20 cricket requires different talents to excel in it, as well as specialized skills (death bowling and power hitting, for example), which is why many successful T20 cricketers don't necessarily do well in other formats. When players are selected in T20 cricket based on their ODI performances and vice versa, it is an example of not respecting T20 cricket as a distinct sport.

If it is baseball that T20 cricket sought to emulate in terms of duration, by all accounts, it has succeeded. Given how much the world has changed in the last decade, and attention spans with it, blaming authorities for Test cricket's inability to draw enough crowds consistently and blaming T20 cricket for it is just silly.

A lot of T20 is high-quality cricket, showcasing a lot of skill and thought. It is here to stay and the game is better for it.

AFTERWORD

Jaideep Varma
Creator, Impact Index

It may seem strange to tell the story of Impact Index at the end of the book. But we didn't want anything to distract from what this book is really about – the retelling of cricket history.

If these stories have indeed made you see things differently, perhaps you are also wondering why an entity like Impact Index or indeed this entire mindset it represents is marginalized in the cricket world.

Impact Index's own story perhaps explains that best.

How it began

Impact Index was created accidentally in March 2009 (via some seemingly directionless doodling) as a result of an invitation to Oxford for the ICC Centenary Conference where I was asked to present a paper on the world's greatest Test cricketers. That invitation had come due to the widespread coverage of an exercise I had led for a website called HoldingWilley on India's greatest Test cricketers, which was also featured on the front page of the *Hindustan Times* nationally. That exercise used qualitative ideas that inadvertently had laid the foundation for Impact Index's core idea – match, and more significantly, series context.

The first version of Impact Index was embarrassingly subjective, yet it threw up some thought-provoking findings, that were well received at Oxford. There were several writers and thinkers on the game there, many of whom were very encouraging. Some of them also suggested that we develop the T20 version and pitch it to IPL, which had already had two seasons by then, as conventional T20 stats are the most meaningless of all.

Back in India, first we worked on making the system much more objective, which was accomplished by basing all calculations on inputs from the scorecard.

And then began a journey that for all practical purposes isn't really over yet.

Impact Index in modern-day India, and the cricket world

The three primary functions, and therefore commercial opportunities, for Impact Index lie in the following: live cricket (where it can comment on the ongoing game with unique observations, in any medium), team consultancy (helping a team select and then squeeze out its full potential, in conjunction with video analysis) and editorial material. This book is just a part of the third function.

We interacted with many entities to try and stand on our own feet commercially. These are some of the highlights of our journey so far – assembled together, it provides as good a portrait of modern-day India as anything else. Some of this may seem to be an excuse for public whining, but there really seems to be no other way to explain the magnitude of the uphill struggle that it is to establish a new idea in this sport, especially in India.

Take, for example, a very senior official I met in 2009 who asked, 'I appreciate the potential Impact Index has, and how it can benefit the game, but why should I build your business?'

The then marketing head of a cricket body told us through a mutual contact in 2010 that they were not too keen on Impact Index because the system was 'too transparent'.

An official in team management once said to me: 'Impact Index seems very interesting no doubt, but I want my team to be the second one to use it, not the first.'

The marketing head of a major mobile company invited me for multiple meetings to his office over four months, even introduced me to his boss, but in the end hinted obliquely that nothing would go forward without a bribe.

Then, there was this sports editor of one of India's biggest newspapers, who after getting into a deal with us, first accused me of plagiarizing someone else's concept (never elaborating on it) and then, mid-tournament, demanded that we reduce our price (as if that was the logical punishment for the crime of 'plagiarizing'). In the end, after considerable unpleasantness, I had to complain to his boss to get my full payment. Curiously, a few years later, that editor was fired for corruption.

There was a premier sports channel that had multiple meetings with us and suddenly, for no apparent reason, just stopped communicating. A couple of months later, they put up an alternative statistical system on their website that had more or less the same parameters as we did, that claimed to do exactly what we had claimed to them. They were even brazen enough to say in their introduction: 'Impact Index is also doing something like this.' Thankfully, their findings were embarrassingly inadequate and they had no choice but to abandon the system. It transpired that three of their employees had actually expected to create something better in two months of working part-time on it than what Impact Index had done in four years of full-time commitment.

Then there was the owner of this massive data analytics company with international interests, who wanted to buy out Impact Index. He was charming and forceful, and told us we could move operations to his office while 'formalities were being completed', which I naively agreed to, as their tech support was ostensibly far superior. Barely three weeks later, he went back on a lot of what he had committed to me, brazenly lying through his teeth later. We feared for the privacy of our data but, despite managing to hire someone from my team eventually, he could not do anything with that. Four years on, he was sued by a former business partner for fraud, with a curious allegation that 'the motivation to commit such deceitful actions sprang partly from his religious beliefs and a perverse mindset – which turned traditional fiduciary duty principles on their head – had its roots in his devotion to the Hindu deity Shiva the Destroyer, whose core philosophy called for destroying or selectively abandoning the past.' This, I kid you not, was actually mentioned in the court papers.

There was also the sports channel where a very senior manager explained to me the objective of the cricket stats system he wanted. 'The numbers you generate cannot be complicated; they have to be understood by my dhobi, my watchman and my driver.' My response – 'You don't need numbers, you need item numbers' – admittedly wasn't the smartest move I ever made, but two years later, when this same channel launched a system that had five numbers for each player with no single reference point (and thus was five times more complicated than ours), I did wonder where that resolve went.

Then, in 2013, a premier cricket website's editor got in touch with me saying he was interested in acquiring Impact Index. Excited about the intellectual possibilities (which included tying up Impact Index scorecards with their own match scorecards), I agreed to a full due diligence of the system without a non-disclosure agreement even. That happened over two days, and we were enthusiastically given the go-ahead. And then came the punchline from their business head: they weren't offering money, just revenue share. The editor who originally approached me expressed surprise and encouraged me to negotiate hard, which I did. But oddly, they suddenly did not seem at all interested any more, and later I heard their attempt at creating their own system had been aborted as well.

A major international technology company tied up with us for World Cup 2015, used our data shabbily, but still managed to create quite a buzz. They did not credit us in their personnel list or internal communications, not even when they won a prestigious media award.

I could tell you about the television news channel that signed us up exclusively for the World Cup, demanded we station two of our team members in their city for the duration of the tournament, and in the end, quite simply did not pay a single rupee.

Or about a prominent cricket coach in Australia whom we offered our services for free on the condition that he took it seriously and valued it, which he enthusiastically agreed to. He asked us for specific recommendations, which we provided before each match. Even though we saw a lot of our suggestions being ostensibly implemented, he gradually stopped communicating. The team, against the odds, reached the semi-final, then won the tournament. After several reminders, we finally heard from him. Even though he conceded that his team had chosen to chase in the final due to the case we made in our document, apparently, our material hadn't been useful otherwise, as there was 'too much jargon' in it, and then claimed that all the other recommendations they implemented were by their club analyst. I prepared a list of all the jargon-free observations we had made; it filled six pages, with the implemented ideas in brackets, and specifically requested him to tell us if any of this had been useful. He never replied.

A senior English statistician with a prominent television channel who was referred to our work came back with the claim that this was 'similar' to the world rankings which he had worked on when he was sixteen in the early 1990s! It is another matter that doing match-by-match data wasn't exactly a DIY computable task then, nor is there any explanation as to why his system did not produce a single insight that has ever been spoken of.

There was also this English journalist who expressed discomfort with a finding of ours because it did not 'chime in' with the 'accumalated wisdom over the years'. There was no attempt to examine how we came to our conclusion; it had to fit his preconceived notions for that to happen.

There are many other stories but you get the drift. What chance can any new idea have in this environment?

And the hostility within the cricket coverage fraternity isn't exactly reassuring either. We are constantly reminded that it is not our place to challenge history, or indeed, even make general observations or express opinions outside the realm of numbers, as if simple logic is only the domain of the 'properly qualified' (which really only means doing time here). The insecurity apart, it is the rancour which is befuddling. So, a young journalist will happily call us 'frauds' on a Facebook forum just a few months after applying for a job with us (when we politely told him there was no vacancy). Or an NRI academic and a self-styled cricket writer/statistician will constantly harangue us for not revealing our system, attack us on Twitter, write articles on private blogs trashing us (even anonymously sometimes), but never actually end up doing anything beyond esoteric trivia himself. I had to name him in an angry piece on our website for him to stop.

In this milieu, with no money spent on PR or marketing, Impact Index still somehow managed the following: coverage on the front page of *The Times of India*, a six-month exclusive tie-up with Yahoo!, to be quoted on BBC World Service, Star Sports and ESPN Cricinfo, to be written about in *Wisden Almanack* (UK), *Forbes* and *International Business Times*, featured on CNN-IBN, CNBC, News X, Zee News and even had two half-hour dedicated specials on NDTV.

Yet, by the beginning of 2014, I had not just emptied out my savings, I was in debt as I struggled to pay my automation partners in Bengaluru. Not to speak of a distinct siege mentality that had developed in me after all this time. Out of all the people who had worked on this with me, only Soham Sarkhel had lasted the obstacle course, which probably had as much to do with this being his first job and not knowing any better, as with his own interest and conviction in the system. What kept me going was the desire to see what the Test findings would reveal; its automation had not been completed, and I could not abandon it after all these years of work.

However, thanks to interest at Wisden India, their holding company Fidelis World finally invested in Impact Index in April 2014, procuring majority stake. I got paid for the first time in five years – and contrary to popular assumption, not exactly a fortune – just enough to recover my whole investment till then, with a modest interest. This acquisition allowed me to redesign and run our website without worry (or interference), and the salient ideas for what constitutes this book came about during that phase.

Still, Impact Index is squarely a part of the corporate world today and anything can happen to it anytime. Like, two of its four-member team can be fired behind its leader's back by a company brought in to 'restructure' with no conversation or idea about different people's roles – the delightful irony of two IIPM graduates causing the firing not being the only surreal touch. The two remaining members then threaten to quit immediately, and the management forced to reinstate the other two, as through the haze of egg on their face they realize no one else can run the system. Secure for the moment perhaps, but with no guarantee that Impact Index will be run authentically in the future – the corporate world isn't exactly known for that.

But hopefully, with a clearer long-term vision, perhaps with more fruitful partnerships, Impact Index can maintain its original intent and continue its search. Hopefully, other entities will join in and perhaps do it even better than us. What matters is that there are more books, more untold stories and more cases of righting history. Cricket needs this clarity more urgently than it ever has.

ACKNOWLEDGEMENTS

Impact Index owes special thanks to R.S. Prakash and Paramvir Singh for unstinting, unconditional support that has often translated to tangible help throughout Impact Index's life-cycle so far.

And to Gokul Chakravarthy, Jatin Thakkar, Monty Desai, Sreeram Ramachandran and Karthik Swaminathan for helping take Impact Index intellectually forward at different times.

Thanks to Anand Vasu, Dileep Premachandran, Nikhil Naz, Subrat Mohanty, Cartwheel/Holding Willey, Ronak Saturia, Prem Panicker, Rajnikanth S., Matt Thacker, Phil Walker, Jo Harman, Rahul Ram, Vistasp Hodiwala, Murali Krishna, Mukul Chadda, Varun Grover, Suhaas Ahuja, Sanjay Kewlani, Avijit Ghosh, Harshad Nalawade, Dhruv Sehgal, T.V. Narayan, Vic Nicholas, Reema Abbasi, Jonathan Cumberbatch, Karunya Keshav, Himanish Bhattacharjee, Sayantan Dasgupta, Mohan Polamar, Rajesh Pant, Abhishek Ranjan Jha, Sethumadhavan Napan, Uday Shetty, Kalpana Rao, Basudev Biswas and Bharavi for support, help or attention.

And to Greg Chappell, Srinivas Bhogle, Lawrence Booth, Simon Sweetman, Sudhir Vaidya, Ramnarayan Venkatraman, Osman Samiuddin, Pat Howard and Andy Zaltzman for votes of confidence at different times; they have meant a lot.

Thanks to Pradeep S., M.R. Raghavendra Rao, Samsul Hoque Choudhury and Sudarshan B. at Innosolv and Rohan Almeida before.

To our literary agent Kanishka Gupta for saving us from peeping out of yet another slush pile.

And to our editor at HarperCollins, Ajitha G.S. for bringing much required balance and poise. Thanks also to S.K. Ray Chaudhuri. And to Jojy Philip (typesetting), Saurav Das (design), Bonita Vaz-Shimray and Divya Saxena (cover design) and Amrita Talwar (publicity).

To Anand Krishnan for giving us the space to do this book.

And to Boria Majumdar for starting this whole journey off, even if inadvertently.

Finally, special thanks to the late Dr Kalyan Mukherjee, sarod maestro and cricket student, whose propensity to be deeply moved while looking at old cricket scorecards planted a seed that perhaps led to all this.